POPE PIUS XII LIB., ST. JOSEPH COLLEGE
3 2528 01343 1608

D1524597

Śiva in Dance, Myth and Iconography

This volume is sponsored by the
Inter-Faculty Committee for South Asian Studies
University of Oxford

Oxford University South Asian Studies Series

ŚIVA in Dance, Myth and Iconography

Anne-Marie Gaston

DELHI
OXFORD UNIVERSITY PRESS
BOMBAY CALCUTTA MADRAS

Oxford University Press, Walton Street, Oxford OX2 6DP

NEW YORK TORONTO
DELHI BOMBAY CALCUTTA MADRAS KARACHI
PETALING JAYA SINGAPORE HONG KONG TOKYO
NAIROBI DAR ES SALAAM
MELBOURNE AUCKLAND

and associates in
BERLIN IBADAN

© Oxford University Press 1982
First published in paperback 1990

SBN 0 19 562595 1

Printed by Pramodh P. Kapur at Rajbandhu Industrial Co.
C-61 Mayapuri, Phase-II, New Delhi 110064
and published by S.K. Mookerjee, Oxford University Press
YMCA Library Building, Jai Singh Road, New Delhi 110001

To my gurus
eastern and western

Contents

List of Tables

List of Plates

Acknowledgements

This research would never have begun without the care and dedication extended to me by my dance masters when instructing me in four classical dance styles of India. In Bharata Natyam: the late Ellappa Pillai, Kalanidhi, K. N. Dakshinamurthy, Swarna Sareswati, Adyar Lakshman, Gayatri Venkataraman, Uma Dandayudapani, Padma Subramanium, and Kiranur Govinda Rajan; in Odissi: Kelucharan Mahapatra, Hari Krishna Behera, and Mayadhar Raut; in Kuchipudi: Raja Reddy, Narasimha and Vasanti Acharya; in Kathakali: P. V. Balakrishna and Balasubramaniam. I should also like to thank my Chhau teachers Krishna Chandra Naik and Madhuri Kamath. They constitute the unacknowledged source of many of my statements concerning the living dance tradition and I am extremely grateful to them.

Two books relevant to this topic have preceded the present study: *Natarāja in Art, Thought and Literature,* by C. Sivaramamurti, and *Indian Classical Dance in Literature and the Arts* by K. Vatsyayan. These provide copious documentation and their authors were major sources of inspiration for this work both through their publications and through personal contact.

I wish to express my gratitude to my supervisor and friend Professor Richard Gombrich, Boden Professor of Sanskrit, who encouraged me from the beginning to take up this study and then helped me to integrate my traditional knowledge based on an essentially oral tradition, with the critical approach appropriate to an academic context

This book is based on my M. Litt. thesis for the Department of Oriental Studies, Oxford University, where for some time I was also guided by Dr Wendy Donniger O'Flaherty. Her infectious enthusiasm and vast knowledge of Hindu myths persuaded me to integrate them into my study.

Others who have read my work and offered criticism, suggestions and encouragement are Dr Sanjukta Gupta (Utrecht University), Dr Derrick Puffet and Dr Michael Carrithers (both of Wolfson College, Oxford) and Gauhar Rizvi (Trinity College, Oxford) and in particular my colleagues and fellow students of Indian art at the Oriental Institute, Oxford: Andrew Topsfield (Assistant Curator of Indian Art, Victoria and Albert Museum, London) and Thomas Maxwell (Assistant Curator of Indian Art, Ashmolean Museum, Oxford). Dr J. C. Harle (Curator of Eastern Art, Ashmolean Museum, Oxford) encouraged me to concentrate on dancing images and guided my study of the sculptures.

I should also like to thank Dr George Mitchell for valuable discussions particularly concerning early images from the Deccani region, and allowing me to consult his extensive collection of photographs. I owe a very special debt to Michael Dudley (FRPS) and Jeff Gorbeck for the skill and labour which they have expended in the processing of the photographs. I would like to thank the following for allowing me to use their photographs: Jeff Gorbeck, for Plates 22, 23, 79; Thomas Maxwell for Plates 47 and 48; and Dr J. C. Harle for Plate 94. The remainder of the photographs were taken by Tony Gaston and myself.

The greatest encouragement came from Tony Gaston, who travelled to the temple sites with me. For both of us the enjoyment of experiencing Indian art as part of a living tradition provided a great source of personal satisfaction as we shared the cultural heritage of the India which we both love.

Genuine appreciation must also be expressed for the financial assistance which I received from the Canada Council and Commonwealth Scholarships Committee for pursuing my artistic career in classical Indian dance; and the Boden Fund, Oxford, towards the production of my thesis.

I should also like to thank the Secretary of my Oxford College, Wolfson, Miss Sheila McMeekin, who ensured that facilities were made available for me to keep up my daily dance practice while I was pursuing my academic research. This was extremely important to me as it allowed me to continue to perform regularly. The encouragement I received from Gwendolyn and General Peacher made it possible for me to continue full-time research at Oxford with performing during vacation periods.

In Madras, Mr Balaram, the Sharma family of Children's Garden School and Y. G. Doraiswamy and in Delhi, the V. Arunachalam family extended tremendous assistance. Akhila Krishnan of Delhi, a Carnatic concert vocalist, was generous with both her time and knowledge in our discussions and performances of songs based on Śaivite myths.

During my stay at the Kerala Kalamandalam Mr Vasudevan and Mr Balakrishna Valathol were extremely helpful.

The members of the Central Sangeet Natak Akademi in Delhi in particular, Messieurs Jivan Pani, Mohan Khokar, Keshav Kothari, and Bansal and D. N. Patnaik of the Orissa Sangeet Natak Akademi all deserve a very special thank you.

The Archaeological Survey of India was most co-operative in extending permission to take photographs at the sites.

Ewart Reid, the late Dorothy Reid, and Liliane and Bill Jenkins also deserve a special thank you for their generosity to me while they were in Delhi. The assistance of my parents Helen and Jim Groves enabled me to continue my work while moving frequently between three continents.

Abbreviations

AC	*Abhinaya Candrika*, in *Oḍissi Dance*, D. N. Patnaik, Cuttack, 1971.
AD	*Abhinayadarpaṇa*, ed. and trans. M. Ghosh, 2nd ed. Calcutta, 1957.
AgP	*Agni Purāṇa*, trans. M. N. Dutt Shastri, 2 vols., Chowkhamba Sanskrit Series, Varanasi, 1967.
ICD	*Indian Classical Dancing: A Glossary*, M. Bose, Calcutta, 1970.
ICDLA	*Indian Classical Dance in Literature and the Arts*, K. Vatsyayan, New Delhi, 1968.
KP	*Kūrma Purāṇa*, trans. a board of scholars, Varanasi, 1972.
LP	*Liṅga Purāṇa*, trans. a board of scholars, Ancient Indian Tradition and Mythology Series, vols. 5 & 6, Delhi, 1975.
Naṭarāja	*Naṭarāja in Art, Thought and Literature*, C. Sivaramamurti, New Delhi, 1975.
NŚ	*Nāṭya Śāstra*, trans. and ed. M. Ghosh, 2 vols., Calcutta, 1967.
NŚ, GOS	*Nāṭya Śāstra*, vol. I, 2nd rev. ed., Gaekwad's Oriental Series, No. XXXVI, Baroda, 1956.
MP	*Matsya Purāṇa*, ed. Jamma Das Akhtar, *The Sacred Books of the Aryans*, Delhi, 1972.
ŚilPr.	*Śilpa Prakāśa*, trans. A. Boner and K. Ramachandra, Leiden, 1968.
ŚP	*Śiva Purāṇa*, trans. a board of scholars, 1st ed., Ancient Indian Tradition and Mythology Series, vols. 1–4, New Delhi, 1970.
SRM	*Naṭarāja in Art, Thought and Literature*, C. Sivaramamurti, New Delhi, 1975.
TL	*Tāṇḍava Lakṣaṇam*, trans. B. V. N. Naidu and others, Madras, 1936.
VDP	*Viṣṇudharmottara Purāṇa*, trans. P. Shah, 2nd ed., Gaekwad's Oriental Series No. 137, Baroda, 1961.
VP	*Vāmana Purāṇa,* trans. a board of scholars, All India Kashiraj Trust, Varanasi, 1968.

Abbreviations of regional names

Be	Bengal
Bi	Bihar
Gu	Gujarat
HP	Himachal Pradesh
Ka	Karnataka
Ke	Kerala
Mah	Maharashtra
MP	Madhya Pradesh
NWFP	North West Frontier Provinces
Or	Orissa
Ra	Rajasthan
TN	Tamil Nadu

Symbols:

* one knee straight

Introduction

A conjunction of several fortuitous events introduced me to the field of Indian dance and sculpture and eventually provided me with the subject matter for this study. The first was the nature of my introduction to Indian art. I began my study of Bharata Nāṭyam, a south Indian classical dance style, in 1964, after being inspired by the sculptures of dance on the temple towers of the Naṭarāja temple at Cidambaram. In the same way, I decided to study Oḍissi, after a visit to the Surya temple at Konarak in Orissa, where the sculptural representations of the dance are numerous. I also watched classical and folk styles of dance throughout India in which the purāṇic legends of Śiva's dance are still depicted.

Most of my teachers were hereditary masters of the dance who had been taught by their fathers or relations or had been temple dancers themselves and were now teaching. Some of their knowledge has been passed on to me and it was this fortunate association that encouraged me to write about the background of the dance. Without the dedicated care extended to me by my dance masters when instructing me in four of the classical dance styles of India I would never have been in a position to undertake this research. They constitute the source of many of my statements concerning the living dance traditions, and I am extremely grateful to them. I have drawn upon my practical training when making comparisons between the depiction of Śaivite myths in dance and in sculpture.

Today the worship of Naṭarāja is almost completely confined to south India. Despite the prevalence of the cult in the south, items currently performed in the southern dance style, Bharata Nāṭyam, include only a limited number on this theme, while those in praise of Kṛṣṇa and Murugan are more numerous. Secular themes are also widespread.

In Orissa, there are numerous sculptural representations of Naṭarāja dating from the sixth to the eighth century, yet in the Oḍissi dance tradition Naṭarāja is almost completely ignored, and during a recital an icon of Lord Jagannātha is usually placed on the stage, in contrast to the Naṭarāja image used during a Bharata Nāṭyam recital. In the Kelucharan Mahapatra school of Oḍissi dance, Naṭarāja is depicted only as the father of Gaṇeśa, who is also a dancer in his own right. No specific item in praise of Naṭarāja is danced. The great Vaisnava poem, the *Gīta Govinda* of Jaya Deva, appears to have superseded former Śaivite themes in the dance.[1]

Although the dance has an ancient tradition it is continually evolving; for this reason I felt it was important to record the richness of the dance vocabulary as it exists today and apply this knowledge to a wider context. Very little is known about the history of dance in India and in the fifteen years in which I have been intimately associated with it I have seen it evolve with the development of new items and new presentations, in response to the changing taste of audiences and the desire of dancers for greater self-expression. Parallel to these changes in the dance is the revival of old dance items and songs, some reconstructed with the help of old masters, others re-choreographed using old songs.

Indian classical dances are often considered to have originated solely as religious performances, but it is apparent from early writings on dance that they also served a secular function. As with many social institutions it is difficult to make a distinction between the religious and the secular, but it is clear that there has been an element of both present throughout the history of the dance. This combination of religious and secular art is reflected in the field of temple sculpture, where strictly iconographic representations of deities often appear side by side with depictions of dancing girls, amatory couples, and other themes whose religious significance is not immediately apparent.

Indian dance is divided into two main sections: pure movement and mime. In comparison with western classical dance the mimetic portions are numerous and more highly developed, with stories mainly drawn from Hindu mythology. As myth became more important in the narrative portions of the dance, a complex system of hand signs, body positions and facial expressions evolved to enable the dancer to express it. Similarly in Hindu iconography, this same complex system of symbols developed to signify particular mythological events. There is a great deal of similarity between these symbols and the language of gesture (*abhinaya*) used in the dance, particularly in Bharata Nāṭyam, to describe the same myths. In this way iconography provides a useful key to understanding the descriptive portions of the dance. Not only do both art forms use much of the same symbolism expressed within the confines of their own medium: the dancer employing hand signs to suggest an attribute, while the icon is depicted actually holding the attribute, but it is highly likely that, since dancers and sculptors have been, so to speak, looking over each other's shoulders for several thousand years, they might actually have influenced each other in determining when a specific attribute is appropriate. It is therefore not profitable to assign priority to a particular art form as originating this symbolism. Moreover, the contest is unequal, because while sculptors have left copious and durable records of the evolution of their art, the development of dance can be traced back no further than the length of living memory, and that filtered through the inevitable romantic distortions inseparable from the oral tradition.

For me the study of dance and sculpture has always gone hand in hand, for it was the pose I was taught in Oḍissi dance for Naṭarāja that first led me to discover its sculptural representations in Orissa, and to appreciate that there were forms of Naṭarāja other than the one so frequently depicted in south Indian bronzes. At that time I was struck by the contrast between the depictions of Naṭarāja in the Oḍissi and Bharata Nāṭyam styles of dance, each imitating the sculptural pose most common to their region of origin. In the Bharata Nāṭyam dance tradition, the pose for Naṭarāja and many of the attributes alluded to are those characteristic of the typical Cōla bronzes of Śiva (Plates 1a, b). In the Oḍissi style, the pose and attributes used are similar to those of the earliest sculptures from Orissa (Plates 1c, d). For example, to portray Naṭarāja with a leg lifted up and across the body would be a grave error in the Oḍissi style, as this is peculiar to the Bharata Nāṭyam dance tradition. Some inconsistency is to be seen, however, in the semi-classical traditions such as Mayurbhanj Chhau in eastern India, which incorporates athletic postures of a dancing Śiva similar to those to be seen in the Kailasanatha temple, Kancipuram, in south India. It may be that they are acceptable in Chhau because this is performed by men, and omitted from the southern dance, Bharata Nāṭyam, because they are considered unsuitable for female dancers.

Observations such as these encouraged me to examine and compare the variety of poses in dance and sculpture adopted in different regions. To this end I have tried to classify images of Naṭarāja and then apply this classification to other images of Śiva and to decorative dancing figures. My classification derives from my experience as a dancer rather than from iconographic considerations such as those employed by art historians. I have drawn on the rich store of evidence relating to various Indian classical dance styles as they are depicted in sculptures of dancers, as recorded in early treatises [in particular the *Nāṭya Śāstra* (*NŚ*), *Abhinayadarpaṇa* (*AD*) and the *Viṣṇudharmottara Purāṇa* (*VDP*)] and taught in the living dance tradition. Because dance remains a living art form, the opportunity to draw on the knowledge of current exponents still exists. This is one of the strengths of my approach. As the classical tradition embodied in the *VDP* affirms that a knowledge of dance is a prerequisite for the practice of iconography[2] it follows that this knowledge should also be fundamental to critical iconographic analysis. I hope that my familiarity with the living dance forms of India[3] where traditional texts find practical application, has enabled me to understand and illustrate the way in which terms are used not only in the dance but also in sculpture and iconographic texts. An understanding of dance terminology should provide a greater consistency where it is applied to sculpture, and facilitate a more exact documentation of the dance in Indian iconography.

Śiva, as one of the principal Hindu deities, is surrounded by an immense body of mythology. His iconography, whether in painting or sculpture, is thus extremely diverse. He is regarded as embodying all aspects of existence and is therefore sometimes portrayed as the Trimūrti: the creator, preserver, and destroyer. These functions are also

Plate 1

1a Bharata Nāṭyam

1c Oḍissi

1b Bronze Naṭarāja, Kivalur, Tanjore Art Gallery (TN), 11th c.

1d Stone Naṭarāja, Mukteśvara Compound, Bhuvaneswar (Or), 7th c.

personified separately in the form of the three gods, Brahmā, Viṣṇu and Śiva, with Śiva here representing only the destructive aspect. The concept of encompassing all aspects of existence is paralleled in the dance by compositions designed to demonstrate the complete range of human emotions in a single item, as in the '*nava rasa*' compositions found in Bharata Nāṭyam.

Śiva as Naṭarāja, the presiding deity at the great south Indian shrine in Cidambaram, is regarded as the lord of the dance, and many of the songs used in Bharata Nāṭyam refer to this association. More than any other deity, dance is associated with the mythology of Śiva, forming in its most exalted aspect a metaphor for the cosmic cycle of creation and destruction and the individual cycle of birth and re-birth. In many other myths too, Śiva is portrayed as dancing, whether for his consort Pārvatī on the heights of Kailāsa, among the spirits in the cremation ground, or on the body of the conquered dwarf, Mūyaḷagan, symbolizing forgetfulness. The greater or cosmic dance, known as *ānanda tāṇḍava*, is implicit in all the other instances of his dance, but the myths themselves, and their depictions in iconography, do not always express this.

An image of Śiva is a veritable encyclopaedia of mythological references. Each attribute, such as the trident, the snake, and the skull in his crown, the unmatched ear-rings, has some story attached of which the beholder is being reminded. The images are normally referred to according to the major mythological strand that they portray; hence Śiva in a dancing pose is referred to as Naṭarāja, but at the same time minor details signify other aspects, which may themselves be represented in full images.

The symbols used in iconography, when translated into the gestures of the dance (*mudrā, abhinaya*), form a useful language by which the dancer can refer briefly to Śiva's different aspects without miming them explicitly. A detailed knowledge of these symbolic gestures allows the audience to appreciate the many facets of Śiva through the presentation of a single theme, thus mirroring the essential unity of the concept of godhead underlying the vast diversity of manifestations. In this way, iconography is a key to understanding references made in the descriptive portions of the dance.

In order to interpret both the dance and the iconography, one constantly falls back on the mythology for explanations, and I have therefore felt it appropriate to include those myths of Śiva which involve dance. Manifestations of Śiva, in addition to his Naṭarāja form, which may be depicted dancing in myth and/or iconography are: Tripurāntaka, Ardhanārīśvara, Kālārimūrti, Gajāsurasaṁhāramūrti, Bhikṣāṭana, Vīrabhadra, Bhairava, and Vīṇādhara. Some of these aspects are frequently depicted in live dance, some only occasionally, and still others never. To show which of these aspects of Śiva are currently considered most important within the living dance traditions of India, I shall refer to their various depictions in different regional dance styles. These dances did not develop in artistic isolation but were influenced by other traditions, both visual and literary. Even today dance masters and dancers return to the texts and sculpture for new ideas and inspiration. Śiva is not the only Hindu god who dances in myth and iconography. He is, however, represented more frequently in a greater variety of dance poses than the other deities. Not only is the mythology of Śiva full of references to his different dances, but it is he who is usually credited with the creation of dance as an art form.[4] The dancing Śiva is therefore an appropriate image to study when comparing dance in iconography, myth, and live dance.

In considering the range of Śaivite iconography I assume that Śiva is dancing wherever he is depicted with either one or both knees bent. This is because the knees are held bent most of the time in both the Bharata Nāṭyam and Oḍissi styles of dance, and the position is maintained whether moving sideways, backwards or turning. This position of the knees is also characteristic of many other Indian dance styles.

Images of Naṭarāja show the full range of body, hand and foot positions. Practically all poses exhibited by sculptures of other dancing figures are also found in the iconography of Naṭarāja. For these reasons, images of Naṭarāja make the most suitable subject for an analysis of iconography.

I have chosen to deal with sculptures from the

earliest times to about A.D. 1450, dividing them chronologically into four different periods, and geographically into four regions.

In embarking on this research I set out to further understanding of development of the iconography of Naṭarāja and other dancing images of Śiva, both regionally and chronologically, and to show how it relates to decorative dancing figures and to the depiction of Śaivite stories in the living dance traditions. Even if I have failed in this rather bold aim, I have at least drawn together many disparate facets of Hindu culture and linked together many things which were previously never connected. I hope that the book will serve this more modest purpose for my readers.

The book is intended to interest scholars of Indian art wishing to broaden their horizons and those interested in Indian classical dance. It should also be of some interest to anthropologists and social historians. Chapters I and II, which deal with dance in its social context and historical perspective, should be useful to all these readers. Chapter III, which introduces different classifications of Naṭarāja images, and IV, which describes the diversity of such images, will mainly be of interest to art historians. In Chapter V different components of the Naṭarāja image are discussed and attributes compared with their depictions in dance through gesture, providing material for art historians and dancers. Other images of Śiva in dancing poses are discussed in Chapter VI, which also describes their associated mythology and the ways in which they are represented in dance. This is probably the most important section for those interested in the interrelationship of mythology, iconography, and dance. The book concludes with a chapter on decorative dancing figures, comparing them with images of Naṭarāja.

CHAPTER I

Dance in Indian Society

Dance in traditional Indian culture permeated all facets of life, but its outstanding function was to give symbolic expression to abstract religious ideas.[1] This is illustrated in the plastic arts by the dancing figure of Śiva as Naṭarāja, in which his dance represents the cosmic cycle of creation and destruction.[2]

The close relationship between dance and religion began very early in Hindu thought, and numerous references to dance include descriptions of its performance in both secular and religious contexts. Since traditional Indian society has never clearly demarcated secular from religious activity, it is difficult and unnecessary to ascertain in which milieu the dance may have originated. It is likely that dance was first practised for the simple joy of movement or as a spontaneous manifestation of devotion[3] before later becoming ritualized in the form of religious ceremonies. This resulted in the two main divisions of dance: the folk (*deśi*), and the more complex and strictly codified classical dance (*mārga*), the latter evolving from the former.[4] It seems likely that the religious association of the dance is older than historical records.

From the present state of Indian classical dance it is difficult to reconstruct its position in Indian society prior to its elevation as a classical art form through transplantation to the concert stage. Few of those who performed the dance in its original setting in temples and royal courts remain alive, and these women are often reluctant to talk about a period when their profession was generally looked upon with disdain. For those who are prepared to reminisce, thirty years have elapsed since their temple performances ended at the time of Indian independence, and much has been forgotten. It is clear, however, that the opprobrium which was attached to dancers in the early decades of this century was not typical of their status in earlier times. Formerly they must have formed an influential element in society, patronized by monarchs and wealthy religious foundations, and enjoying an independence open to few women in other branches of society. Today many of this group have either stopped performing, or died, and with modernization and caste mobility their sons (who were dancers and musicians) are going to school for a 'respectable' education which will lead to secure positions.

In the last few years we have again seen a rise in the status of certain dance styles, as they have become more and more the preserve of young girls from wealthy, influential families. In fact, the attitudes to Indian dance may be likened to the western attitude to ballet dancers at the turn of the century, which was considered an accomplishment for most little girls, but discouraged as a full-time profession. The popularity now experienced by Indian classical dance has existed only in the last twenty years. The form in which the dance survives today however has been altered to suit contemporary tastes. This was evident when I watched a former *devadāsī*, Muthulakshmi, holding a class in the old palace of Pudukkottai in Tamil Nadu, and compared her *abhinaya* with Muthulakshmi's own rendering of a song (*padam*). When questioned about this, Muthulakshmi conceded that she was teaching something different, but said in defence that it was necessary to adapt to the demands of the public.

Throughout this book I shall be referring to two styles in particular: Bharata Nāṭyam and Oḍissi. Bharata Nāṭyam is the classical dance style of Tamil Nadu and south Karnataka, particularly around Mysore city and Bangalore. Today it is probably the most popular of all dance styles and is performed regularly in major cities all over India.

Bharata Nāṭyam was formerly performed by a caste of female dancers called *devadāsīs* and constituted a normal part of daily ritual in the temples of south India. It was also performed on secular occasions in the courts of the southern states and during festivals. A number of items regularly performed in Bharata Nāṭyam are based on Śaivite mythology and I have used many of these in making comparisons between depictions of Śiva and his attributes in live dance and sculpture.

Oḍissi was originally a more localized style, developing in what is now the state of Orissa. Before it became popular some fifteen years ago, it was performed by *maharis* (female temple dancers) and *gotipuas*[5], pre-pubertal boy dancers who travelled in troupes performing dance dramas throughout Orissa. Many former *gotipuas* now teach the dance. Out of the traditional repertoire of this style, in so far as it has survived, only one or two invocatory prayers and one particular piece (*Batu Nṛtya*) include references to Śiva. The latter piece includes numerous poses reminiscent of those illustrated in sculpture on the Surya temple at Konarak. During the last few years, several other Śaivite items have been choreographed.

In the past, although dancing girls were found all over India, the profession developed to the fullest in the great temple cities of southern India, where the daily ritual surrounding the god came to resemble a royal court. Both kings and god required many servants, and in the case of the temples these became known as *devadāsīs* (literally, female slaves of god). The term included all female servants employed for the upkeep of the temple and service of the deity. Through usage, however, the term *devadāsī* has become almost exclusively associated with temple dancers, and it is from this tradition that the classical dances performed on the stage today originally derive. The tradition has been aided by the survival of a small number of dancers and teachers who grew up and were trained in the traditional manner. In the translations of the early inscriptions and literary references, courtesans, prostitutes, 'public women', 'harlots' and 'temple dancers' have been synonymous, and we shall see that all these interpretations may be correct.

A definition of the term *devadāsī* given in the *1901 Madras Census Report* is probably a fair indication of the attitude of westernized Indians towards the dance: 'Handmaidens of the gods, [they] are dancing girls attached to the Tamil temples, who subsist by dancing and music and the practice of the oldest profession.'[6] Dr Muthulakshmi Reddy speaking in the Madras Legislature at about this time, was also explicit: 'Now the appellation [of *devadāsī*] as every one of us here knows, whatever the original meaning may have been, now stands for a prostitute. None of us in the south who are too familiar with their customs can dispute the fact.'[7] At this time many different regional names were in use for the institution of *devadāsī*. Thurston's *Castes and Tribes of Southern India*,[8] the *1901 Census Report of India*,[9] and the legislative debate for 27 February 1922[10] are only three of many sources that give regional names of *devadāsīs* all over India. From these it becomes clear that *devadāsīs* had both secular and religious functions.

Perhaps the outstanding feature of the system was the formal marriage of the *devadāsī* to the god of the temple to which she was attached. According to all available records, this ceremony was nearly always performed, whether or not the duties as dancer were combined with that of a courtesan and prostitute. The legislative debates of 1922 on the abolition of the *devadāsī* system describe the marriage ceremony of dedication thus: 'Above the age of sixteen, the religious tenets prohibit their enrolment. A girl to be dedicated according to the rules observed from time immemorial must be a virgin... No temple authority would think of dedicating a girl above fourteen.'[11] But in the same debate it was also pointed out that there was no scriptural basis for this tradition.[12]

New applicants to the temple authorities were mainly the daughters of *devadāsīs*. Others were dedicated by parents for religious motives; it was not unknown for parents without children to promise to dedicate their first daughter to the temple.[13] Girls were purchased for this purpose as late as 1912–13 and it is reported that up to Rs 2000 was paid. In other cases girls were kidnapped and introduced to the profession. The collectors of Belgaum, Dharwar, and Bijapur districts reported that a total of 2,623 girls had been 'seduced from their homes for this purpose'.[14] Other temple records speak of women dedicating themselves.[15] Among some castes, such as a sect of weavers (*Kakatias*) from Kancipuram[16] and a caste of musicians from Coimbatore (the *Kaikolan*), it was traditional to make one daughter a *devadāsī*.[17]

As soon as a girl was accepted she would register with the temple authorities and start drawing her pay.[18] The Śucindram temple granted her a house.[19] The marriage to the deity (*tālikeṭṭu*) took place slightly later, on an auspicious day, according to traditional Hindu rites with a sword, drum, dagger, or another *devadāsī* dressed as the husband, representing the groom.[20] Once the symbol of marriage, the *botti*, was tied, the *devadāsī* could never legally marry again,[21] and since the wedding ceremony usually took place at 6, 8, or 11 years of age, the girls were unable later to revert to the life of an ordinary married woman. (Of course, marriage before puberty was common; indeed as the *Madras Census Report* of 1911 states: 'In south India, a girl may marry an arrow, or a tree, perhaps to escape the reproach of attaining puberty unmarried. She may marry an idol, which generally implies that she becomes a prostitute.'[22] It wasn't marriage at an early age, but the fact that the girls had to devote themselves to the temple and to all persons who visited it that prompted government inquiry.) After the marriage ceremony the chief dancing master initiated the *devadāsī* into the art of dancing.[23] He too was supported by the temple.

The children of dancing *devadāsīs* formed the artistic community of singers, dancers, and musicians. It was, and is, through these repositories of an oral tradition that we understand how to perform the gestures and follow the instructions enumerated in the texts, because dance as a living art form can only be maintained through practice and imitation. It would otherwise be difficult, if not impossible, to reconstruct solely from the texts the type of movement found in Indian dance.

Today the dance, in particular the Bharata Nāṭyam style, is no longer restricted to the particular group for whom it was once a vocation, but has largely become an accomplishment for young ladies of reasonably wealthy families. These girls are usually discouraged from adopting the dance as a profession and in most cases their dancing careers are terminated at marriage. The dance was earlier performed in both courts and temples, but when it left the confines of the temple for the stage, much of the religious content was maintained, including such rituals as seeking protection from the eight guardians of the quarters, and offering obeisance to mother earth.

There has always been some ambiguity surrounding the secular and religious components of the dance tradition but the earliest references in the *Ṛg Veda* and the early law texts such as the *Laws of Manu* and the *Arthaśāstra* stress the secular function. Descriptions of the dance by early European travellers, particularly the Portuguese, mention both court and temple performances, often by the same girls, emphasizing the difficulty of dividing the secular from the religious in India.

Early literary references to dance are also ambiguous about the purpose of the dance. The *Ṛg Veda* employs a dancing girl as a metaphor when describing dawn,[24] but no attempt is made to link dance with religious activity, nor is there any indication of the disrepute in which dancers were later held. Although this first reference is from a religious text, it is no more than a poetic metaphor, and lends no support to the idea that Indian dance began as religious ritual.

The secular importance of dance is affirmed very early in the *Arthaśāstra*[25] and the *Laws of Manu*, which list dance as one of the many accomplishments of courtesans. However, while Manu deals harshly with them and advises kings: 'Gamblers, dancers and singers . . . let him instantly banish from his town',[26] his advice seems to have been largely ignored and they were often given a respected place in society on account of their accomplishments. One such example is Ambapali, a courtesan during the time of the Buddha, who was considered one of the treasures of the city of Vaisali.[27] Dr. Short, a medical officer in Tamil Nadu during the nineteenth century, also observed that the *devadāsīs* were, in general, far more educated than married women, and formed the chief magnet of Hindu society, so that a wife considered it honourable for her husband to visit them.[28] These are not isolated examples; the sixteenth-century writer, Domingos Paes, describes the privileged social position of the dancers in the court of Vijayanagar thus: 'These women (are allowed) even to enter the presence of the wives of the king, and they stay with them and eat betel with them, a thing which no other person may do, no matter what his rank may be.'[29] Auboyer writes that dance usually accompanied the toilet of a princess.[30]

The importance of dancers is shown in many of the plays written during the classical period, which often include a dancer as one of the main characters, particularly since a dance recital was considered an essential part of the play.[31] These dramas provide further information about the social position of dancers and courtesans,[32] but they are also important because they describe dance in temples, while the *Arthaśāstra* and *Laws of Manu* restrict their discussion of dance to courtesans. Kālidāsa (5th c.? A.D.) in his *Meghadūta* describes temple dancers during the evening worship of Śiva at the temple of Mahākāla in Ujjain in this way: 'The temple girls' cinctures tinkling with the dance steps, their hands weary with the yak-tail fans.'[33]

The *Purāṇas* acknowledge the role of the temple dancer to be synonymous with that of courtesans and prostitutes, and several *Purāṇas* recommend dedicating girls to temples.[34]

The *Vāmaṇa Purāṇa* indicates the hazards of trying to remain pious while on pilgrimage in the holy city of Banaras: 'Where the vedic accents of great Brahmans mingling with the sounds of the girdles of sportive women, are transformed into sounds of great sanctity.'[35]

Dance was not restricted to Hindu temples; it appears to have been performed in the temples of all the three indigenous faiths of the subcontinent. An inscription dated A.D. 1270 at Gaya records dance in a Buddhist shrine: 'Worship is here (offered) three times a day by means of instrumental music in the highest key (*pañchama gata*)[36] and Rambhā-like (a celestial dancer) Bhāvanīs[37] (dancing girls attached to the temples)...dancing round wonderfully.'[38] Somadeva, the eleventh century Kashmiri writer, in his *Kathāsaritsāgara*, tells the story of Isvaravarman, who went to the Hindu temple at Kanchanapura (not to be confused with Kancipuram in south India) and saw Sundari, a *devadāsī*, dancing there. At the end of the dance he sent a friend there to solicit her, and she bowed and said: 'I am highly favoured.'[39] The eleventh-century Jain reformer, Jinavallabha, in his *Saṅghapaṭṭaka* was concerned about the large numbers of dancing girls distracting monks in the Jain temples of Rajasthan.[40]

Just as dancers formed part of the court of Indra, the celestial king, it became the custom for kings to have certain ceremonial activities performed by dancers, such as holding the royal umbrella, fanning the royal couple with yak-tail fans, and being present at state occasions like royal consecrations.[41] Many of the customs continued and Abbé Dubois, a priest working in south India in the nineteenth century, records that when a king or distinguished visitor made a formal visit to the temple, he should properly be accompanied by a certain number of *devadāsīs*.[42]

In the royal courts the king assumed god-like powers and the same ceremony was accorded to him as to the god in the temple. In fact, temple ritual was modelled on court ritual, and while dancers were important adornments to a court, the royal *devadāsīs* could be transferred to religious duties or vice versa. It is recorded of King Jalauka of Kashmir that: 'A hundred out of his seraglio who had risen to dance [in honour of the god] at the time fixed for dancing and singing he gave out of joy to Jyestharudra [Śiva].'[43]

This practice was not restricted to the Hindus: a twelfth-century inscription records the transfer of a dancing girl from one of the Buddhist 'temples' (stupa or cave) at Salonapura to the harem of a local king.[44]

In Tamil Nadu in the twelfth century, Rajendra Cōḷa ruled from Tanjore; under his orders four hundred temple dancers were brought from nearby temples to be attached to the Bṛhadīśvara temple of Tanjore. The inscription that records the event is important as it names all the temples, both Śaiva and Vaiṣṇava, that had dancers attached to them.[45] Undoubtedly Rajaraja's centralizing of the dance tradition around his temple and court made Tanjore a focus of culture in south India and it was this early patronage of the Cōḷa kings that led to the standardization of the Bharata Nāṭyam form of dance as it is known today.[46]

Without patronage, either by rulers or temples, the professional dancing class *devadāsīs*, which included teachers (*naṭṭuvans*) and musicians, could not have developed the art to the high standard that it achieved. From the time of the *Cilappatikāram* (fourth to sixth century A.D.)[47] in which Madavi, the dancer and courtesan, receives a garland from the king after her first public performance,[48] there are numerous references to dancers receiving royal recognition for their excellence. The Cōḷa king Vira Rajendra 1 (1063–70)[49] 'ordered some land at Tiruvorriyur to be reclaimed and the produce used for services in the temples including . . . maintenance . . . of dancing masters and girls.'[50] Kings seem to have been generous in their support, and records of their generosity can be found in inscriptions. Aditya II (10th c. A.D.)[51] gave land for a dance performance during Tai Pūśam, and three dances to take place beginning the day after the festival of Vaigāśi Tiruvādirai, for which the dancer was to receive some paddy.[52] Rajendra Cōḷa Deva (1012–44)[53] and Vikrama Cōḷa (1118–35)[54] also gave some land to support the cost of dance recitals at certain festivals.[55]

Some kings did not limit their encouragement to professional dancers but encouraged members of their own family, of high birth, to learn the dance. This was probably to give them grace in deportment and they performed for their own entertainment as well as that of other courtiers. Perhaps the standards of the dance altered when it was thus performed by amateurs. One of the Portuguese travellers who visited Vijayanagar records that the royal ladies of Vijayanagar were taught the dance.[56] Two other Portuguese travellers, Nuñiz and Pietro della Valle (1623–4), record seeing dance. The stick dance described by della Valle, which he saw being performed at Ikkeri near Dharwar,[57] is illustrated on many of the sculptural friezes at Vijayanagar, particularly at the base of the king's throne.[58] (This stick dance is still performed today in south India.)[59] Krishna Deva Raya, Acutya's son, had a dance hall in his palace[60] which no longer exists.

The *devadāsīs* were economically independent; they were not part of a man's household, and many of them became wealthy in their own right. It was not unusual for these women to own houses and lands, which were often given to them by the temple. However, while the *devadāsīs* were rewarded by land, food and privileges for their services, they too contributed generously to religious institutions. This practice was in accordance with the *Kāmasūtra*, which stated that money gained by courtesans should be used 'to construct temples, tanks, gradens . . . and other religious gifts'.[61]

Queens were not the only women who enjoyed economic independence. A Canarese inscription on the Mahakutesvara temple of Mahakut near Badami, during the time of the Calukyan king, Vijayaditya (A.D. 696–743) records: 'Hail! The heart's darling of Vijayāditya-Satyāśraya, . . . the harlot Vinopati . . . having at this very place bestowed the entire gift of a *hiranyagarbha* and having set up its silver umbrella . . . may he who destroys this grant be guilty of the five sins.'[62] A Telegu inscription dated A.D. 1053 mentions Kasadi Suramadevi, a concubine of the Kōta chief, Ketarāja, giving some money to keep a lamp burning in the temple of Ramesvara of Velpunuru.[63] During the time of Rajaraja III (A.D. 1298–1322)[64] a dancer constructed high walls inside the temple of Vellaimurti Alvar, for which she and her descendants received certain temple privileges, such as waving yak-tail fans before the deity in processions and a daily gift of rice.[65] The duty of waving yak-tail fans must have been a coveted one because the granting of this honour to *devadāsīs* was recorded in several inscriptions. The performance of this ritual is recorded as early as Kalidasa's *Meghadūta* in his description of worship at the Mahakala temple at Ujjain.[66] A dancing girl holding a yak-tail is a common sculptural motif throughout India.[67] One of the stories associated with the temple of Madurai 'refers to a *Dāsī*, or dancing girl named Hema of Śrī Pushpavana Tirupuvana who was an ardent devotee of Śiva . . . The idol which bears the dancing girl's kiss is placed in the temple of Madurai.'[68]

In addition to dancers being used in both temple and court, they were also an important part of festival celebrations, which were ostensibly religious, but also secular in function.[69] King Jogaladeva of Nadol in Rajasthan was insistent that all festivals be celebrated with dance. In A.D. 1147 at the temple of Laksmansavamin at Nadol, in Rajasthan, he decreed: 'The order is that when a festival of any particular god commences, the courtesans attached to the temple of other gods must also put on their ornaments and best garments . . . to celebrate it by instrumental music, dancing and singing and so forth.'[70]

Jogaladeva then states that anyone who tries to abolish dance at festivals will be dealt with by the ruler, and the inscription ends with a curse on any prince who does not maintain this practice.

According to European travellers, dance remained popular at festivals.[71] Fray Sebastien Manrique in the seventeenth century wrote of the car festival in Bengal during Durgā pūjā: 'This strumpet [Durgā] is carried along in a highly ornamental triumphal car with a large band of dancing girls, who besides dancing, gain a livelihood by prostitution. These dancers go in front, dancing and playing various musical instruments and singing festal songs.'[72]

Abbé Dubois in the nineteenth century also saw dancing during the car festival at Tirupati and he recorded that at this time Lord Venkaṭeśvara through his Brahmins selected new dancing girls from the crowd that came to celebrate his festival.[73] During the car festival the *basavis* (a group of women from the Konkan area, not dedicated temple dancers yet dedicated to the temple through the same type of marriage ceremony), could, according to custom, change their mates.[74]

Abbé Dubois saw that the harvest festival of south India, Pongal, was celebrated with dance,[75] a feature that is being revived today. As late as 1910 *devadāsīs* were displayed in the floating festival at Dohnavur, Tinnevelly district: 'On the dais of the barge, in the place of honour, nearest the idols, stood three women and a child.'[76]

The marriage festival has usually been a time for dance.[77] Kālidāsa in his *Kumārasambhava* records it at the wedding of Śiva.[78] Dance as part of the festivities at Hindu weddings during British rule in India has been portrayed in woodcuts and painting, and after its decline in popularity during early and post independence days, this practice is being re-introduced.[79]

There were not always religious reasons for kings encouraging temple dancing; Alberuni, writing in the eleventh century observed that in the temples of north India 'No Brahmin priest would suffer in their idol temples the women who sing and dance and play. The kings make them an attraction for their cities... By the revenue they derive from the business both as fines, and taxes, they want to recover the expenses which the treasury has spent on the army.'[80] Tavernier writing in the seventeenth century observed that for the same reasons the king of Golconda encouraged public women, because they promoted heavy consumption of alcoholic drinks, over which the government had a monopoly. While the number of dancers seemed to have declined in the nineteeth century from the 20,000 described, with possible exaggeration, by Tavernier at Golconda,[81] they were still very important and their numbers considerable. Those attached to temples were listed in the temple records; the Sucindram temple in Kerala recorded seventy-two[82] in 1819. Certainly temple dancers were very much in evidence in south India when Dr Buchanan and Abbé Dubois wrote in the nineteenth century. Abbé Dubois stated that every temple of importance had eight to twelve *devadāsīs* attached to it,[83] while Buchanan observed that the two large temples of Kancipuram had about one hundred dancing girls attached to them.[84] The local government reports of 1912 stated that *devadāsīs* existed in Assam, Madras, and the Jagannatha temple in Orissa, but not in Bengal, Sind, United Provinces or Gujarat.[85] Even in 1932, by which time dancing in temples had been declared unlawful in British India, P. G. Sundaresa reported at the annual conference of the Madras Music Academy: 'We all know that today, even in Pandaripur, daily worship is being done in the temple accompanied by *nāṭyam* (dance); similarly in Srirangam, during the ten days preceding the Mukkotai Ekadasi day, worship is generally accompanied by *nāṭyam*.'[86]

Paying royal honours to a deity made up the chief part of the duties performed in the temple by the *devadāsīs*.[87] These depended on the region: those from Kerala swept the temple, while in Tamil Nadu sweeping was considered beneath their status. Most accounts list holding lights in front of the idol as one of the main duties. Abbé Dubois describes this ceremony and records that it took place twice a day,[88] as do the accounts in the Sucindram[89] and Ramesvaram temples.[90] Dance as part of the ritual in divine worship was listed as fifteenth in the sixteen acts of honour and homage paid to the deities.[91] An inscription dating to the reign of Kulottunga III (1205–18)[92] records 'the assignment of a fixed period in the day for every dancing girl to perform her services by turn to the temple'.[93]

In the thirteenth century, Marco Polo reported that in the temple of Tanjore[94] dancers performed while food was placed in front of the idol.[95] Paes in the sixteenth century also observes this at Vijayanagar: 'The brahmins feed the idol every day, and when he eats, women dance before him.'[96]

Abbé Dubois told of singing and dancing twice a day in temples of importance.[97] This practice continued into the twentieth century as the *Travancore State Manual* of 1906 records Tamil *devadāsīs* dancing and singing before the deity.[98] The ritual of dance was recorded with some accuracy at the Ramesvaram temple in 1920:

> At 4.30 or 5 am [the puja begins] . . . the dancing girls [muraikari] officiating for the day, with rudrāksha beads in place of jewels, dressed up as a Brahmani and her hair uncombed . . . open up all the doors up to the mahāmaṇḍapa. Later the god is taken in procession preceded by musicians and attendant dancing girl . . . the dancing girl at the door repeats a tevara ujal or verse in honour of Śiva.[99]

In the former state of Travancore there were two classes of *devadāsīs*: one group performing as part of daily worship, another being reserved for performances during festivals.[100] However, this delegation of duties was not always followed, particularly in Tamil temples. The Sucindram temple in Travancore, with many customs linked with Tamil Nadu, records a division of duties that first began with those *devadāsīs* who were the best dancers being selected to dance in front of the principal deity; but later this duty became a hereditary one.[101] Perhaps the outstanding difference between Tamil *devadāsīs* and those from Travancore is that those from the Tamil areas would dance at secular functions, particularly at private gatherings, while the Travancore *devadāsīs* would not.[102] This gave the latter a much higher social position,[103] but it is generally accepted from the living tradition that survives today, that the Tamil *devadāsīs* achieved a higher degree of proficiency in dance than those from other areas.

We saw earlier that by the twentieth century dance had been banned in the temples of British India, but no such official restriction existed in princely states such as Pudukkotai until they became part of India with independence in 1947. Two *devadāsīs*, Muthulakshmi and Saraswati, told me in 1973 that they had been actively attached to the temples and courts of Pudukkottai and had shared responsibility both for performing at festivals, as well as daily worship in temples. It is from such *devadāsīs* that the tradition has been passed on.

Many dancers continued to perform well into old age. Kamakshi (1810–90) one of the dancers attached to the court of Tanjore, danced until she was seventy-five,[104] and Balasaraswati, one of Kamakshi's descendants, is now well into her fifties, still performing, and acclaimed in the seventies as the greatest living exponent of Bharata Nāṭyam. Not all dancers continued to dance into later life, however, and a retirement ceremony is mentioned in the records of the Sucindram temple for *devadāsīs* who had reached an advanced age or become chronically ill.[105] Facing the assembly of priests (as at her enrolment), the *devadāsī* unhooked her earrings and presented a gift of money. The earrings were returned to her, but she no longer wore them. Thurston also records the removal of jewellery on retirement, and a reduction in salary.[106] Dubois writes that at the Tirupati temple the women could be 'divorced' by the God if the Brahmins no longer found them pleasing.[107] However, with this one exception, the *devadāsī* system does seem to have afforded some security, since after dedication the girls were given a house, food and sometimes land.[108]

Amy Carmichael, a missionary working in south India, wrote that the temple not only provided bare subsistence but that after being dedicated, the girl's funeral expenses were assured.[109] The *Gazetteer* of the Godavari district records in 1907 that the funeral pyre of every girl of the dancing caste (*sani*) should be lit with fire brought from the temple.[110] The same source noted that a similar practice was to be found in the Srirangam temple near Tiruchirapalli.

It should be clear from these scattered references that dance and dancers have always formed an integral part of Indian culture, and to differentiate between the strictly religious or secular functions is impossible. For *devadāsīs* too, dance was a fundamental condition of existence; something so important that it brooked no questioning. This is poetically illustrated by a story from the *Rājataraṅgini*:

Once a king (Lalitāditya Muktapida) (A.D. 699-736)[111] took out himself alone an untrained horse into a waste land in order to break it in. There, far away from men, he saw one maid of lovely form singing and another dancing. He observed they came to the same spot several days later so he came up and questioned them. They told him: 'We are dancing girls belonging to a temple... By the directions of our mothers, who got their living here, we perform at this spot dancing ... This custom handed down by tradition has become fixed in our family. Its reason we cannot know nor can anyone else.

Later the king has the spot excavated and an old temple is discovered.[112]

CHAPTER II

The Formalization of Indian Dance

We have seen that dance was considered important enough to become the *dharma* of certain castes.[1] No doubt one of the factors which contributed to dance forms becoming regulated and systematized was that it was considered a craft to be studied and mastered.

The rules of the dance were formalized in the *Nāṭya Śāstra* (*NŚ*), 4th–5th c. A.D.?[2] which recorded a complex system which had presumably been in existence earlier as an oral tradition. The *NŚ*, a text on dramaturgy of which dance forms only a part, also includes discussions on the aesthetics of music, rhetoric, grammar, and other allied subjects. Although many of the traditional masters do not have first-hand knowledge of this text, or indeed of any others, their knowledge, usually acquired by rote, encompasses the practical application of the theory of the texts. The *NŚ* is still the final authority for all the regional variations of the existing numerous classical schools of dance.

Dance according to the *NŚ* has two aspects: *nāṭya* and *nṛtta*. The original meaning of *nāṭya* was mime, not acting in the modern sense, but it was often used in classical Sanskrit theatre[3] which continues to the present in the form of Kudiyattam, performed in Kerala. *Nāṭya* also survives today in folk theatre[4] and in the various dance traditions as one of the characteristic features of Indian dance. Its other component, *nṛtta*, pure dance or aesthetic movement, would be considered dance in the western sense. The *Abhinayadarpaṇa* (*AD*), a later text on dramaturgy and dance (13th c.?),[5] mentions a third form of dance, *nṛtya*.[6] The *NŚ*, however, does not use the term *nṛtya*, but only divides the dance into *nṛtta* and *nāṭya*, a practice also followed by other early dance texts. For our purpose it is sufficient to know that both mime (*nāṭya* and *nṛtya*) and pure dance (*nṛtta*) are important elements in Indian classical dance. Throughout this work the word dance will be used in the Indian sense, and hence include both *nṛtta* and *nāṭya*/*nṛtya*.

According to the *Viṣṇudharmottara Purāṇa* (*VDP*)[7] both dance and its static representation in sculpture should convey *rasa*.[8] *Rasa* pervades all the classical Indian arts (except temple building or architecture)[9] and results from the awakening of latent psychological states (*sthāyī-bhāvas*) in the beholder by the use of appropriate formalized imagery. While the methods and particular imagery comply strictly with convention, they can assume infinitely subtle variations in the hands of the skilled artist.[10] The expression of certain *bhāvas* by a dancer was considered an important way to worship God, and was one of the reasons dance became a necessary and integral part of religious worship. 'When a man worships God, the best method adopted by him for showing his feeling is by *bhāvam* [*bhāva*] i.e. word of mouth or facial expression or the movement of the limbs.'[11] The dancer employed all three: she sang the religious songs (*padams*),[12] externalized her feelings with facial expressions (*abhinaya*),[13] and danced using stylized movements.[14] The *VDP* states that the aesthetic effect of sculpture should be achieved in a similar way.[15] In this case, the position of the limbs, the attributes, and the facial expression are only three of the many elements used to evoke an emotional response in the beholder.

The expression of *bhāva* through dance, as an important means of worshipping god and as an acceptable expression of the ecstatic joy of divine communion, was common in Tamil Nadu in the period prior to the construction of existing temples (before the seventh century).[16] For Appar, one of the early Śaiva *bhaktas* of south India (Nāyaṉmārs), 'the whole world seemed to dance and sing and play' (*viḷaiyāṭu*).[17] While the songs of the Nāyaṉmārs provide an insight into the mystical and devotional life of south India (from the sixth to the twelfth centuries)[18] for our purposes the *bhakta* songs[19] are more useful sources of information concerning the early iconography of Śiva since they describe the god's appearance.[20] This is particularly valuable because only a limited number of Naṭarāja figures survive from the earlier part of this period.[21] Many of the specific occasions in mythology on which Śiva danced were well known[22] before that time, but the attributes of Śiva and their various interpretations, though mentioned in earlier texts, are more fully explored in *bhakta* poetry. The *bhakta* tradition continues to flourish in south India up to the present day,[23] and although the *devadāsīs* whose duty it was to express *bhāva* to the deity through dance no longer perform in temples, the deities' attributes are still enacted in the *nāṭya/nṛtya* portions of the dance as it is performed today on the stage.[24] It is from these songs in praise of Śiva that the illustrations for Śiva's attributes in dance given in Chapters V and VI, are drawn.

The *VDP* reiterates much of the material found in the *NŚ*, but adds (what appears to be taken for granted in the *NŚ*), that the ideal conditions necessary for producing good sculpture would include mastery of dance.[25] The close connection between the dance movements suggested in sculpture, and the successive poses which cumulatively constitute the movement in Indian classical dance as it is performed today, suggest that the sculptors were familiar with the practice of dance. Today these sculptures provide documentation and a basis for comparison of the dance as it was in the past, with its present form. With the recent trend to create new compositions, however, many sculptural poses are being re-introduced into the dance, the choreographers claiming to be discovering and recreating an older more authentic form than has previously been seen. This has to be borne in mind in any comparison of present-day dance with sculpture.

The simplest combinations of dance movement discussed in the *NŚ*, Chapter IV, are *karaṇas*, of which one hundred and eight are described. The *NŚ* defines a *karaṇa* as the combined [movement of] hands and feet in dance[26]. The translation by Bose, however, adds the proviso that for a movement to constitute a *karaṇa* it must be aesthetically pleasing.[27] Although the *NŚ* contains the earliest descriptions of *karaṇas*, they are also mentioned in the later texts, which either follow the *NŚ*, in some cases elaborating upon its directions, or offer independent interpretation.[28] The *VDP* mentions 108 *karaṇas* but names only ninety,[29] and does not discuss them. Their sequence differs slightly from that in the *NŚ*. Sivaramamurti believes that the earlier sculptural representations of *karaṇas* that still remain are from the eighth century,[30] during the time of Dantivarman Pallava.[31] These have been identified as stray sculptures of women dancing, incorporated in the reconstructed temple at Bahur near Pondicherry, but unfortunately very few remain and Sivaramamurti does not include any photographs.[32] He gives illustrations of dancing figures from the ninth century temple of Prambanam, in Java,[33] as the earliest carvings of *karaṇas* that are still *in situ*.

The earliest carvings still *in situ* in south India are inside the main shrine of the Brhadisvara temple at Tanjore (A.D. 985–1014).[34] Here only eighty-one of the *karaṇas* are represented,[35] but it is believed that they are in the order given in the *NŚ*[36] and can be identified despite the fact that they were neither numbered nor accompanied by *ślokas* from the *NŚ*. Here it is important to remember that other texts known at this time such as the *VDP*, listed some of the *karaṇas* in a different order from the *NŚ*.

The use of *karaṇas* as sculptural motifs remained popular in later centuries. The dance figures carved on the west (twelfth century),[37] east (twelfth to thirteenth century)[38] and south (thirteenth century)[39] *gopuras* of Cidambaram (Plate 2) were no doubt imitated in the sculpture which was carved slightly late on the *gopuras* of the Sarangapani temple at Kumbakonam (1350),[40] the Vrddhagirisvara temple at Vrddhacalam[41] (Plate 3) and the Arunacalesvara temple at Tiruvannamalai[42] (Plate 4). The northern *gopura* of the sixteenth century at Cidambaram also contains carvings of *karaṇas*.[43]

The representations of *karaṇas* on the Naṭarāja temple at Cidambaram are the most important, not only because all four *gopuras* are decorated with representations of dancers, but because there are inscriptions from the *NŚ* carved above the plaques on the east and west *gopuras*.[44] Vatsyayan contends that these *karaṇas* and also the dancing figures carved on the frieze of the Devi shrine (fourteenth century)[45], demonstrate that the sculptors were familiar with the *NŚ*, and *Śilpa*

Plate 2

Gopura Carvings, Naṭarāja Temple, Cidambaram (TN)

Plate 3

Gopura Carvings, Vrddhagirisvara Temple, Vrddhacalam (TN)

Plate 4

Gopura carvings, Arunācalesvara Temple, Tiruvannamalai (TN)

Śāstras, as well as the actual dance.[46]

At Cidambaram most of the dancers represented are women: these are not restricted to the *gopuras* but are found in the hall of one thousand pillars, the Devī shrine (Sivakāmi/Amman court), and Subramaṇya shrine, and on all fifty-six of the eight-foot pillars in the dance hall. Fergusson remarked that the latter were 'most delicately carved';[47] unfortunately they have been disfigured by whitewash.

Raghavan and Sivaramamurti interpret the Tanjore *karaṇa* panels as depicting Śiva with four hands, two of which 'dance' while the other two hold Śiva's various emblems such as the *ḍamaru*, fire, snake, etc.[48] Only two of them, numbers sixty-one and seventy-two,[49] are represented as being executed by women dancers, not by the male Śiva figure, possibly because they depict movements ritually associated with females.

Sivaramamurti identifies the dancing figures in the *karaṇa* panels at Kumbakonam as Viṣṇu in the form of Kṛṣṇa[50] (Plate 120) with occasional depictions of Siva. Raghavan writes that there is no basis for assuming that these sculptures depict Viṣṇu, since the Sarangapani temple and the nearby Somesvara Śiva shrine originally formed a single temple.[51] An inscription on a pillar of the shrine which was probably part of the Sarangapani temple, is from the time of the Cōḷa king, Rājarāja I,[52] but the actual Sarangapani temple and the *karaṇa* figures on the *gopuras* are dated to the mid-fourteenth century.[53] In several depictions a *gaṇa* is present, a feature associated with Śiva, not Viṣṇu. In fact, Sivaramamurti acknowledges that certain *karaṇas* such as the *lalāṭa tilaka* can only show Śiva since the *karaṇa* is drawn from a particular incident in Śaivite mythology.[54] The names and numbers of the *karaṇas* shown at Kumbakonam are covered with whitewash which can be scraped away. However, the name does not always accord with the *karaṇa* depicted, because when the *gopura* underwent reconstruction the *karaṇas* were not replaced in the same order given in the *NŚ*.[55] There are ninety-five *karaṇas*, some on the outside, others on the inside wall of the *gopura*.[56]

The Vrddhacalam and Tiruvannamalai sculptures of *karaṇas* are in the Vijayanagar style, and are carved on the inside of the *gopuras*[57] (Plates 3, 4). Those at Vrddhacalam are of particular interest because there are two figures included in each panel, suggesting the beginning and end of a movement. *Karaṇas* are not depicted on the *gopuras* of the south Indian temples,[58] but dancers form a major part of the decorative motifs on most temples throughout India, providing extensive illustrations of the possibilities of movement and variety of dance poses.

The practical application of dance sculpture was recorded by Paes, the Portuguese traveller who visited Vijayanagar during the reign of Krishna Deva Raya (1509–29).[59] His observations of the dancing figures, probably *karaṇas*, in the dance hall, make it clear that these carvings were not merely decorative but used as a source of instruction by contemporary dancers:

> The designs of these panels show the position at the ends of dances in such a way that on each panel there is a dancer in the proper position at the end of the dance; this is to teach the women, so that if they forget the position in which they have to remain when the dance is done, they may look at the panels when it is the end of the dance. By that way they keep in mind what they have to do.[60]

The figures described by Paes have unfortunately not survived; only the decorative friezes around the base of the king's throne now remain.[61]

Let us briefly compare the *karaṇas* which appear in sculpture in Tamil Nadu, with the body positions used at present in Bharata Nāṭyam, the classical dance style from the same southern region, and Oḍissi from Orissa state from the eastern region. These two dance traditions share certain characteristics with sculptures of dance poses: knees bent, shoulders kept at right angles to the audience, and similar hand and foot positions. There are, however, differences in the treatment of the torso, both in contrasting dance styles and in the representations of *karaṇas* in sculpture from different periods. In the early *karaṇa* representations on the Brhadīsvara temple at Tanjore (eleventh century)[62] the torso is usually shown with one side raised (*udvāhita*) and the hip deflected to one side of the mid-line, normally the opposite side to that on which the torso is raised. This position is known as *tribhaṅga*, and is one of the characteristic body positions for Oḍissi[63] (Plate 8d).

Plate 5

A comparison of the poses for Naṭarāja in the Bharata Nāṭyam and Oḍissi dance traditions and those typical of sculptures from the same region.

Plate 5a

Plate 5b

Plate 5c

Plate 5a

Representations of the *lalita karaṇa* at Cidambaram (*NŚ*, Gos, Plate VI, *karaṇa* 33). The right arm is in *Gajahasta/karihasta* (Plate 9h) and the left hand is in *alapadma* (Plate 9a), by the ear.

Plate 5b

Depicting an elephant in the Oḍissi dance style. The right arm is in *gajahasta/karihasta* symbolizing the trunk, with the hand in *mṛgaśīrṣa hasta* (Plate 9s), indicating tusks. The left hand in *dola*, is held by the ear to indicate the flapping ear of the elephant (Plate 9g). The position of the arms is the reverse of the directions given in the *NŚ* for the *lalita karaṇa* but the same as shown in the sculpture of the *karaṇa* at Cidambaram. The foot positions are the same as for the *karihasta karaṇa* (Plate 5c).

Plate 5c

Representation of the *karihasta karaṇa* (*NŚ*, Gos, Plate XV, *karaṇa* 87) at Cidambaram. The feet are in the position specified by the *NŚ* (*NŚ*, 4.148). Although this sculpture comes from the southern region, the position is almost identical with that seen in the Oḍissi dance style from the eastern region (Plate 5b).

The main body position for the Bharata Nāṭyam dance style, with the torso perpendicular to the ground (*sama*) (Plate 8b) is in contrast to the deflected hip or the *tribhaṅga* body position as seen in Oḍissi (Plate 8d), and it is this treatment of the torso which constitutes perhaps the most outstanding difference between the two dance styles. In the Oḍissi dance tradition the torso can move independently of the lower body, and in static positions, the independent movement of the torso, to one side, forces the hip on the opposite side to protrude. In contrast, the torso in the Bharata Nāṭyam style should not move independently of the hips.

The way in which the torso is held is also a major difference between earlier and later sculptures of *karaṇas*. The *karaṇas* depicted on the temples at Cidambaram, Tiruvannamalai and Vrddhacalam are closer to the Bharata Nāṭyam body position, any deflection of the hips being less marked than in the Tanjore *karaṇas*, or in other early illustrations of dancers. Through a comparison of the *karaṇas* depicted on temples (Plates 5c, 119) and other sculptures of dancing figures with contemporary Indian classical dance styles, it is evident that in the treatment of the torso the current Bharata Nāṭyam style differs considerably from that depicted by the earlier *karaṇas*. It is possible to see in the change of body position from the earlier to the later *karaṇas*, the gradual development of the angular, twentieth-century Bharata Nāṭyam style.

The dances performed in Orissa, geographically isolated from the south, appear to have maintained a form closer to that illustrated by the earliest *karaṇas*. Dancing girls carved on the Surya temple at Konarak (Plates 6, 122, 123) are contemporary with the early *gopuras* at Cidambaram (Plates 2, 5c, 119) but illustrate the same *tribhaṅga* position which is still current in Oḍissi dance, and is observed in the majority of the early sculptures of dance all over India. The fact that Oḍissi, as performed today, preserves the same shape exhibited by early sculptures, indicates that this style may have undergone less alteration than Bharata Nāṭyam with the course of time.

Archaeological and historical evidence suggests that Indian dances have maintained their principal characteristics over the last two millennia. Their persistence probably owes much to the authority of the early texts such as the *NŚ* and the *AD* which laid down clear instructions for the conduct of the dance. The foundations of Indian dance movements rest on the descriptions of the *karaṇas* in these texts, and illustrations of these in sculpture occur on a number of major temples dating back to at least the eleventh century A.D.

Plate 6 **Dance Hall, Surya Temple, Konarak, Orissa**

CHAPTER III

A Classification of Naṭarāja Images

Ananda Coomaraswamy in 1912 was the first art historian to write about Śiva's dance, and the first to attempt a classification of the iconography of Naṭarāja. Coomaraswamy recognized that many different forms of dance were ascribed to Śiva, but he limited his divisions to three: evening, *tāṇḍava* and *nādānta*—all based on mythological events.[1]

Gopinath Rao's slightly later classification (1916), in his *Elements of Hindu Iconography*, has been more influential and is generally accepted without question. He was the first to use a system based upon five of the 108 *karaṇas* described in the *NŚ: lalita, catura, kaṭisama, talasaṃsphotita,* and *lalāṭa tilaka*.[2] *Karaṇas* are the simplest combinations of dance movements described in the *NŚ*, combining movements of hands and feet.[3] Rao makes only passing references to their pictorial representation on the *gopuras* of the Naṭarāja temple at Cidambaram, where the appropriate verses from the *NŚ* accompany each image on the east and west *gopuras*.[4] This is unfortunate since these sculptures are intended to illustrate the description of one of the phases of the various movements which make up the *karaṇas*. Although K. Vatsyayan assigns the names of *karaṇas* to dancing figures, she also recognizes the limitations of such an approach: 'The *karaṇas* of Bharata are cadences of movement and the sculptor can only depict a moment in a cadence and not the entire cadence. It is important to point that out because scholars have misinterpreted the term *karaṇa* by considering it a static pose.'[5]

Unfortunately, however, when Rao assigns an image to a *karaṇa* category, apart from not recognizing this limitation, he does not analyse each image systematically, and his justification for assigning an image to a particular *karaṇa* is based on frequently incomplete, and occasionally incorrect evidence. For instance, if the foot requirements for a *karaṇa* are satisfied, Rao often omits discussing the hand requirements, or *vice versa*. In fact Rao himself concedes that his assignment of *karaṇas* to pieces of sculpture is somewhat inaccurate because of inadequate knowledge of the traditions and practical application embodied in the *NŚ*.[6] Despite this, other writers have followed his terminology, usually without reservation.[7]

Another classification of dance poses used by G. Rao, Pattabiramin, and V. Raghavan, was based on those in the *āgamas,* south Indian Śaivite texts which include descriptions of iconography.[8] The origin of the twenty-eight *āgamas* is obscure; according to tradition they come from the nine manifestations of Rudra.[9] Winternitz assigns their date to the seventh–eighth[10] centuries A.D. but Rao believes some may have been composed as late as the twelfth century A.D.[11] Raghavan writes that these *āgamas* (along with the *sthalamāhātmyas*, religious texts pertaining to south Indian Śaivite shrines) were based on the *NŚ*, and this accounts for the overlap of terminology used for the sculpture.[12] Like the *NŚ* the *āgamas* list 108 dance modes of Śiva, but the names sometimes differ.[13] Rao limits his *āgamic* divisions of images to the southern *nṛttamūrtis*.[14] Pattabiramin and Raghavan, however, include illustrations from all over India in their discussions.[15]

Alice Boner has classified Orissan Naṭarājas (Naṭāmbaras) into three categories on the basis of descriptions in the Śilpa Prakāśa, but these divisions are highly imprecise, mainly because the term '*kuṭṭitam*' which she employs refers to an up and down movement of the feet.[16] Classification of the iconography of Naṭarāja by other authors mainly follows the criteria discussed above. Problems with classifications based on the *karaṇas* stem largely from the fact that they were intended originally as instructions for movement rather than static poses, and hence there is room for wide differences in interpretation.

The *āgamas*, which might be expected to provide the most useful basis for classification of sculpture, describe only southern images and hence are of limited value in a system embracing images of Śiva from all over India. The mythological context of dance though occasionally clear, provides a very broad criterion by which to classify images and is too liable to subjective interpretation.

In reviewing the various classifications of Naṭarāja it became apparent to me that for my purpose I required a system which was solidly based on static positions and that none of the existing classifications were suitable. Another problem with previous classifications is that very few writers have acknowledged their sources for descriptive iconographic terms. Moreover, since their nomenclature may be chosen from various sources such as *āgamic* texts, the *Śilpa Śāstras*, the *NŚ*, or even from philosophic interpretations placed on the position of the different parts of the body, confusion is almost inevitable. Table 1 illustrates that the same image may be classified differently by different writers and sometimes even assigned different names by the same writer.

In view of the confusion already present in the literature I felt it necessary to present my own classification, viewing it strictly from the point of view of a dancer.

Starting from first principles, it is evident that as Naṭarāja is the embodiment of dance (*NŚ, AD*)[17], we should look to his main sculptural representation for the basis for such a classification. The positions of the feet have been chosen as the main criteria for this classification because they are fundamental in determining the pose adopted; once the feet have assumed a certain position, the weight must be adjusted accordingly. While the body position may vary slightly within each type of foot position, the foot position according to this classification can be unequivocally identified. Images of Naṭarāja can be divided on this basis into five types (Table 2). The images fall into two broad categories: in one, some part of both feet, or one foot and one knee, are in contact with the ground, and both knees are bent; in the others only one foot touches the ground, and both knees are bent, the other leg being either bent and slightly raised or raised with the foot higher than the head. Illustrations and definitions of foot positions given in the *NŚ*, *AD*, and *VDP*, are presented in Plates 7a–7f.

In all types the shoulders are parallel with the wall of the temple behind them. To allow this the torso is often twisted, or raised on one side. For types A, B and C the knee of the leg(s) in contact with the ground is bent unless indicated with an asterisk (*). Some of the foot positions portrayed in sculpture are anatomically impossible and these are indicated thus: (x).

Plates 7a–7f identify the foot positions and Plates 8a–8t demonstrate the range of variation possible within the five main types. The terminology used is taken from the *NŚ, AD*, and *VDP*. The strong visual evidence that the iconography of sculpture and the repertoire of dance are closely related, makes the use of these texts a logical one.

According to my classification, the feet are divided into five types (A–E), but from Table 3 it is clear that Rao provides for only three: A, B, and D. Another weakness is that Type A.III TAg is classified under both *catura* and *kaṭisama*. Possibly the most serious limitation is that the examples for *catura* fall into two different categories (Types A and B). My own classification has the advantage of distinguishing more accurately the wide range of poses used in the depiction of Naṭarāja and other dancing images, and allows very little latitude for differences in interpretation. With the Type A category, the exact placement of the feet, whether turned outwards in *tryaśra* or pointing straight ahead in *sama*, may sometimes be difficult to distinguish. In addition, particularly where the stone is weathered, it is hard to tell whether it is the tip of the toe touching the ground (*agratalasañcara*) or the ball of the foot (*kuñcita*). As all these poses fall within Type A.III, however, it affects the resulting classification only slightly. It is not possible to make meaningful comparisons between the dance poses exhibited in different areas and from different periods, without some uniform and unequivocal classification.

In describing individual pieces, I have employed terminology from the texts used for the feet, to describe the positions of hands and arms. The *Abhinayadarpaṇa* is preferred except where it does not include an appropriate term. Other authors have also used terminology from these texts but because of differences in the definitions given for particular hand positions in different texts, there is danger of confusion where sources are not ack-

Table 1. *Summary of synonymy among the names of dance poses according to various texts*

Karaṇa classification in NŚ	*TL*	*NŚ GOS*	*NŚ Cal*	*VDP*	*Agamic text*	*Agamic name of same pose*	*Mode acc. to G. Rao*	*Alternative name of same pose*	*Classification*
bhujangāñcita	40	40	40	40	*Aṃśumādbhed-āgama*	*bhujangalalita*	1		Type C-I
						bhujangatrāsita	7		
					uttarakāmikāgama	*bhujangatrāsita*			
					karaṇāgama	*sabhāpati*		*ānandatāṇḍava*	
					mayamata	*bhujangatrāsita*		*nādānta*	
						bhujangalalita		*sadānṛtta*	
					mayamata	*sandhyātāṇḍava*		*āḍavallān*	
					silpasangraha			*sadātāṇḍava*	
					no specific *āgama*	*bhujanga-naṭana*		evening dance	
					" "	*ānandatāṇḍava*		*sabhāpati*	
					no text given	*umātāṇḍava*		*gaurītāṇḍava*	
						gauritāṇḍava			
						kalikatāṇḍava			
					Śilparatna	*tripuratāṇḍava*	5,6		
					no text given	*samhāratāṇḍava*	7		
*lalāṭatilaka**	50	50	50	47	no text given	*ūrdhvatāṇḍava*	5	*kālitāṇḍava*	
						kalikatāṇḍava	6	according to the *Vataranya Mahatmya Samhāratāṇḍava*	Type D
						candaṭāṇḍava			
*talasamsphotita**	69	69	69	not in *VDP*					
urdhvajanu	25	25	24	24	*Śivaparākrama*	*bhujangalalita*			
*catura**	39	39	39	39		*sandhyātāṇḍava*			
					no specific *āgama*	*bhujangatrāsita*			
					Śilparatna	mode 9			
					no text given	mode 9			
					no text given	*bhujangatrāsita*		*Kaligatāṇḍayam* (sic)	
*kaṭisama**	19	19	19	19			6		Type A
*lalita**	33	33	33	33			6		
alīdha sthana*				*sthana* in *VDP* only					

* =Rao's *karaṇa* classification.
Sources:
Banerjea, J. N., *The Development of Hindu Iconography,* pp. 472–5; Barrett, D., *Early Cola Architecture and Sculpture,* pp. 99, 101, 110–13; Boner, A., *Principles of Composition in Hindu Sculpture;* Coomaraswamy, A., *The Dance of Shiva,* pp. 81–95; Dass, R. K., *Temples of Tamilnad,* p. 190; Harle, J. C., *Temple Gateways in South India,* Plates 131, 132, 133, p. 100; Lippe, A., 'Some South Indian Icons', *Artibus Asiae,* Vol. XXXVII3, 1975, pp. 169–208; Pattabiramin, P. Z., *Trouvailles de Nedoungādou*, pp. 25–71, and all Plates; Rao, G., *Elements of Hindu Iconography,* Vol. II. Part I. pp. 223–270; Sivaramamurti, C., *Naṭarāja in Art, Thought and Literature*; Srinivasan, P. R., 'The Naṭarāja Concept in Tamil Nad Art', *Roopa Lekha,* Vol. XXVII, No. 1, Summer, 1956, pp. 24–35; Srinivasan, P. R., 'The Naṭarāja Theme in Cōḷa and Subsequent Period' (sic). *Roop Lekha*, Vol. XXVII, No. 2, Winter, 1956, pp. 4–11; Srinivasan, P. R., Bronzes of South India, 1963, *Bulletin of the Madras Government Museum,* No. 8, New Series; Sastri, Krishna, H., *South Indian Images of Gods and Goddesses,* pp. 77–89.

Table 2. *A general classification of sculptures depicted in dance poses, based on the main positions of the feet exhibited by images of dancing Śiva.*

Type A. Some portion of both feet in contact with the ground. All the illustrations have both knees bent (*kṣipta*) unless otherwise indicated by an asterisk (*). Type A is divided into five poses and these are illustrated in Plates 8a–8o.

Type B. One knee bent and raised so that the foot is clear of the ground. The other leg is also bent normally (Plate 8p).

Type C. One leg raised and lifted across the body and the foot extended. The other leg is normally bent. Type C is divided into two poses, given in Plates 8q–8r.

Type D. One foot raised and lifted to the level of the head or above. The supporting leg may be bent or straight (Plate 8s).

Type E. Kneeling on one knee with the lower part of that leg raised behind. The other foot is flat on the ground (Plate 8t).

In all types the shoulders are parallel with the wall of the temple behind them. To allow this the torso is often twisted, or raised on one side. For Types A, B, and C the knee of the leg(s) in contact with the ground is bent unless indicated with an asterisk(*). Some of the foot positions portrayed in sculpture are anatomically impossible and these are indicated thus (x).

Table 3. *A comparison of images illustrated by Rao using his classification and the classification proposed here*

Table 1 clarifies the diversity of terms previously employed by other writers. As Rao's classification is the most widely used and he provides illustrations of his classification, I refer to his illustrations in presenting the argument in favour of my own classification. To eliminate further confusion over interpretation, only those of the *karaṇa* categories that are illustrated are referred to.

Name of the karaṇa	*Rao's only illustration in* Elements of Hindu Iconography, *Vol. II, Part I*	*My classification*
Lalāṭa tilaka	Plate LXIV, figs, 1 & 2	Type D
	Plate LXV, figs, 1 & 2	Type D
Talasaṃsphoṭita	Plate LXVIII	Type B
	Plate LXIX	Type B
Catura	Plate LXVII	Type B
	Plate LXVI, figs. 1 & 2	Type A. III TAg
Kaṭisama	Plate LXII	Type A. III TAg
Lalita	Plate LXIII	Type A TKu

nowledged. To clarify the situation these alternative names are presented in Plates 9a–9jj, alongside illustrations of the different hand positions. The term 'main arms' is used to describe the foremost pair of arms in images possessing more than one pair.

The technical term for hand positions is *mudrā*, or *hasta*, while for a position of the whole arm, usually only the word *hasta* is employed. J. N. Banerjea states that a *hasta* means the whole arm with a hand in a particular pose such as *gajahasta* and *daṇḍahasta*, but the two terms have come to be used interchangeably.[18] The *AD* and *NŚ* call the hand signs *hasta*. The *VDP* uses both *mudrā* and *hasta*, but while it reserves *mudrā* for those hand positions that have a secret or mystic meaning, it uses the term *nṛtta hasta mudrā* for the hand poses used in dancing. Many of the *hastas* in the *NŚ* are included in the *mudrā* section of the *VDP*.[19] *Mudrās* form an important topic in Tantric texts.[20] R. K. Poduval states that *mudrās* in works of art may be compared with *nṛtta hasta mudrās* in that they are only decorative.[21] Grunwedel has noted that in Buddhist art, certain hand postures attached themselves to particular legends and the position of the hands in the chief figure becomes an indication of the legend.[22]

Dance masters use both the terms *hasta* and *mudrā*. These *hastas* are used in dance as decorative positions in the *nṛtta* portions or as a language of gesture in the *nāṭya*/*nṛtya* portions. While some hand signs are restricted to one category it is more common for the same hand sign to be used in both the *nṛtta* and *nāṭya* sections. The hand signs are further sub-divided into single and double hand gestures.

Definitions of terminology for foot positions in the *Nāṭya Śāstra* (*NŚ*), *Abhinayadarpaṇa* (*AD*) and *Viṣṇudharmottara Purāṇa* (*VDP*)

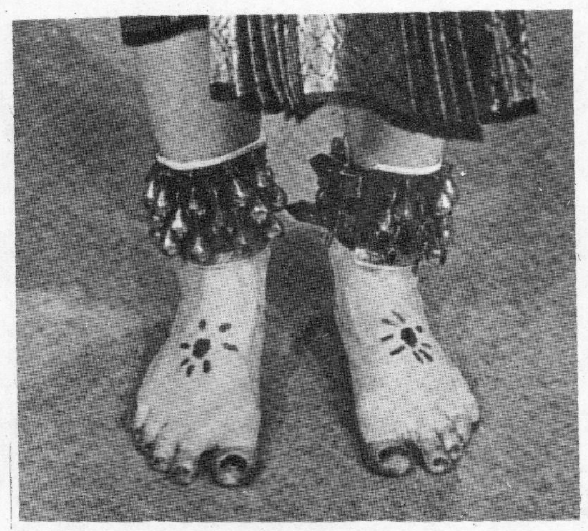

Plate 7a
Feet flat (Type 1)

Sama (S). The foot is flat and points straight ahead.

Sama: (natural) feet placed on an even ground. It relates to representing a natural position.' (*NŚ* X. 41–50)

'Two feet are in a natural position on the ground with even placing.' (*VDP*)

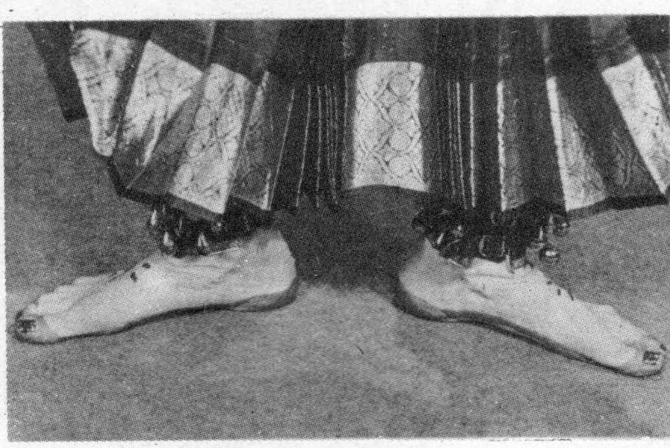

Plate 7b
Feet flat (Type 2)

Tryaśra (T). The foot is turned outwards. This position is not included in the Calcutta edition of the *NŚ*, but is in the GOS.

'The dancer rests her feet in *sama* with the heels inward and the big toes stretched out.' (*NŚ* IX. 270–2)

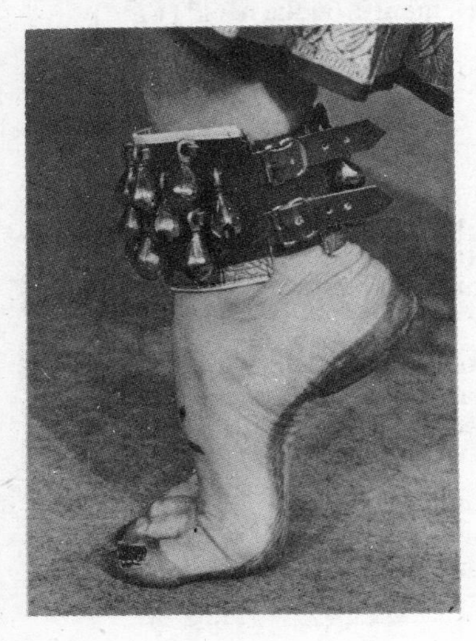

Plate 7c
Heel raised (Type 1)

Kuñcita (K). The foot is bent and the weight rests on the ball of the foot.

'The heels thrown up, toes all bent down and the middle of the feet bent too.' (*NŚ* X. 41–50)

'The middle part of the foot is contracted.' (*VDP*)

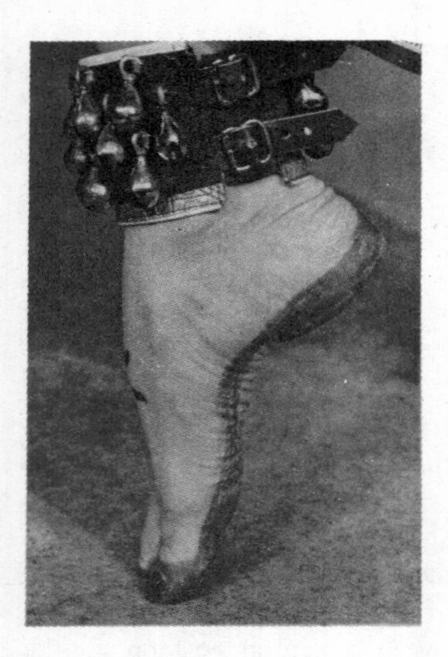

Plate 7d
Heel raised (Type 2)

Agratalasañcara (Ag). The heel is lifted and the weight rests on the tip of the big toe.

'The heel thrown up, the big toe put forward and the other toes bent.' (*NŚ* X. 41–50)

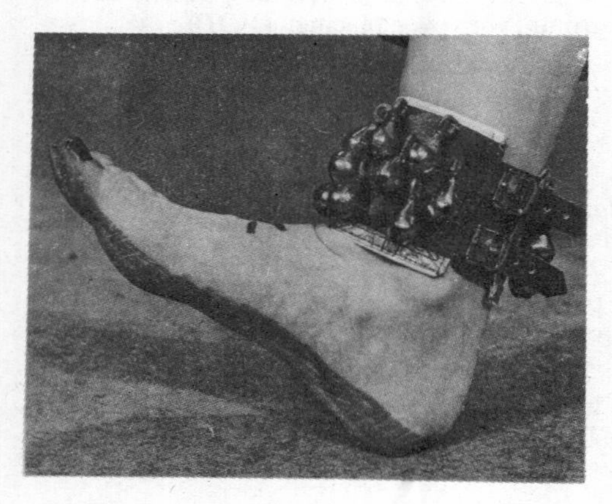

Plate 7e
Toe raised (Type 1)

Añcita (Añ). The heel is on the ground and the rest of the foot is raised.

'The heel on the ground, the forepart of the foot raised and all the toes spread.' (*NŚ* X. 41–50)

'The forepart of the foot is raised. This means that the movement is on the heel.' (*VDP*)

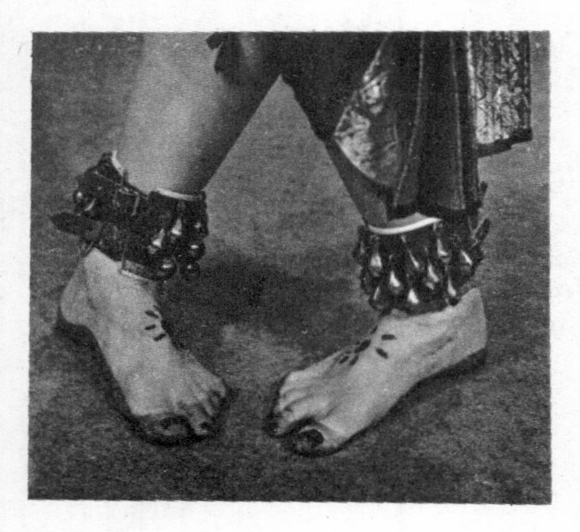

Plate 7f
Feet crossed (Type 2)

Svastika (Sv). The feet are crossed. Only one illustration is given here, but in Plates 8n–o several variations incorporating the *sama*, *kuñcita*, *tryaśra* and *agratalasañcara* foot positions will be given.

'The right foot should be put across the left and the right hand should be put across the left hand; this would be the *svastika* posture.' (*AD* 267–71)

Svastika is not listed in the *NŚ* or *VDP* as a *maṇḍala* or standing posture, but appears throughout these texts when the movement of crossing or releasing the feet is required.

Illustrations of the five types of foot positions described in Table 2 and different poses possible within Types A and C

Type A.1

Plate 8a

Sama, sama (SS). Both feet are in *sama*. If both knees are bent this is anatomically impossible, except if the weight is placed on the outside of the feet. Such a position is assumed in the Kathakali dance style.

Plate 8b

Tryaśra, tryaśra (TT). Both feet are in *tryaśra*. With the heels almost touching, this is the traditional starting position for the Bharata Nāṭyam dance style and is called *ardhamaṇḍalī*.

Plate 8c

If the heels are about nine inches apart this position is called *chowk* in the Oḍissi dance style.

Plate 8d

Tryaśra, tryaśra (TT, Tribh). Both feet are in *tryaśra*, but one (either) is slightly in front of the other. This foot position usually accompanies the *tribhaṅga* body position, one of the main positions in the Oḍissi dance style.

Note the similarity between the body position used in Oḍissi dance and the illustration of the *kaṭisama karaṇa* at Cidambaram (Plate 119). The similarity between Oḍissi and early sculptural representations of dance from other regions was discussed in Chapter II.

Plate 8e

The sculpture depicted in Plate 8e is discussed in Chapter VII, Plate 119.

Type A.II

Plate 8f

Kuñcita, kuñcita (KK). Both feet in the *kuñcita* position.

Plate 8g

Agratalasañcara, kuñcita (AgK). Both feet are turned outwards, one in *agratalasañcara* and the other in *kuñcita*.

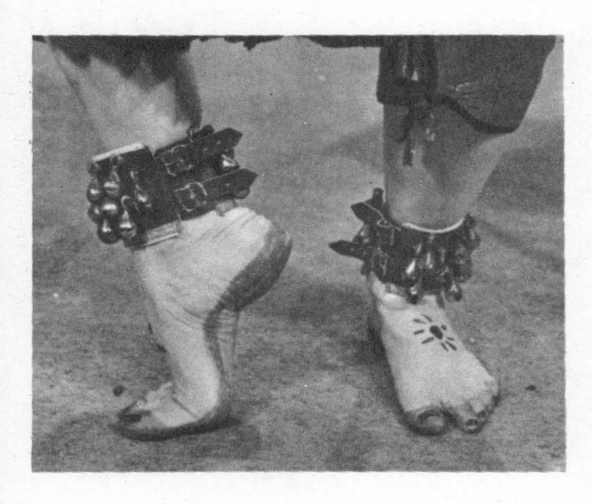

Type A.III

Plate 8h

Sama, kuñcita (SK). One foot is in *sama*, the other in *kuñcita*.

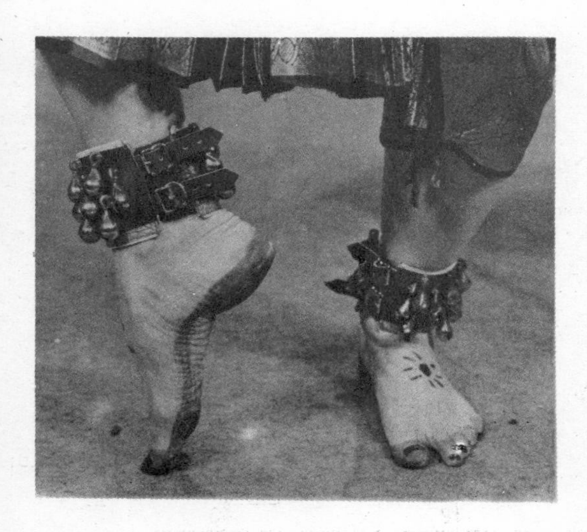

Plate 8i

Sama, agratalasañcara (SAg). One foot is in *sama* the other in *agratalasañcara*.

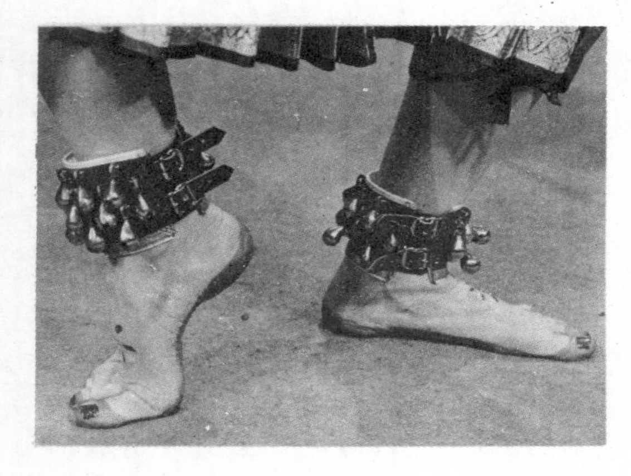

Plate 8j

Tryaśra, *kuñcita* (TK). One foot is in *tryaśara*, the other in *kuñcita*.

Plate 8k

Tryaśra, *agratalasañcara* (TAg). One foot is in *tryaśra*, the other in *agratalasañcara*.

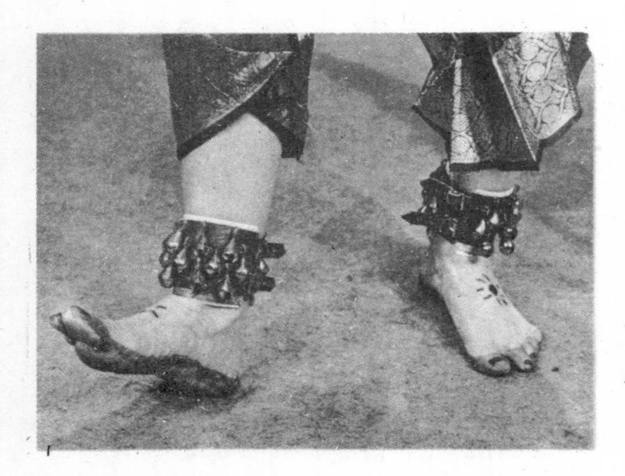

Type A.IV

Plate 8l

Sama, *añcita* (SAñ). One foot is in *sama*, the other in *añcita*.

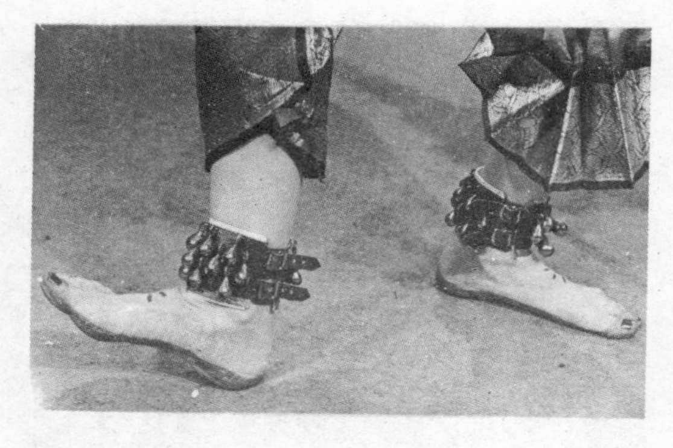

Plate 8m

Tryaśra, *añcita* (TAn). One foot is in *tryaśra*, the other in *añcita*.

Type A.V
Plate 8n

Svastika (Sv). The feet are crossed in various combinations of *kuñcita*, *agratalasañcara*, *sama* or *tryaśra*.

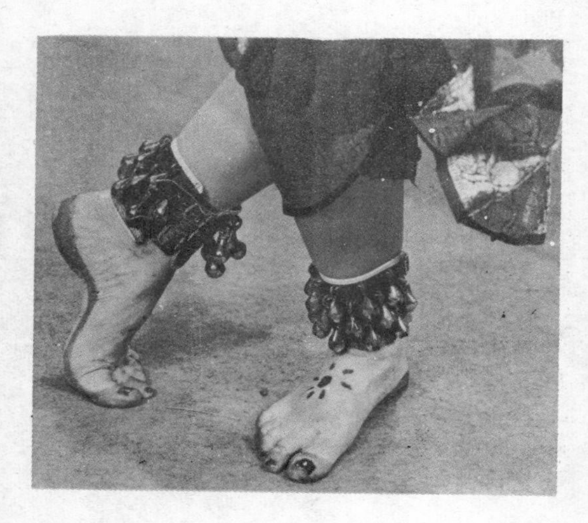

Type A.V
Plate 8o

Svastika (Sv). The feet are crossed in various combinations of *kuñcita*, *agratalasañcara*, *sama* or *tryaśra*.

Plate 8p

Plate 8q

Plate 8r

Type B

Plate 8p

One foot is flat in either *tryaśra* or *sama* and the other knee is bent and raised so that the foot is clear of the ground.

Type C.I

Plate 8q

One leg is lifted across the body and the foot extended. The other leg is bent, with the foot usually in *tryaśra*.

Type C.II

Plate 8r

One leg is bent and lifted so that the knee points in the same direction as the supporting foot.

Type D

Plate 8s

One foot is raised and lifted to the level of the head or above. The supporting leg may be either straight or bent (x). This image is discussed in Chapter IV, Plate 35.

Type E

Plate 8t

Kneeling on one knee with the lower part of that leg raised behind. The other foot is flat on the ground.

Comparison of names used for *hastas* / *mudrās* in the *Abhinayadarpaṇa* (*AD*), *Abhinaya Candrikā* (*AC*), *Nāṭya Śāstra* (*NŚ*), *Viṣṇudharmottara Purāṇa* (*VDP*) and Iconography (Ic)

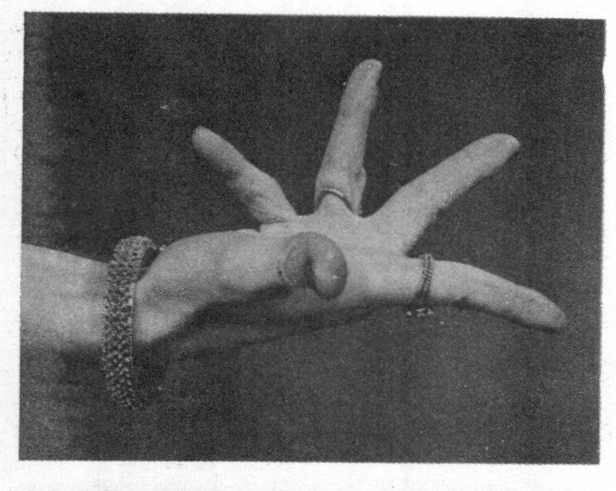

Plate 9a

NŚ. Alapallava Añcita	*NŚ.* IX. 90–1, p. 181; IV. 100, p. 54
AD. Alapadma	*AD.* 146–9, p. 56
VDP. Kolapadma	*VDP.* p. 76
Ic. *Vismaya*	Rao, G., I. I., p. 16 Banerjea, J. N., p. 260

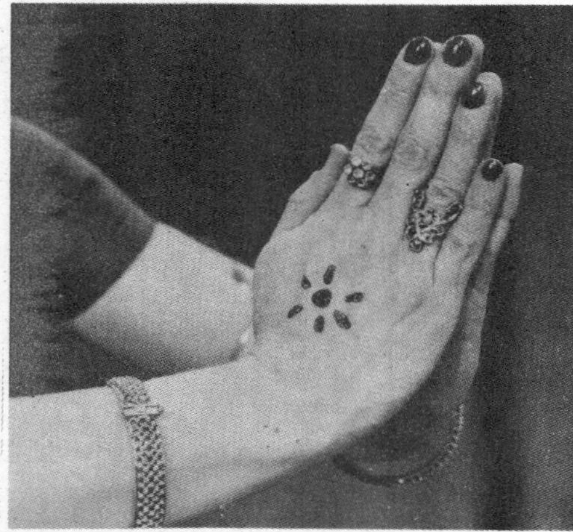

Plate 9b

NŚ. Añjali	*NŚ.* IX. 127–8, p. 185
AD. Añjali	*AD.* 176–7, p. 59
VDP. Añjali	*VDP.* p. 73
Ic. *Añjali*	Rao, G. I. I., p. 16
Ic. *Vandanī, namaskāra*	Banerjea, J. N. p. 251

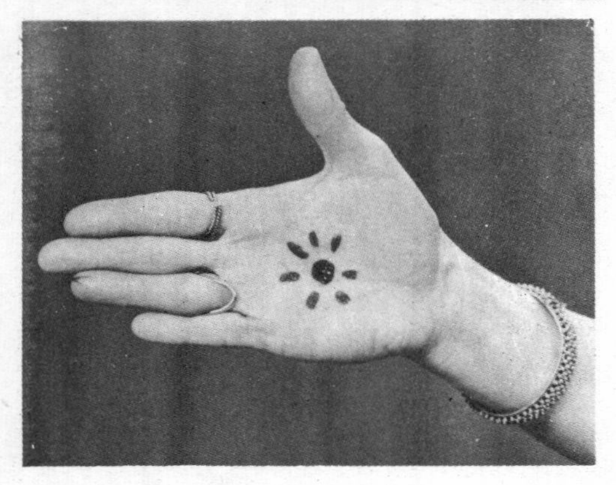

Plate 9c

NŚ. Ardhacandra	*NŚ.* IX. 42–4, p. 176
AD. Ardhacandra	*AD.* 111–13, p. 54
Ic. *Abhaya*	Rao, G. I. I., p. 14
Ic. *Varada*	,, ,,

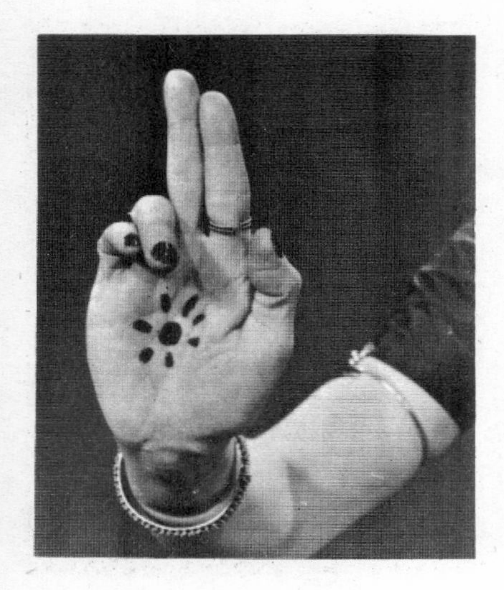

Plate 9d

NŚ. —	
AD. Ardhapatāka	*AD.* 103–4, p. 53
Ic. *Vismaya*	Banerjea, J. N., p.260
Ic. *Vitarka*	,, ,,

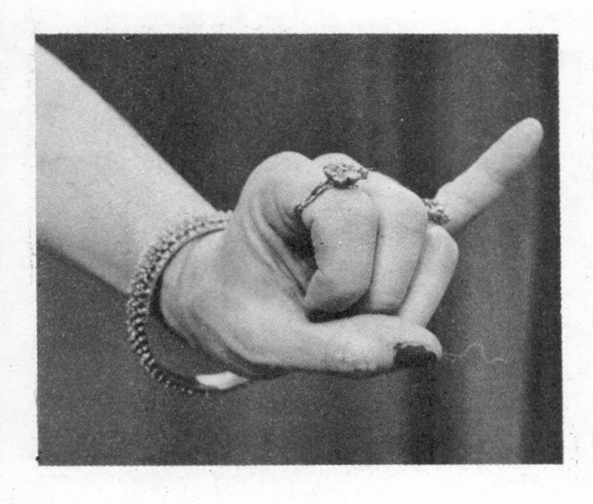

Plate 9e

AC. Bāṇa	Patnaik, D. N., 1971 (no page)

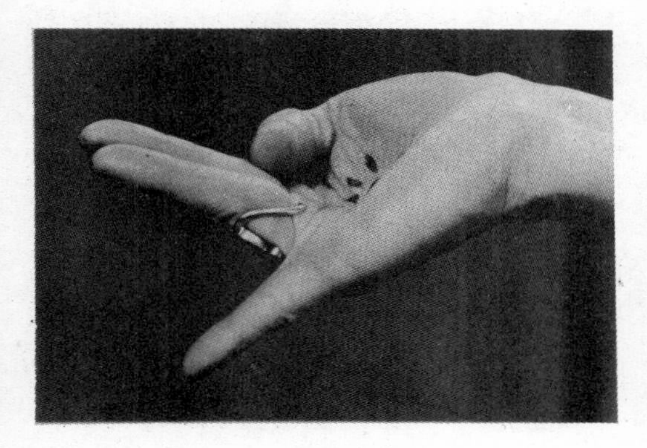

Plate 9f

NŚ. Catura	*NŚ.* IX. 92–9. pp. 181–2
AD. Catura	*AD.* 149–52, p. 57
VDP. Catura	*VDP.* p. 72

Plate 9g

NŚ. Dolā	*NŚ*. IX. 141–2. pp. 186–7
AD Dolā	*AD*. 181–2, p. 60 'When the *patāka* hands are placed on the thigh.' Today, however, it is taught as specified in the *NŚ*.
VDP. Dolā	*VDP*. p. 74

Plate 9h

Ic. *Gajahasta* *Daṇḍahasta* *Karihasta* *Latāhasta*	Rao, G., I. I., p. 191 Banerjea, J. N., p. 258 Ragavan, V., *NR*, p. 95
NŚ. Karihasta	*NŚ*. IX. 187, p. 191

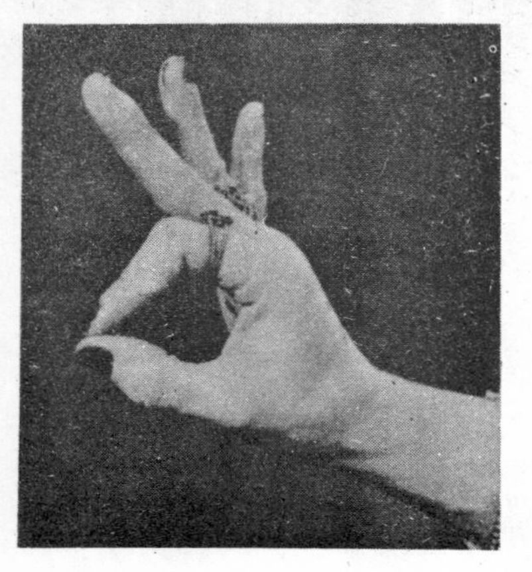

Plate 9i

NŚ. Haṃsāsya	*NŚ*. IX. 103–4. pp. 182–3 The position described is not used in Bharata Nāṭyam or Oḍissi.
AD. Haṃsāsya	*AD*. 154–7, p. 57
Ic. *Cin-mudrā* *Vyākhyāna-mudrā* *Sandarśana-mudrā*	Rao, G., I. I., pp. 16–17. Banerjea, J. N., p. 255

Plate 9j

NŚ. Haṃsapakṣa	*NŚ.* IX.105–8, p. 183
AD. Haṃsapakṣa	*AD.* 157–9, p. 57
VDP. Haṃsapakṣa	*VDP.* p. 72

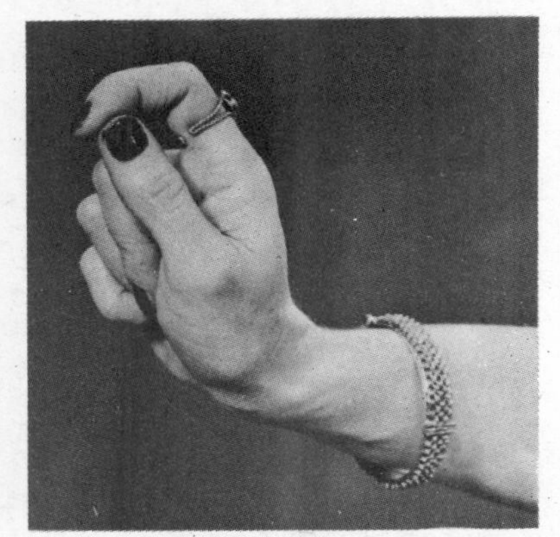

Plate 9k

NŚ. Kapittha	NŚ IX.58–9, p. 178
AD. Kapittha	*AD.* 121–4, p. 55.
VDP. Kapittha	*VDP.* p. 71

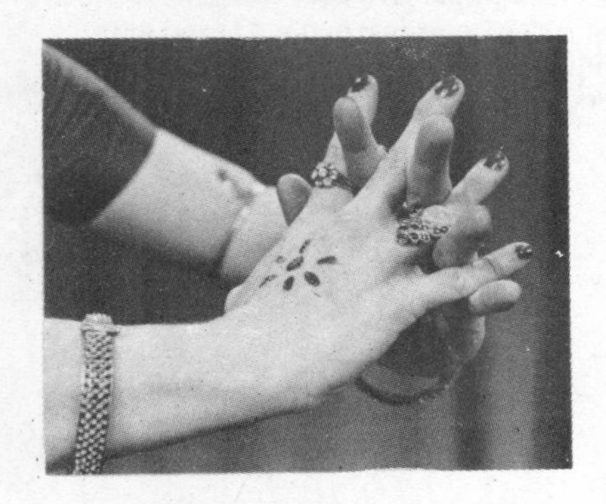

Plate 9l

NŚ. Karkaṭa	*NŚ.* IX.132–3, p. 185
AD. Karkaṭa	AD. 178–80, p. 60
VDP. Karkaṭa	*VDP.* p. 73

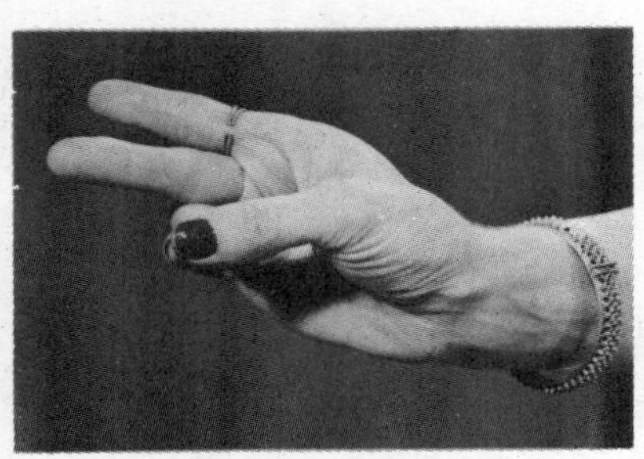

Plate 9m

NŚ. Kartarimukha	*NŚ.* IX.38–42, p. 176
AD. Kartarimukha	*AD.*105–7, p. 53
VDP. Kartarimukha	*VDP.* p. 70
IC. Kartarimukha	*ICDLA* p. 81

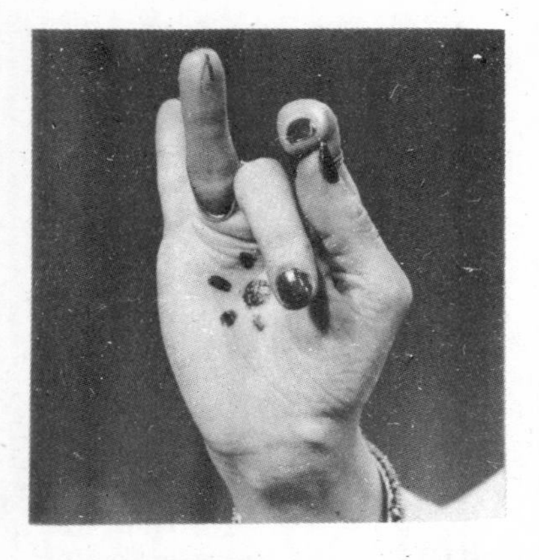

Plate 9n

NŚ. Kaṭakāmukha	*NŚ*.IX.60–3, p. 178
AD. Kaṭakāmukha	The hand sign described under this name in the *AD* is different (see below)
VDP. Kaṭakā-mukha	*VDP*. p. 70. Rao, G., I. I. p. 15
Ic. *Siṃhakarṇa*	Banerjea, J. N. p. 258

Plate 9o

AD. Kaṭakāmukha AD 124–7, p. 55
The hand sign described in the *AD* and the one taught by traditional Bharata Nāṭyam teachers differ. The latter is shown here.

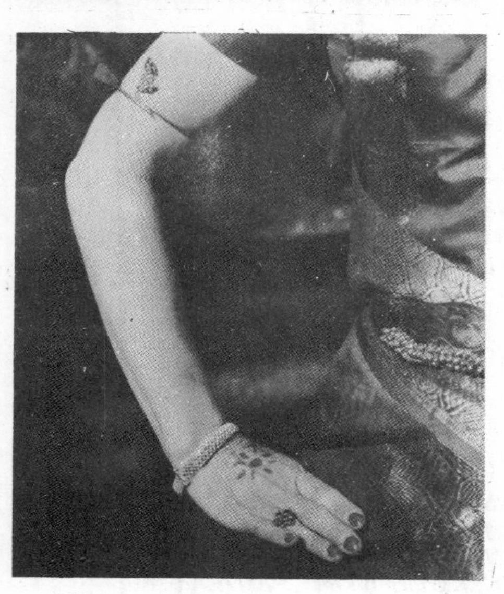

Plate 9p

Ic. *Kaṭyavalam-bita*	Rao, G., I. I., p. 16
Kaṭisaṃsthita	Banerjea, J. N., p. 256.

Plate 9q (See also *Plate 9g*)

NŚ. Latā	*NŚ*. IX.186, p. 191
VDP. Latā	*VDP*. p. 75

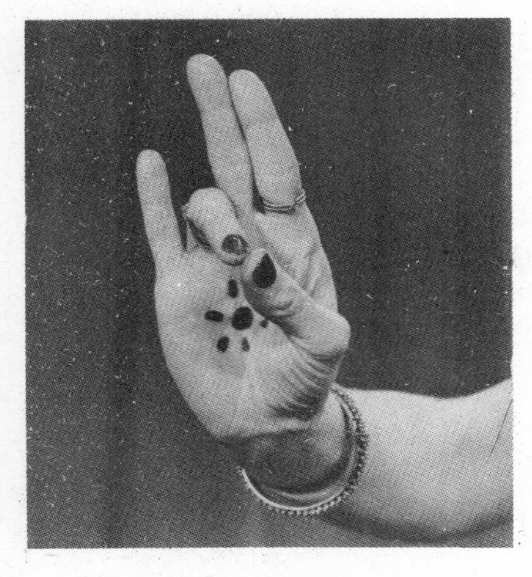

Plate 9r

NŚ. —	
AD. Mayūra	*AD*. 108–10, pp. 5–54

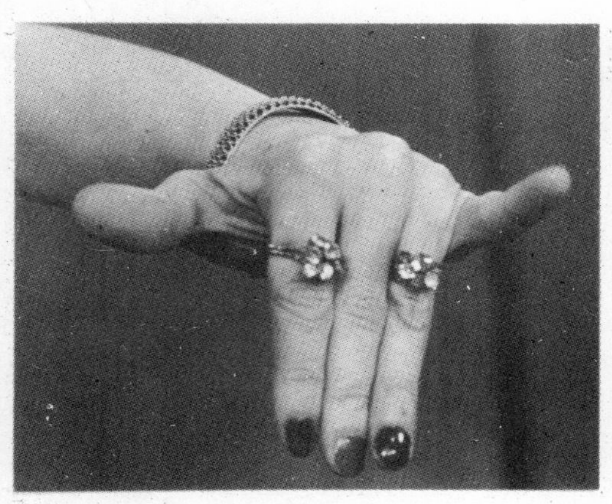

Plate 9s

NŚ. MLMṛgaśīrṣa	*NŚ*. IX.86–7, p. 181
AD. ML Mṛgaśīrṣa	*AD*. 139–42, p. 56
VDP. ML Mṛgaśīrṣa	*VDP*. p. 71

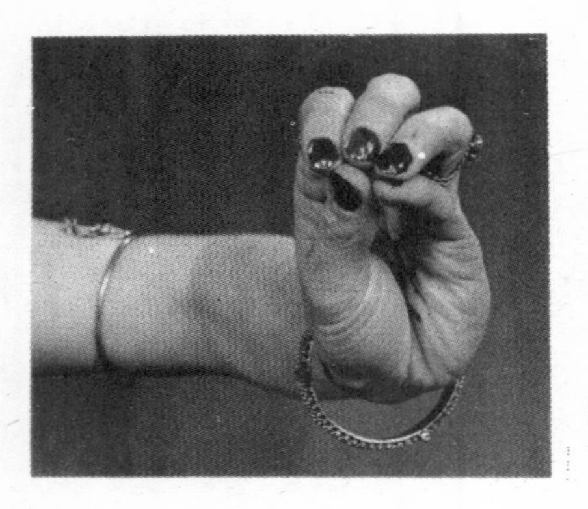

Plate 9t

NŚ. Mukula	*NŚ*. IX.116–18, p. 184
AD. Mukula	*AD*. 161–3, p. 58
VDP. Mukula	*VDP*. p. 73

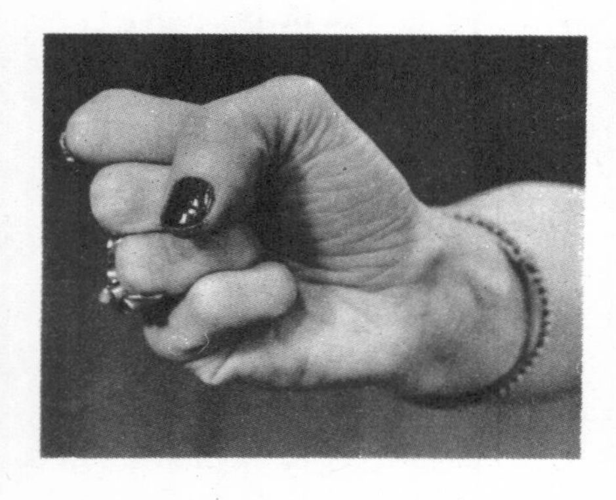

Plate 9u

NŚ Muṣṭi	*NŚ*. IX.54, 56
AD. Muṣṭi	*AD*. 161–3, p. 58
VDP. Muṣṭi	*VDP*. p. 71

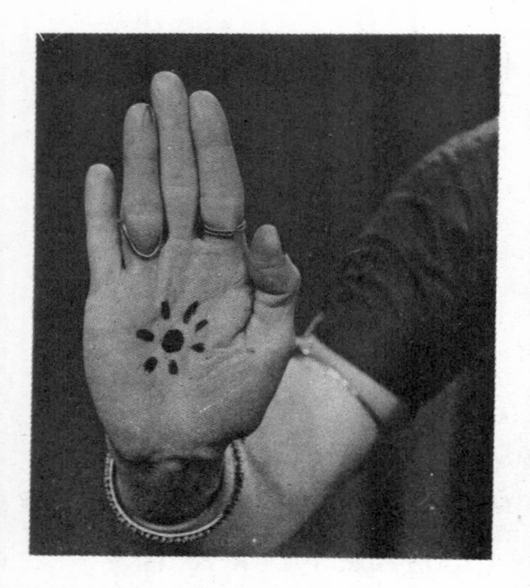

Plate 9v

NŚ. Patāka	*NŚ* IX.17–25, p. 174
AD. ,,	*AD* 88–99, p. 52–3
VDP. ,,	*VDP*. p. 70
Ic. *Abhaya*	Rao, G., I. I., p. 14
Varada	
Dhyānamudrā	
Yogamudrā	Banerjea, J. N., p. 254
Samādhimudrā	
Bhūmisparśa-mudrā	Ibid., p. 262
Bhūmisparśa-mudrā	

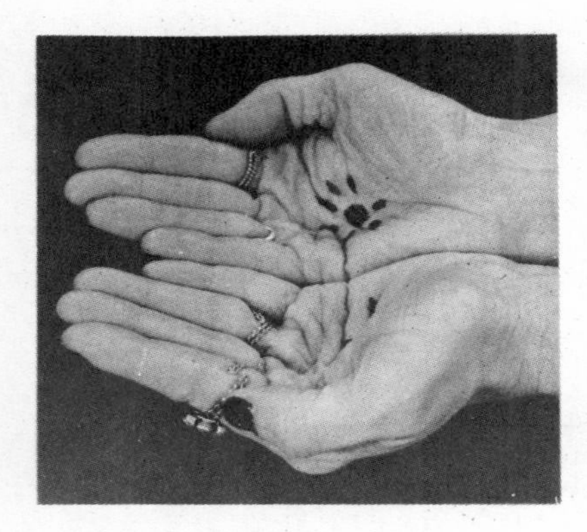

Plate 9w

NŚ. Puṣpapuṭa	*NŚ,* IX. 143–5, p. 187
AD. Puṣpapuṭa	*AD.* 182–4, p. 60
VDP. Puṣpapuṭa	*VDP.* p. 74

Plate 9x

NŚ. Recita *NŚ.* IX. 181, p. 190

As given in the *NŚ*, this *hasta* describes a movement, but this is not used in dance or identifiable in iconography. Sivaramamurti uses the term to describe an arm raised obliquely upwards, as illustrated (*SRM.* pp. 203. 227).

Plate 9y

NŚ. Saṃdaṃśa	*NŚ.* IX. 109–15, pp. 183–4
VDP. Saṃdaṃśa	*VDP.* p. 72
Ic. *Siṃhakarṇa*	Rao, G., I. I., p. 15
Cinmudrā	ŚRM. p. 180
Vyākhyāna-mudrā	

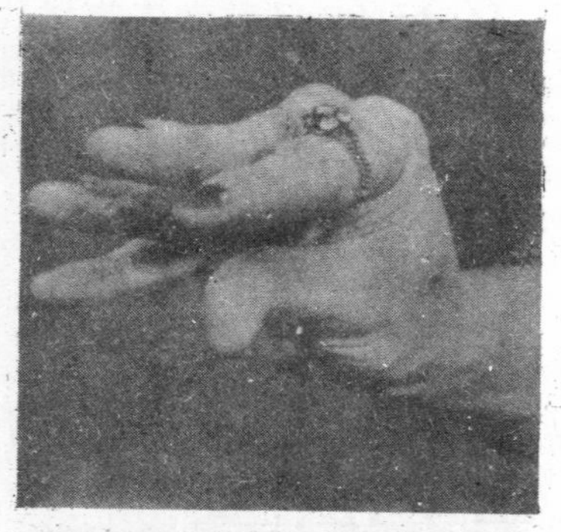

Plate 9z

AD. Saṃdaṃśa	*AD.* 159–61, p. 57–8

This describes a movement of the fingers from closed to open.

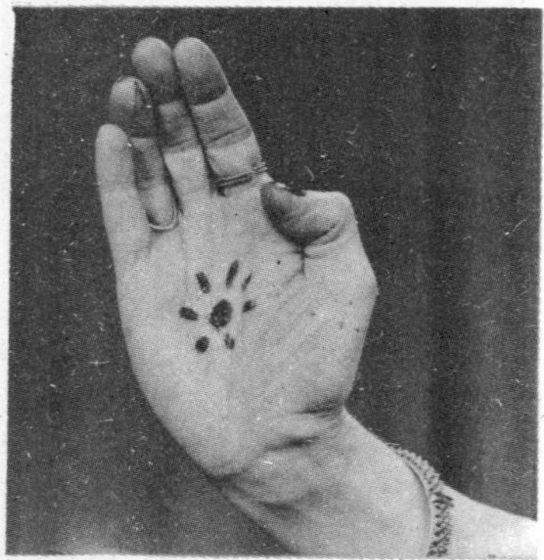

Plate 9aa

NŚ. Sarpaśīrṣa	*NŚ.* IX. 84–5, p. 181
AD. Sarpaśīrṣa	*AD.* 137–9, p. 56
VDP. Ahiśiras	*VDP.* p. 71

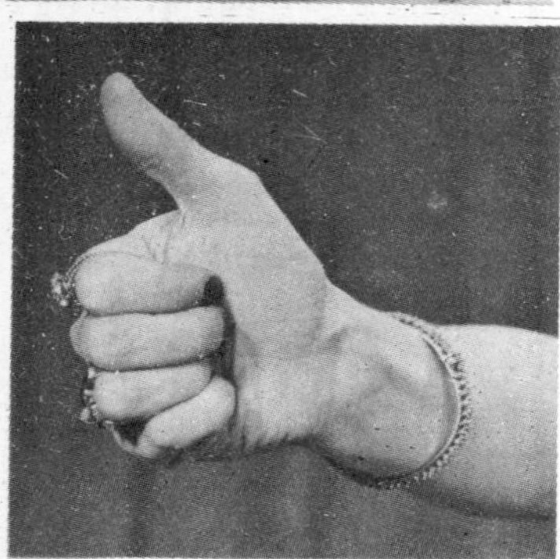

Plate 9bb

NŚ. Śikhara	*NŚ.* IX. 56–8, p. 178
AD. Sīkhara	*AD.* 188–21, p. 54
VDP. Sīkhara	*VDP.* p. 71

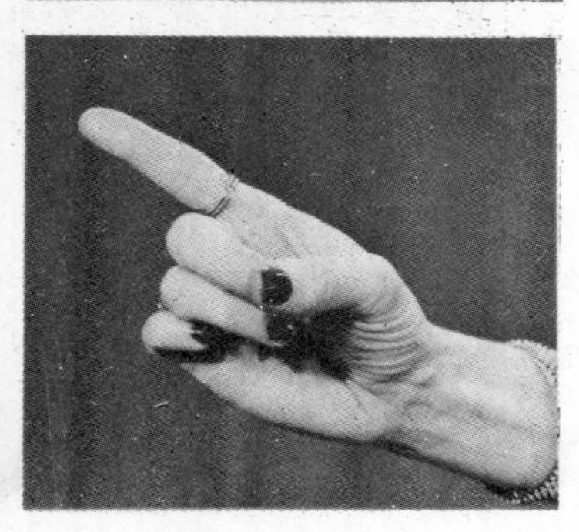

Plate 9cc

NŚ. Sūcī	*NŚ.* IX. 65–79, pp. 178–80
AD. Sūcī	*AD.* 127–31, p. 55
VDP. Sūcī	*VDP.* p. 71
Ic. *Tarjanī*	Rao, G., I., p. 15
	Banerjea, J. N., pp. 259–60

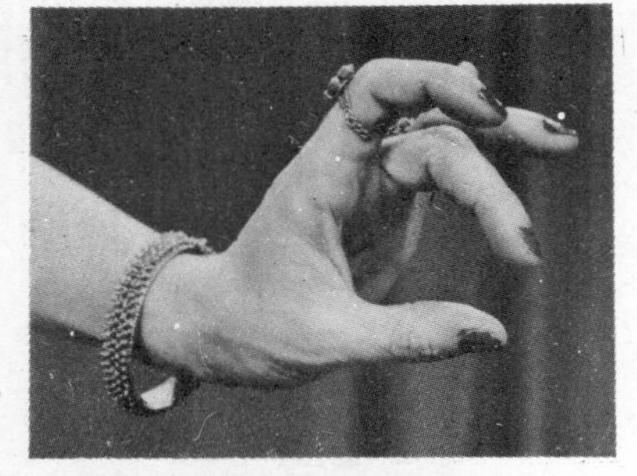

Plate 9dd

AD. Śukacañcu	Patnaik, D. N. 1971 (No pagination)
Ic. *Siṃhakarṇa mudrā*	Rao, G., I. I., p. 15

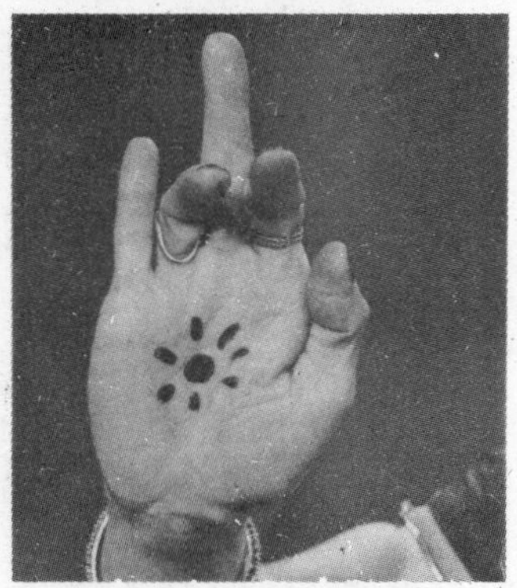

Plate 9ee

NS. Sukatuṇḍa	*NŚ*. IX. 51–3, p. 177
AD. Sukatuṇḍa	*AD*. 115–16, p. 54
VDP. Sukatuṇḍa	*VDP*. p. 71

Plate 9ff

NŚ. Svastika	*NŚ*. IX. 134–5, pp. 185–6
AD. Svastika	*AD*. 180–1, p. 60
VDP. Svastika	*VDP*. p. 73

The picture illustrates the *hasta* as given in *AD*; instructions in the *NŚ* and *VDP* differ slightly.

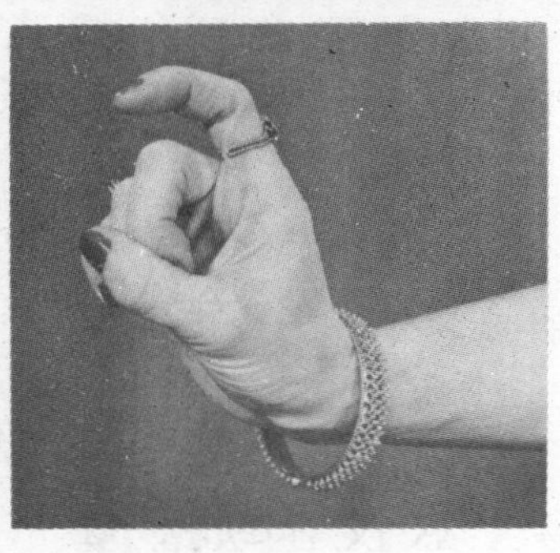

Plate 9gg

NŚ. Tāmracūḍa	*NŚ*. IX. 121–5, p. 184
AD. Tāmracūḍa	*AD*. 163–4, p. 58

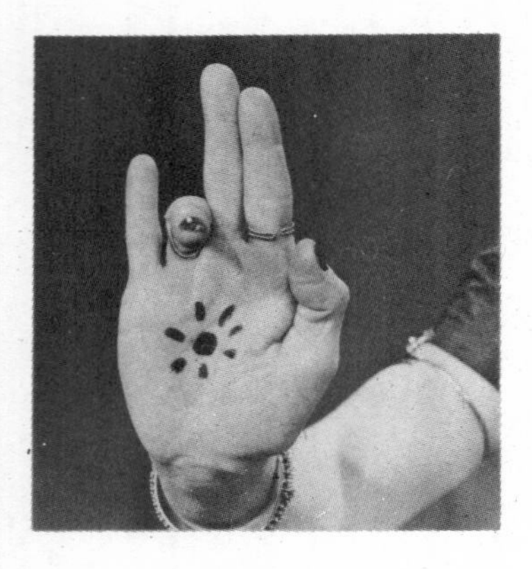

Plate 9hh

NŚ. Tripatāka	*NŚ.* IX. 26–37, pp. 175–6
AD. Tripatāka	*AD.* 100–2, p. 53
VDP. Tripatāka	*VDP.* p. 70

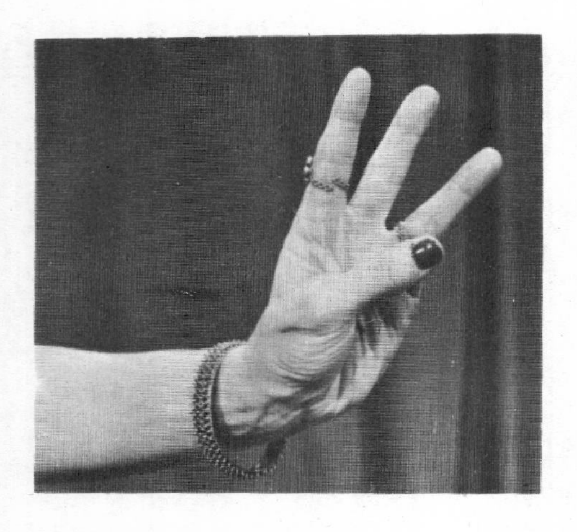

Plate 9ii

NŚ.	
AD. Triśula	*AD.* 165, p. 58

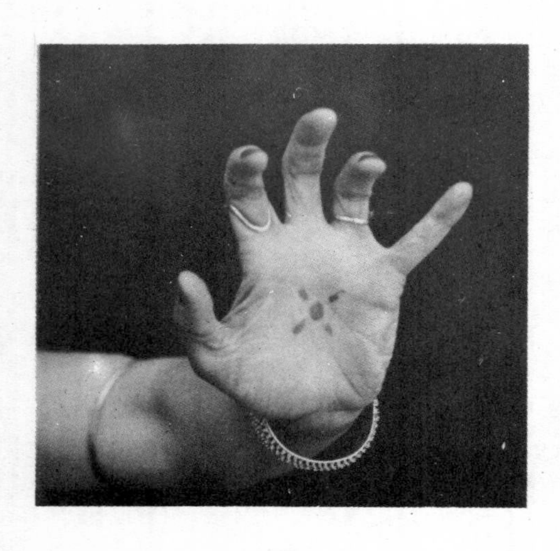

Plate 9jj

NŚ. Urnanābha	*NŚ.* IX. 119–20, p. 184

CHAPTER IV

Varieties of Naṭarāja

Naṭarāja is literally 'King of dancers'. While there are many features that are characteristic of most Naṭarājas, there are no exact criteria for identifying all Naṭarāja images. Generally speaking, all images of Śiva dancing are described as Naṭarāja unless they possess attributes specific to other forms of Śiva. Dominant attributes characteristic of various other manifestations of Śiva which may occur in dance poses are as follows: Tripurāntaka, wielding the bow and sometimes shooting an arrow; Ardhanārīśvara, a figure exhibiting female secondary sexual characteristics on the left side, and male characteristics on the right; Kālārimūrti, usually dancing on the personification of death; Gajāsurasaṃhāramūrti, dancing on an elephant hide or head which is either held behind or supports the figure; Bhikṣāṭana, wearing sandals and carrying a begging bowl—the figure sometimes emaciated; Vīrabhadra, dancing with Sati, his dead wife, on his shoulders; Bhairava carrying a club surmounted by a skull, with protruding canine teeth and frequently three-headed, with a halo of flames; Vīṇādhara, holding a *vīṇa*. These manifestations of Śiva in dance postures will be discussed in Chapter VI.

The complex symbolism which is embodied in the most famous representations of Naṭarāja, with the left leg lifted up and across the body, constitutes one of the world's most beautiful iconic concepts. I shall, however, make no attempt to discuss the philosophic implications of this dance as they have already been dealt with at length by Coomaraswamy, Sivaramamurti and others.

The most important myth involving Śiva as Naṭarāja is that related in the *Cidambaram Māhātmya* (A.D. 1313).[1] Śiva apprehends that certain sages no longer pay him homage. He therefore instructs Viṣṇu to appear in the form of a seductive dancer, Mohinī, to distract them, and meanwhile himself appears before their wives as a *sadhu*. The wives, lured by his beauty, follow him into the forest. To destroy Śiva the sages prepare a sacrifice and from the fire emerge a tiger, trident, snakes, and finally a malignant dwarf, Mūyaḷagan or Apasmāra. (Apasmāra is the term normally used to refer to the dwarf on which Naṭarāja dances in many images.) Each of these Śiva subdues, tying the tiger's skin round his waist, decorating himself with the serpents, and then dancing on the back of the dwarf. This myth is normally associated with the south Indian bronze Naṭarājas of the Cōḷā period, the pose generally referred to as *Ānanda Tāṇḍava* 'the dance of bliss' (Type C.I). Plates 62a-e (pp. 119–20) illustrate this story as shown in Bharata Nāṭyam.

Coomarsawamy and other scholars have discussed this pose at such length that it is often accepted as the typical form of Naṭarāja. The images are usually of bronze and have four arms, the two main or foremost pair of hands in *gajahasta*, and *abhaya*, while the other two hold the fire and the *ḍamaru*.

It is in this form that Śiva is the presiding deity of the temple at Cidambaram, and it was in such temples that the Bharata Nāṭyam style originated. According to mythology it was at this spot that Śiva performed his dance of *Ānanda Taṇḍava* at the request of his devotees. Practically all Bharata Nāṭyam items invoking Naṭarāja refer to Cidambaram, or Tillai as it is also known.[2] Although this pose is the form of Naṭarāja most familiar to most people, it is not in fact the most widespread, being more or less confined to south India. Even in south India a wide variety of dance poses of Naṭarāja can be seen, particularly on the Pallava temples at Kancipuram. Some of these, like many of the poses depicted in carvings of dancers are not often seen in the current repertoire of dance (Types D and E).

Another myth which involves Śiva dancing is that of his *Sandhyā Tāṇḍava* or evening dance for his consort on the heights of the Himalayas. The poses used to depict this dance are less formalized than those showing the myth of the *Cidambaram Māhātmya*, and therefore cannot be assigned to a particular category, but must be individually assessed. Here Śiva is frequently shown surrounded by his family while he dances in gay abandon. This is a favourite theme of many Pahārī miniatures[3] and the impression is one of true movement, rather than the suspended animation of *Ananda Taṇḍava* with the feet in Type C.I.

Chronology and Regional Distribution of Naṭarāja Images

Sculptures of Naṭarāja will now be discussed in relation to their type, date and location. For the chronology of most of the sculptures I have relied on the authority of previous writers, but where they disagree I have had to choose between them, relying on stylistic criteria. The images dealt with are divided into four periods (Gupta and three later periods), since this was found to be the most convenient manner in which to divide the images under consideration. Precise dating will be given where known.

Gupta: Images made within the boundaries of the Gupta empire up to the sixth century A.D.

Period 1: A.D. 550 up to *c*. A.D. 800

Period 2: A.D. 800 up to *c*. A.D. 1100

Period 3: A.D. 1100 up to *c*. A.D. 1450

The images are also classified on the basis of their origins in four regions (See p. 213). The regional divisions were based on stylistic grounds, and confined to four, so that a sufficient sample of sculptures was available from each region.

Deccani region: Karnataka, Maharashtra, and part of Andhra Pradesh.

Eastern region: Orissa, Bengal, Assam, Bihar, and parts of Andhra Pradesh, Madhya Pradesh. and Bihar.

Northern region: Himachal Pradesh, Gujarat, Rajasthan, Bihar, Uttar Pradesh and part of Madhya Pradesh.

Southern region: Tamil Nadu, Kerala, and coastal Andhra Pradesh.

Gupta Images

The most common symbol for Śiva is the *liṅga*, representing both the generative force of the universe and the personification of Śiva. This duality in interpretation finds expression in Bharata Nāṭyam where *śikhara hasta* represents both the *liṅga* and the personification of Śiva (Plates 10a, b). *Liṅgas* vary from natural rock formations (*svayambhū*) to formed and semi-personified examples bearing one or more faces *(mukhaliṅga)* which were the most common representation of Śiva during Gupta times (Plate 11).[4] Certain of Śiva's facial attributes were represented, and from this point iconographic conventions recognizable in later works became established. Some of these attributes disappear completely, and some disappear only to re-emerge later as attributes associated with Naṭarāja (particularly in Type C.I), or other aspects of Śiva dancing. For instance, an Ekamukhaliṅga from Mathura (Uttar Pradesh)[5] has matted locks of hair gathered tightly to his head, the third eye is vertical, and the face sports a moustache.[6] Another Ekamukhaliṅga from Udayagiri (Madhya Pradesh)[7] also has a third eye, but does not have a moustache, and the matted locks, tied up in a knot, flow down to the shoulders.

Naṭarāja images rarely have a moustache, which is a Gupta feature that appears later only in isolated examples of Śiva from the southern region. While both examples of Ekamukhaliṅgas have a vertical third eye, the illustration here of Naṭarāja from the Gupta period (Plate 12) does not, nor do the other examples of Gupta Naṭarājas which are discussed. There are, however, images from the eastern region, from all periods (Plates 14, 15, 16, 17a) and the Deccani region (Plates 22, 26) from the first period that have a third eye, as do some of the second period images from the northern region (Plate 43). Many stone (Plates 50, 52) and most bronze images from the southern region[8] from the second and third periods have this feature (see also Plate 66c, Chapter VI).

Both the Ekamukhaliṅga examples have matted hair falling to the shoulders, a feature shared with some Naṭarāja images from the Deccani region at Ellora (Madhya Pradesh)[9] while second and third period images of Naṭarāja (particularly bronzes) from the southern region, have some locks falling to the shoulders, most extend outwards(Plates 64g, h).

Although Marshall has identified a torso from

Symbols within symbols

Plate 10a

Depending upon the context of the story being enacted, *śikhara hasta* represents either the *liṅga* or Śiva himself. (Any male character is also shown with *śikhara*). The right hand in *śikhara* and the left in *patāka* symbolizes the *liṅga* and the *yoni*. This latter combination is employed when Śiva is being worshipped.

Plate 10b

The right hand in *śikhara* represents Śiva. The left in *simhamukha* represents Nandi, the bull, Śiva's mount.

Harappa as a possible Naṭarāja,[10] it is not until Gupta times that we can positively identify images of Śiva dancing. By the time of the Guptas, dance had become an accepted part of worship in Hindu temples and during this period the variety of representations of Śiva increased. In fact, Śiva is the first god depicted in iconography as dancing, although it is the Vedic god Indra who pre-dates him in mythology as the great dancer.[11]

Images identified as Naṭarāja dancing in Type C.I, and dancing on Apasmāra in poses other than Type C.I., appear in sculpture well before the generally accepted date of the *Cidaṃbaram Māhātmya* (A.D. 1313), and outside the geographical confines of the southern region. Many of the first period images from the Deccani region for instance have Apasmāra present in a variety of poses (Plates 62a–e).

An image of Type C.I from Bhumara (Uttar Pradesh) in the northern region, is the earliest example of this pose, and probably the earliest Gupta image to be identified as Naṭarāja.[12] It is placed in a *caitya* window or medallion. This image predates (fifth to sixth century) the first southern representation of Type C.I which is the seventh century Naṭarāja in the Pallava cave temple at Siyamangalam (Tamil Nadu),[13] to be discussed later. These are isolated examples of a pose that does not become widespread until the later part of the second period, particularly in bronze images of the southern region[14] (Plates 61a–d).

A bust of Śiva from Nachna Kuthara (near Bhumara, Uttar Pradesh), is the only Gupta Naṭarāja which is illustrated (Plate 12). It shows the right arm across the front of the body in *gajahasta*. This arm position which is also exhibited by a dancing *gaṇa* from Bhumara[15] is typical of many later Naṭarāja images and strongly suggests that the figure is dancing. Both the *gaṇa* and the bust of Śiva have one left hand thrown upwards in *alapadma*, the palm facing backwards. The *gaṇa* is two armed, but the Nachna Kuthara bust probably had four arms of which three remain, the third being held beside the head in *muṣṭi*, gripping an object resembling a pestle. At Sakore (Madhya Pradesh), also in the northern region,[16] Naṭaraja dances in Type A. V., as the central figure on a door lintel. The image is multi-armed.

Probably the best example of a dancing Śiva

from the Gupta period is from Sirpur (Madhya Pradesh) in the eastern region.[17] The image is of Type A.III and is eight-armed. It is one of the most important examples of an early Naṭarāja, because it establishes characteristics that keep appearing much later and I shall therefore describe it in detail. The main right arm is in *gajahasta*, rotated at the wrist to allow the hand in *hamsasya* to face outward, while the main arm on the left is bent at the elbow; but the hand is broken. The dancing figure between the legs, also of Type A.III, has the right hand in *gajahasta*, and the left in *saṃdaṃsa*. If we interpret this figure to be imitating Śiva's dance we could assign the same *saṃdaṃsa hasta* to the broken left hand of Naṭarāja. The remaining eight arms of the Naṭarāja image hold Śiva's main attributes: in the right hands the trident and the drum (*ḍamaru*); while one left hand holds a skull and another in *mṛgaśīrṣa* touches Devī's chin. Two hands hold a snake overhead.

Sivaramamurti identifies the figure between the legs as probably being Taṇḍu or Bharata, Śiva's first disciples of the dance.[18] This figure has normal physical proportions and will be discussed later in this chapter as well as in Chapter V. Images of Naṭarāja from the Gupta period are concentrated within the areas covered by the Gupta empire. So far, I have discussed images of Naṭarāja from the Gupta empire of Types A and C, all dated no later than the sixth century A.D. Just as some of the attributes of the *mukhaliṅga* representations from this period set trends that are often continued or re-emerge centuries later, so too do certain attributes of standing Śiva images from the Gupta period appear in later images of Naṭarāja. They are portrayed with notable clarity and simplicity. For example, the standing Śiva from Samalaji, north Gujarat, is one of the rare examples in sculpture of Śiva with a tiger skin, complete with head, tied about his loins. This attribute is prominent in the later miniature paintings of the Punjab hill schools[19] (Plates 62a-e).

Two other areas for first period images, which definitely do not fall within the sphere of the Gupta empire, are both within the southern region. Possibly the earliest Naṭarāja of Type B is found outside the Mugalarajapuram Cave,[20] near Bezwada, Andhra Pradesh, while the earliest depiction of Type E is found in a *kuḍu* on the Shore Temple at Mahabalipuram (Tamil Nadu). These have been included in Table 4 and will be discussed under non-Gupta images. Table 4 gives what are possibly the earliest examples of stone Naṭarājas of the five types (and in most of the poses), as well as possibly the earliest bronze representations of four types (the bronze reprsentations do not include Type E). The table demonstrates that all the main types have been represented in stone by the first period (Types A and C are from the Gupta period). The bronze representations are of Types A, B, C, and D, and belong to the second period. Representations of *gaṇas*, small dancing figures associated with Śiva's dance in both literature and sculpture,[21] are also included in this table. They have been included because their sculptural representations pre-date, or are at least contemporary with, sculptures of Naṭarāja, and they display all the five types of dance poses. These will be discussed in detail in Chapter VII.

First period, A.D. 550–800, non-Gupta images of Naṭarāja

While figure sculptures from the Gupta period are uncommon, the next period affords a much wider range of examples to choose from. By the first period, images of Śiva dancing in forms other than Naṭarāja begin to appear, and images of his Vīṇādhara, Ardhanārīśvara, and Gajāsurasaṃhāramūrti aspects are depicted in dance poses (see Chapter VI).

Eastern region

Examples from the eastern region come from four temple sites in Bhubaneswar (Orissa): from a shrine in the compound of the Muktesvara temple (Plates 13a, b), from the Parasuramesvara temple (Plate 14), the Vaital Deul temple (Plate 15) and the Sisiresvara temple (Plate 16), and from the Madhukesvara temple at Mukhalingam in Andhra Pradesh (Plates 17a, b).

The Orissan Naṭarājas, with the exception of the isolated piece from the Muktesvara compound, are all sculpted in medallions (*kūḍus*) and the circular frames probably influence the nature of the composition. All have either ten or twelve

Table 4. *Poses used in the depictions of Naṭarāja and associated gaṇas during the first period and their regional distribution (see also Table 2 and Plates 8a–t, in Chapter III)*

Type	Pose	Period	Region	Example in stone	Period	Region	Example in bronze	Period	Region	gaṇa
A.I		1	E	Parasuramesvara temple Bhubaneswar(Or) Plate 14			—	1	D	Cave II, Badami Plate 99
A.II		1	E	Bharatesvara temple Bhubaneswar (Or) (ARB. Plate 42)	2	E	Amrtagatesvara temple Melakkadambur (TN) (SRM. p. 303. 181) The bronze is eastern but the temple southern. See below under Siva dancing on Nandi.			
A.III	SAg	G	D	Sirpur (MPr) (SRM, p. 172.9)			—			
A.III	SK	1	E	Muktesvara compound Bhubaneswar (Or) Plate 13a			—			
A.III	TAg	1	D	Outside Cave I, Badami (Ka) Plate 18	2	S	Virupaksa, temple Kilakkadu (TN) (SRM p. 206.54)			
	TK				2	S	Delhi Museum Tiruvarangulam (TN) (SRM 228.79)	1	D	Cave I, Badami (Ka) Plate 100
A.IV				—			—			—
A.V		G	N	Sakore (MPr) (SRM p. 171.6)						
B		1	S	Outside Mugalarjapuram Cave, Bezwada (AP) (SRM p. 177.15)	2	S	Nallur (TN) Madras Museum (SRM p. 205.53)	1(G)	N	Dasavatara temple Deogarh (MP) Plate 97
					2	S	Kuram (TN) (SRM. p. 204.52)			
C.I		G	N	Bhumara (MPr)[1]	2	S	Okkur (TN) (SRM p. 227.78)	1	S	Ajanta (Mah) (Plate 98)
C.I		2	S	Tiruvalisvaram (TN)				1	S	Kailasanatha temple Kancipuram (TN) (SRM p. 199.46)
C.II[2]		2	S	Muvar temple Kodumbalur (TN) (Plate 65)	2	S	Valuvur (TN) (SRM. p 104.9)	1	S	Kailasanatha temple Kancipuram (TN) (SRM p. 199.46)
D		1	S	Kailasanatha temple Kancipuram (TN) (Plate 35)	2	S	Tiruvalangadu (TN) (SRM p. 251.108)	1	D	Cave I, Badami (Ka) (Plate 100)
E		1	S	Shore temple Mahabalipuram (TN)			—	1	D	Cave II, Badami (Ka) (Plate 99)

[1] Banerji, R. D., 'The Temple of Śiva at Bhumara', *Memoirs of the Archaeological Survey of India*, No. 16, 1924, Plate XIIIb.

[2] This pose, Type C.II, is the only one in which Śiva is depicted in aspects other than Natarāja: Tripurạntaka, Plate 65 and Gajāsurasamhāramūrti, Plate 83. 84. 85, 86.

arms—a relatively large number; and hold a snake either overhead in two hands or in a single hand held to one side. All the images stand in the *tribhaṅga* position, with one hand resting on the thigh on the side where the hip is thrust out. In all cases one arm is held across the body in *gajahasta*. This may be either the left or right arm, but it is always on the same side as the raised foot. The other main arm may be in *haṁsāsya* (two examples), in *saṁdaṁśa* (two examples), or in *patāka* (one example). In two instances the arm in *gajahasta* crosses above the wrist of the hand in *haṁsāsya*, while in the other examples the more normal arrangement of the arm in *gajahasta* passing below the opposite hand is seen. In all cases, except in the image from the Muktesvara compound, the uppermost pair of arms is raised and flexed at the elbows, with the hands in *alapadma*, the palms facing inwards. This creates the effect of framing the head and may be influenced by the circular shape of the medallion.

A rosary held in one hand is depicted in the Naṭarāja images from the Muktesvara compound (Plate 13a), Bhubaneswar, and the Madhukesvara temple, Mukhalingam (Plate 17a), as well as in two Ardhanārīśvara images from this same period and region, one on the Satrugnesvara temple (Plate 69), and another on the Parasuramesvara temple (Plate 70). These are discussed in Chapter VI. The rosary as an attribute of Naṭarāja appears again in the Deccani region during the third period (Plates 53, 55, 57).

In four of the images Śiva holds a trident, and in three a bowl made from a half skull. Other attributes included in one or two examples are the axe and bell. All images have a third eye and all are ithyphallic. The erect penis is one of the Gupta characteristics maintained by Orissan images of Śiva in his dancing aspects as Naṭarāja (Plates 15, 16) Ardhanārīśvara (Plate 70) and Vīṇādhara (Plate 91), from the first period. There are no early examples of Naṭarāja images from Bengal, but Naṭarājas from this area from the second period (Plate 38) are also ithyphallic.

Devi appears as a subsidiary figure in three of the images but the Muktesvara compound image is the only one with a drummer on its left and Gaṇeśa dancing on its right. In fact this latter image has many similarities with one from the Deccani region, outside Cave 1 at Badami (Plate 18), which belongs to the same period. Both are multi-armed and have many of the same attributes such as the axe, trident, and snake held overhead. Other characteristics they share are the halo behind the crown and the presence of Gaṇeśa and a drummer. The overall impression created by these two images is very similar.

Stylistically the Orissan images resemble Gupta Naṭarājas more closely than the first period images from other regions, but unlike the Gupta images which depict a wide variety of foot positions there is little variety in the foot positions and *hastas*, which remain characteristic of Orissan images throughout all periods. We will see that the southern and Deccani images of Naṭarāja from Period I have nearly the same diversity of foot positions as Gupta images. Nandi is not present in the Naṭarāja images from the earliest part of this period (Muktesvara compound and Parasuramesvara images), but is depicted in the two images from the later part of the period (on the Vaital Deul, Sisiresvara and Madhukesvara temples) (Plates 15, 16 and 17a) and Ardhanārīśvara images from the first period (Plate 69).

Deccani region

From the Deccani region I have chosen fourteen images: one from Badami (Plate 18), two from Aihole, from the Cave and Hucchappaya temples (Plates 19, 20), and seven from Pattadakal: from the Papanatha (Plates 21, 22), Jumbulingesvara (Plate 23), and Virupaksa temples (Plates 24–7). All these sites are in Karnataka. One image is included from the Kailasa temple at Ellora in Maharashtra (Plate 28), and three from Alampur in Andhra Pradesh: from the Svarga (Plate 29), and Brahmesvara temples (Plate 30), and from the Alampur museum (Plate 31).

Of all three periods, the first period is the most prolific for Naṭarājas, the majority of which come from Pattadakal. Many of the Naṭarāja images from the region, particularly those from the first part of the period, have common characteristics with representations from the eastern region, such as the snake held overhead in one or both hands.

Images of Naṭarāja from the first period from the Deccani region vary considerably in the number of arms. The Badami image has eighteen arms

(Plate 18), while images from the Papanatha and Virupaksa temples at Pattadakal have only four (Plates 22, 24). One of the main arms is often in *gajahasta*, but unlike the eastern images there are variations, and several images which have one main hand held beside the shoulder in *abhaya*, have the other hanging in *dola* (*NŚ*) (Plate 19) or flung upwards (Plate 21).

The foot positions for the Deccani images from this period are all of Types A and B, and within Type A include all poses except IV[22]. The arm in *gajahasta* is on the same side as the foot in *kuñcita* or *agaratalasañcara* when the image is of Type A, but for images of Type B, the opposite leg is raised to the arm in *gajahasta*.

In images from the first period, Devī is present at Aihole in the Cave temple and Hucchappayya temple (Plates 19, 20), and in several representations from the Papanatha temple (Plates 21, 22). Only in one illustration on the Papanatha temple does Naṭarāja rest the heel of his hand against her head (Plate 21). In the sculptures on the Virupaksa temple (Plates 24–7) however, Devī is incorporated into the Naṭarāja image by Naṭarāja touching her either under her chin (as in an image from the Vaital Deul, Plate 15) from the later part of this period from Bhubaneswar (eastern region), or with his arm encircling her shoulders (Plate 24). Gaṇeśa is also an attendant figure in images from this region. Musicians are depicted only in some of the Deccani images, and Nandi often stands behind or to one side. Apasmāra is present in half the illustrations.

The snake when represented is held in two positions: over the head in both hands or to one side in one hand. Two other attributes that are common are the trident and the drum. The axe is not depicted as often (Plates 18, 23), but since many images hold the handles of broken implements, these could have been axes or tridents. In fact many of the hands are without attributes, as is true of examples from the eastern region from this period. The most common position for the lowermost hands is for one to rest on the hip, and the other on the thigh, the typical arrangement for the *tribhaṅga* pose in Oḍissi dance (Plates 8d, e)[23]. Two other hand signs, *dola* (Plate 18), and one arm thrown upwards (Plates 20, 27), are depicted in Deccani Naṭarājas from this period.

The Virupaksa temple at Pattadakal provides examples of three types of Naṭarāja images: A, B and E. The majority of the images are of the first two types (A and B), with only one example of Type E. This temple has the greatest diversity of poses for Naṭarāja of any single temple in the Deccani region.

Southern region

In the southern region, four images are included, all from Kancipuram, Tamil Nadu. Two are from the Muktesvara temple (Plates 32, 33), and two from the Kailasanatha temple (Plates 34–5), one of the latter being of Type D and included in Table 4 as among the earliest representations of this pose. The variety of poses adorning the Pallava temples of Kancipuram, in Tamil Nadu, is comparable with that found on the Virupaksa temple at Pattadakal, including poses of Type A, B, and E. At Kancipuram poses of Type D are also found, and the diversity of dancing images on these temples is unrivalled elsewhere either during the first or later periods.

The Type B image from the Kailasanatha temple is probably slightly later than the image from the Mugalarajapuram Cave listed in Table 4. The latter is not illustrated here but is probably the earliest example of Naṭarāja in Type B. It is eight-armed and although badly damaged, a trident can be seen in one right hand, while one of the left hands holds a pot of fire, another a *ḍamaru*, and another in *dola* (*NŚ*), rests on the knee of the uplifted leg. Naṭarāja dances on a kneeling Apasmāra.

A Type C.I image from the southern region, from Siyamangalam,[24] has four arms: the two main ones in *dola* (*NŚ*) and *ardhacandra* resting by the shoulder; the two rear hands hold a pot containing fire and an axe. The axe is also found in Deccani and eastern Naṭarāja images. This is possibly the second-earliest representation of Type C.I, the earliest being the Gupta image at Bhumara.

Another southern image from the Bhairavakonda Cave (Andhra Pradesh)[25] is eight-armed and holds the same attributes as Śiva from the Deccani region outside Cave I at Badami (Plate 18); trident, axe, and snake; however, the snake is held in one hand and not overhead. The feet are of Type A.III.

Unlike the first representation of Type C, which is in the northern region, but later becomes restricted to the southern region, Type D images on the Kailasanatha are probably the first depictions of this type for images of Naṭarāja, and the type continues to be restricted to the south. The Kailasanatha temple has several Type D[26] images but Plate 35 is particularly interesting and unusual because Nandi is included dancing beside Naṭarāja, possibly the only representation of him dancing. The unique iconography of images on the Kailasanatha temple has been discussed by Khokar.[27]

The iconographic similarities between Naṭarājas from the Deccani and southern regions are particularly noticeable during this period. The unusual depiction of a Type E Naṭarāja is found in both regions; in the southern region on the Shore temple at Mahabalipuram, and the Kailasanatha temple at Kancipuram (Plate 34) and in the Deccani region on the Virupaksa temple at Pattadakal (Plate 27). A Naṭarāja from the Virupaksa temple (Plate 26) at Pattadakal holds a firepot of similar design to that held by the Naṭarāja from Avanibhajana's cave at Siyamangalam, and the staff with Nandi seated on top (*nandi dhvaja*) is carried by images from both regions: from the Deccani region, on the Virupaksa temple, and from the southern region in the Cave temple at Tirupparamkunram, and on the Kailasanatha temple at Kancipuram.

Sivaramamurti has discussed the possible influence of dynastic conquests on the stylistic affinities of these two regions.[28]

Second period (A.D. 800–1100)

The nineteen images from the second period are from three regions. The eastern—Muktesvara temple, Bhubaneswar, Orissa (Plates 36a, b, c) Khichingesvara temple, Khiching, Orissa (Plate 37), Karachi Museum (Plate 38); the northern—Sas temple, Nagda, Rajasthan (Plate 39), Śiva temple, Arthuna, Rajasthan (Plates 40, 41), Sukhmahal, Bundi, Rajasthan (Plate 42), Gwalior Museum (Plates 43, 44), Udayesvara temple, Udaiypur, Madhya Pradesh (Plates 45, 46), Lakhamandal, Uttar Pradesh (Plate 47), Jageswar, Uttar Pradesh (Plate 48); and southern—Brahmapurisvara temple, Pullamangai (Plate 49), Kuranganatha temple, Srinivasanallur (Plate 50), Brhadisvara temple, Tanjore (Plate 52), Karunasvami temple, Tanjore (Plate 52), all in Tamil Nadu.

Eastern region

The five eastern images come from three areas: Bhubaneswar (Muktesvara temple), Khiching, and an unidentified spot in east Bengal (Karachi Museum). The four Naṭarājas from the eastern region with the feet intact are of Type A and all resemble first period images from the same region in holding a snake overhead with two hands (Plates 36a–c, 38). Four of the images hold a drum (Plates 36a–c, 37) and two hold a trident (Plates 36c, 38). All the examples appear to have one main arm in *gajahasta* and all but one have the other bent so the hand rests by the shoulder; the fourth has the arm thrown up (Plate 38). In all cases the arm in *gajahasta* is on the same side as the foot in *agaratalasañcara* or *kuñcita*. None of the examples have one hand on the hip, the other on the thigh, which are the hand positions for the *tribhaṅga* pose seen in first period images from the eastern and Deccani regions, as well as in Oḍissi dance. Only one Naṭarāja from the Muktesvara temple touches Devi under the chin (Plate 36c).

Northern region

There are ten images from the northern region: one from Lakhamandal, and one from Jageswar, in Uttar Pradesh; two in the Gwalior Museum; two from the Udayesvara temple at Udaypur, Madhya Pradesh; one from the Sas temple at Nagda, two from Arthuna, and one from Bundi, all in Rajasthan. Three of the images from the northern region are of Type A.III and seven are of Type B. All the Type A, but only two of the Type B images have one main arm in *gajahasta*. In all examples the foot in *kuñcita* is on the same side as the arm in *gajahasta*. All the images in Type A and three in Type B hold a snake, in all but one instance supported overhead with two hands. All but two of the images hold a trident, and two of the Type A images and one Type B hold a drum. The four images from Madhya Pradesh (Plates 43–6)[29] all originally had ten arms, and nearly all of these except the main pair, carry attributes. These include the bow, trident, sword, bundle of sticks, half-skull, bell, snake, and *khaṭvāṅga*. Three are placed in a *kūḍu*, and one is in a main niche.

All the images from Rajasthan are of Type B. The compositions are distinctive in that they have the main pair of arms encircling the major weapons, held half upright at the chest. These include, in the Arthuna images, the *khaṭvāṅga*, and in the Bundi image, the trident. The unbalanced height at which the elbows are held, seen clearly in Plate 41, is reminiscent of poses adopted in the north Indian dance style of Kathak. This device gives the figure the impression of lateral movement.

Devī, Gaṇeśa, and Kārttikeya are present as attendant figures only in the image from Jageswar (Plate 48) while in the image from Lakhamandal (Plate 47), Devī is replaced by a lute player whom Naṭarāja touches under the chin as in some of the first period Orissan images. Musicians are present in all but one of the examples.

The tiny figure seen between the legs of the Gupta Naṭarāja at Sirpur, appears again, imitating Śiva's pose in some images of the northern region (Plates 41, 43).

Southern region

The four images from the southern region all come from different sites in Tamil Nadu: the Brahmapurisvara temple at Pullamangai, the Kuranganatha temple at Srinivasanallur and the Brhadisvara and Karunaswami temples at Tanjore. In these images the number of arms varies from four to eight and they are of Type B (two examples) and C.I (two examples). Three have the main arms in *ardhacandra/patāka* and *gajahasta* (Plates 49, 51, 52) and the fourth has the arm thrown upwards, the other resting by the shoulder in *ardhacandra* (Plate 50). The image of Type B, with one arm in *gajahasta*, has the *gajahasta* arm on the side opposite to the uplifted foot. Two of the four images hold a trident and all hold a drum on the right. Three images hold fire in the left hand and one an axe. Apasmāra is present in the Type C.I images. There are musicians in three of the four examples.

Third Period

Eight images from the third period are illustrated here: five from the Deccani region; where four examples come from the prolific sculptures of Śiva on the Hoysalesvara temple at Halebid, Karnataka and one from Palampet in Andhra Pradesh (now exhibited in the National Museum, New Delhi). Three examples from the southern region come from the Naṭarāja temple at Cidambaram (two examples) and from the Airavatesvara temple at Darasuram, both in Tamil Nadu.

Examples of Naṭarāja from the northern and eastern regions are much less common in the third period than during earlier periods, perhaps because the arrival of Islam in northern, western, and later eastern India led to a general decrease in temple building activities. The Surya temple at Konarak in Orissa, which dates from this period, does include a sculpture of Naṭarāja (now in the British Museum, London), but this forms a relatively minor part of the decoration. In common with many earlier Orissan images, the Naṭarāja from Konarak holds a snake overhead and is ithyphallic. Apasmāra is absent.

The Deccani images are all of Type B and the positions of the legs are remarkably similar. In contrast, the combinations of the two main arms are different in each case. Three images have the main right hand held in *ardhacandra/abhaya* by the breast, and in each case the hand holds a string of prayer beads. In the other images the right arm hangs in *dola*. The main left arm crosses the body in *gajahasta* in one example (Plate 54), while in the case of the two ceiling pieces from Halebid (Plates 55, 56) it is flung up in a loose *patāka*, the palm facing backwards. The Kakatiya image from Palampet holds a fruit in this hand.

Southern region

The three southern images from the third period include two in Type D and one in Type A, all with four arms. In each case the main right hand is in *patāka* by the shoulder. In the two Type D images the main left hand is held above the head, balancing the uplifted leg, while in the Type A image the arm crosses the body in *gajahasta*. All carry the drum in one right hand and the fire in one left hand. In one image (Plate 58) the fire is held as a torch in contrast to contemporary bronze sculptures which normally support the flames on the bare palm. The ear-rings are dissimilar, the one on the left being heavier, a feature common to contemporary bronze Naṭarājas.

The image from Darasuram (Plate 60) includes a *gaṇa* on Śiva's left dancing in Type B. A four-armed deity accompanies Śiva on a drum. Apasmāra is present in the Type D images but not in the Type A image.

Conclusions

A chronological survey of the images considered suggests a gradual reduction in the variety of poses used for Naṭarāja between the first and third periods. The profusion of types seen among the Pallava images of the southern region and the Calukyan images of the Deccan becomes condensed in the third period to regional stereotypes; the Type C.I and Type D images of the later Cōḷa period in the south and the Type B images of the Hoysaḷas in the Deccan.

While the number of arms does not increase after the first period, being reduced to four in many second and most third period images from the south, the attributes carried tend to increase in number, so that practically every hand holds some kind of weapon in the northern images of the second period and the Hoysala sculptures of the third period. This results in a reduction of the number of identifiable *hastas*.

The continual diffusion of styles and creative ideas in the iconography of Śiva is evident from many inter-regional similarities; the connection between the southern and Deccani regions during the first period being particularly notable. Other indications appear in the similarity between the crowns of second period images from Orissa and contemporary images from the northern region suggesting there were contacts between these two regions. This is further supported by the similarity in sculpture and architecture between the Rajarani temple at Bhubaneswar in Orissa, and the contemporary temple group at Khajuraho in Madhya Pradesh.

The modern tendency to think of Naṭarāja as essentially a south Indian deity is clearly unfounded, since images of Śiva in dancing poses come from all parts of the Indian subcontinent, including Kashmir and the Himalaya. The popularity of this dancing form has varied with time, however, depending on the fortunes of Śaivism relative to other Hindu cults, and during the third period, Naṭarāja images are common only in the southern region and adjacent parts of the Deccan. Later, depictions of Naṭarāja are found only in south India where they tend to concentrate on the two typically Cōḷa types, C.I and D, often with a profusion of arms.

Eastern region

The sculptures of Orissa form a distinctive group, probably because Orissa was an independent kingdom throughout most of the period under consideration.[30] Although many of the iconographic features characteristic of Orissan images can be found in Naṭarājas from other parts of India, the relative frequency with which certain features are included makes the Orissan style distinctive. Dancing Śivas from Orissa are called Naṭāmbara, and Boner in her translation of the *Śilpa Prakāśa* has divided this form of Śiva into three types of images.[31] Her three divisions represent two varieties of leg positions: the first example is of Type B and the other two of Type A. Our examples only illustrate Type A.

The *dhyānas* (mnemonic verses) from the *Śilpa Prakāśa* are important as they mention specific iconographic features that frequently occur in Orissan Naṭāmbras as well as in images of Śiva dancing from other areas. Boner's second type of Naṭāmbara is particularly noteworthy because it illustrates the left hand in *gajahasta*, with the hand turned at the wrist so that the palm faces outward. The lowermost left hand is in *sarpaśīrṣa*, with the palm held upwards, and it is this hand that often touches Devī under the chin whenever she is present in sculptures (Plate 16).

Devī is not depicted in Boner's example. One hand rests on the hip for Boner's second type, a feature seen in our examples from the first and second periods from this region. The uppermost hands hold a snake overhead, which is characteristic of our examples for this region from all periods. The pedestal is plain. The *dhyānas* from the *Śilpa Prakāśa* do not mention the minor figures that usually accompany the Naṭāmbara images, yet in actual representations there are many instances where Devī, Nandi, and musicians are present. Boner's first example is her only ithyphallic representation whereas most Naṭāmbaras from this region and all periods are ithyphallic.[32]

A popular site for Naṭāmbara images is on the sides of the *śikhara*, usually high up and encircled by a medallion (*kuḍu*) or sometimes affixed to the plain wall: This preference for carving a dancing image of Śiva on the front of temples, and in particular in the centre of a medallion, is also evident at Pattadakal and Udaipur. At the former site there is a strong preference for showing the feet in Type A as in Orissan Naṭāmbaras, whereas in the latter, Type B is more common.

The Naṭarāja image from Sirpur, Gupta period, is the most complete representation of Śiva known to me, and comes from an area close to the border between the eastern and Deccani regions. Although it is very early, it includes all the main characteristics of Naṭarāja from the eastern region: a snake is held overhead, one arm is in *gajahasta* and the other rests by the shoulder, and the phallus is erect. The image holds a trident and Devī is being touched under the chin, Naṭarāja characteristics found only in the first and occasionally the second period in the eastern region. The small figure dancing between the legs,however, is not found in Orissan images, but occurs in some Deccani images of the first period. Several other features, such as the snake held overhead and the position of the arms, are also found in Deccaṇi images, so that the Sirpur image forms a link between these two regions.

Images of Śiva dancing are not found all over Bengal, but only in the south-eastern districts roughly comprising the ancient divisions of Vanga and Samtala.[33] Haque has recorded seventeen sculptures of Naṭarāja from Bengal, sixteen in stone, of which eleven were discovered in Bangladesh. Seven of the eleven from Bangladesh were concentrated within the bounds of the ancient capital of Vikrampur, Dacca district, and three from the adjoining district of Comilla.[34] Village names such as Natesvara, near Vikrampur and Natghar (from which there is an image of Vīṇādhara illustrated, see Plate 94) give evidence of the importance of Śiva in his dancing aspect.

Some writers have attributed the Naṭarāja cult to the Sena kings bringing Śaivism with them when they arrived in Bengal from the Deccan.[35] Bhattasali, however, gives one example of an image from Bharella that has been assigned the date A.D. 939, earlier than the Sena dynasty.[36] The inscription on this image has unfortunately been mostly destroyed.

> His glorious majesty Layahachandra-deva . . .
> caused to be made the Lord Nartteśvara (*sic*)[37]

The regional name for Naṭarāja in Bengal is Narteśvara.

The images from Bengal are of interest because they conform to many of the requirements laid down in the *MP*, such as dancing on Nandi. This Śiva does in his aspects of both Narteśvara and Vīṇādhara (see chapter VI). However both these figures show more than the required two arms that the *MP* specifies:

> When He is about to dance on His bull, He has two hands.[38]

The only bronze image of Naṭarāja from Bengal is also found dancing on a bull, and is currently worshipped in the Amrtagateśvara temple, Tanjore district, Tamil Nadu, in the southern region. The generally accepted explanation for this removal to south India is that it was part of the booty carried away by the forces of Rajendra Cōḷa in about A.D. 1023.[39]

Amongst the earliest and most numerous sculptures of Naṭarāja from the Deccani region are those from Karnataka, Maharashtra, and part of Andhra Pradesh. While they form an easily recognizable group, they are found only in the first and third periods and share characteristics with the other three regions.

Because the early Deccani Naṭarājas from Aihole, Badami, and Pattadakal show many features that were later incorporated into images from other regions, it seems likely that this area acted as a centre for transmission of ideas in the iconography of Naṭarāja. Its location in the middle of the continent makes it well suited to be a centre for the dissemination of creative ideas.

Characteristics that Deccani images have in common with contemporary images from other regions are:

the snake held overhead or in one hand, which is also found in images from the eastern region;

the incorporation of Devī into the image, seen in eastern images from Orissa;

the trident and drum, which are found in all regions;

the presence of Apasmāra, also found in the southern region;

the *tribhaṅga* position for the hands which is also found in the eastern region;

the Type B position of the feet, which is also found in the southern region in the first period.

Features which are found in images from the Deccani region in the first period and continue in sculptures from other regions of a later period are: the snake held in one hand, which appears in images from the northern and southern regions; and Apasmāra, which continues to appear in the south, while largely, but not completely, disappearing from the Deccani area. Type B images, found in first period Deccani sculptures, appear later in the northern region. A lute player is sometimes incorporated into northern Naṭarāja images, as is the case with Devī in early Deccani ones. First period Deccani images carry relatively few attributes, but third period images, like those of the second period from the northern region, have numerous different attributes. Many first-period images are carved in *kuḍus*, as are first period images from Orissa and second period images from the northern region.

Southern region

Naṭarāja is today principally a southern deity, and the form in which he is most famous, Type C.I, is restricted to the southern region (with the exception of Vijayanagar images from the Deccani region). While Type A images are found throughout India, and Type B images from the earliest period are found in the Deccani and southern regions, it is only in the southern region, in the first period, that all five types of Naṭarāja are represented; four of these, Types A, B, D and E, being on the Kailasanatha temple at Kancipuram. The earliest Type C image from the south is found at Siyamangalam.

The Naṭarāja images on the Virupaksa temple at Pattadakal and those on the Kailasanatha temple have certain iconographic similarities and in addition, both have Naṭarāja images of Types A, B, D and E. The Kailasanatha temple has a Naṭarāja image of Type D, but neither has a Type C image. Types C and D do not appear regularly outside the southern region (except for images from the Vijayanagar period). Type E images, which are unusual, provide a link between the Naṭarājas of the southern and Deccani region. This pose is found in a *kuḍu* on the Shore temple at Mahabalipuram, on the Kailasanatha temple at Kancipuram (Plate 34) and also on the Virupaksa temple at Paṭṭadakal (Plate 27). Some attributes that the southern images share with Deccani images are the vessel of fire and a *nandi dhvaja* (see Plates 64i–j).

Northern region

The illustrations of Śiva dancing from the northern region begin with the Gupta period. At Bhumara there is the first and only illustration from this region of Śiva dancing in Type C.I. Another Gupta image, the bust from Nachna Kuthara (Plate 12), while badly damaged, does illustrate the one arm in *gajahasta*, which continues in later periods. Śiva's matted locks flow down to his shoulders, but in later images from the northern region they are tied up to form a crown. All the northern images illustrated here are of the second period, and although they possess a characteristic style, no attributes are exclusively northern, and many characteristics are shared by images from the Deccani region.

Plate 11
Gupta
Northern region Uttar Pradesh National Museum, Delhi
Liṅga with representation of Viṣṇu, Śiva, Brahmā and Sūrya, 'Surya Catur-mukha'

Plate 12 Naṭarāja
Gupta Nachna Kuthara
Northern region Uttar Pradesh National Museum, Delhi

Plate 13a	Naṭarāja	
Period I	Type A.III (SK)	10 arms
Eastern region	Muktesvara compound temple	Bhubaneswar (Or)

Plate 13b Detail of Plate 13a

Plate 14 Naṭarāja
Period I Type A.1(?)
Eastern region Parasuramesvara temple Bhubaneswar (Or)

The main right hand in *gajahasta* is thrown over the left in *haṃsāsya*. See also Plates 13a, b. One of the right hands is in *haṃsāsya* while another holds a snake that hangs downwards. One hand on the left is also in *haṃsāsya,* while below it another holds a trident. The two lowermost hands rest on the thighs. The image is located in a medallion.

Plate 15	Naṭarāja	
Period I	Type A.III (SKu)	12 arms
Eastern region	Vaital Deul temple	Bhubaneswar (Or)

The main right hand is in *saṃdaṃśa* and the main left in *gajahasta* on the same side as the foot in *kuñcita*. The two uppermost arms are held beside the head in *alapadma,* palms facing inwards. One left hand in *sūcī* is dipping into a half skull *(kapāla),* held by another left hand and the lowermost left hand, in *sarpaśīrṣa* is cupped under Devi's chin. Another left arm bent at the elbow, has the hand at shoulder level in *saṃdaṃśa,* a position which is also seen in the Naṭarāja from the same period on the Madhukesvara temple at Mukhalingam, eastern region (Plates 17a–b).

The hands on the right hold a trident, and a snake and the lowermost rests on the thigh. Nandi peers between Śiva's legs and the image is ithyphallic.

Plate 16	Naṭarāja	
Period I	Type A.II	
Eastern region	Sisiresvara temple	Bhubaneswar (Or)

The right main hand is in *patāka,* palm facing outwards and the left main hand is in *gajahasta,* palm facing inwards. The two arms held overhead are partially broken. One right hand holds a snake, one left hand a half skull and another left hand touches the top of Pārvatī's head. Naṭarāja has a third eye and is ithyphallic, a feature that is emphasized by having Nandi looking upwards.

Plate 17a

Period I	Type A.III (TKu)	14 arms
Eastern region	Madhukesvara temple	Mukhalingam (AP)

The main right hand is in *saṃdaṃśa,* the main left in *patāka,* palm facing inwards. Four arms are held overhead: two hold a snake, whose head peers around the corner and two are held just above his crown. The right hands hold a trident, and a rosary, and two rest on the thigh. One left hand in *saṃdaṃśa* balances the main right one, also in *saṃdaṃśa,* one left hand holds a half skull, another touches Pārvatī under the chin, and another in *sūcī hasta* points inwards. The image is ithyphallic and Nandi between its legs looks upwards.

Naṭarāja dances in a medallion flanked by a drummer, Bhṛṅgī, and Gaṇeśa dancing (see also Plate 17b).

Plate 17b	Naṭarāja and Bhairava/ Gajāsurasaṃhāramūrti	
Period I	Type A	
Eastern region	Madhukesvara temple	Mukhalingam (AP)

The image of Bhairava/Gajāsurasaṃhāramūrti dances in *ālīḍha* below the image of Naṭarāja. The horizontal thrust of the left knee and the trident draws the eye to the right, making the sculpture unbalanced in keeping with its portrayal of only Śiva's destructive power. This is in strong contrast to all the images of Naṭarāja in which the figure is poised in equilibrium, symbolizing the balance between creation and destruction. The uppermost hands support the elephant hide and the left hand holds on to a half skull. A garland of skulls and a horrific expression on his face make a contrast with the serenity of Naṭarāja's above. Like Naṭarāja he is ithyphallic and Nandi stands between his legs looking upwards.

Plate 18	Naṭarāja	
Period I	Type A.III (TAg)	18 arms
Deccani region	Outside Cave I	Badaṁi (Ka)

The main left hand is in *saṃdaṃśa* and the main right, with the palm facing outwards, is in *gajahasta* on the same side as the foot in *agratalasañcara*. The two uppermost arms in *muṣṭi* hold a snake with hood erect. The other right hands, from top to bottom are: extended upwards, in *muṣṭi* holding a *ḍamaru, patāka* bent backwards at the wrist, *patāka* palm facing outwards, *sarpaśīrṣa*, and *dola (NŚ)* (see also Plate 19, Naṭarāja, Cave temple, Aihole, Karnataka).

On the left side, again from the top, the first hand is in *muṣṭi* beside the halo, the second is unidentifiable, the third, also in *muṣṭi*, supports an axe, the fourth, in *patāka*, rests against it and the fifth, in *muṣṭi*, holds a trident. The lowest two rest on the thigh.

Gaṇeśa and a drummer are on Śiva's left and Nandi on his right. Despite its large number of arms, the image carries relatively few weapons; only the axe and the trident. Later images from the same region (Hoysala, Period 3) carry a much wider variety.

Plate 19

Period I	Type A.II (KAg)	10 arms
Deccani region	Cave temple	Aihole (Ka)

The two uppermost hands in *muṣṭi* hold a snake. The right hands, from top to bottom, hold a *ḍamaru,* axe, an unidentifiable object and *haṃsāsya.* The left hands, again from the top, are in *patāka,* holding an unidentifiable object, in *dola* (*NŚ*), and resting on the thigh in *kaṭyavalambita* respectively. A snake with erect hood forms the sacrificial thread and a snake is tied at the waist. A halo surrounds the crown, as in the Naṭarāja outside Cave I at Badami (Plates 13a & b). The seven mothers are nearby, some of them in dance poses.

Plate 20	Naṭarāja	
Period 1	Type A.III (TK)	8 arms
Deccani region	Hucchappayya temple	Aihole (Ka)

Of the two main hands, the right is in *muṣṭi* and the left is thrown upwards. The uppermost right holds a *ḍamaru*, the next is extended upwards (see also Plate 18) and the next, in *muṣṭi*, holds a snake with hood erect. The lowermost left hand rests in *kaṭyavalambita* on the hip and another holds a club.

Pārvatī stands on Śiva's left, her right hand pressing down on the head of a dwarfish female figure. Gaṇeśa, Nandi and an orchestra, including a skeleton, are on Śiva's right. Śiva dances on Apasmāra.

Plate 21	Naṭarāja	
Period 1	Type A.V (Sv)	8 arms (?)
Deccani region	Papanatha temple	Pattadakal (Ka)

The main arm on the right is in *patāka/ardhacandra* by the shoulder, while the other three, from top to bottom, are: two in *muṣṭi*, one holding a *ḍamaru* and the other a staff destroyed at the top, and one resting on the thigh. The arms on the left are broken, although one is extended upwards and another, in *kartarīmukha hasta*, rests against Pārvatī's head. Pārvatī stands in Type A.V*, as seen in Plate 22 from the ceiling of the same temple. She stands on a lotus pedestal with one hand in *sūcī* and the other in *dola* (*NŚ*).

A snake emerges from behind Śiva's right thigh, in a similar position to the one which also serves as sacrificial thread on the Naṭarāja from the Cave temple, Aihole (Plate 19). Śiva stands on a badly damaged Apasmāra. A musician with cymbals sits between Śiva and Pārvatī and another figure, on Śiva's right, observes the performance.

Plate 22	Naṭarāja	
Period 1	Type A.III (TK)	4 arms
Deccani region	Papanatha temple	Pattadakal (Ka)

Naṭarāja dances on the back of a kneeling Apasmāra. The two main hands are in *patāka* (right) and *gajahasta* (left). *Gajahasta* is on the same side as the foot in *kuñcita*. The other right hand holds a trident and the other left hand, in *muṣṭi*, holds a snake with hood erect. Devī stands on Śiva's left in Type A.V* on a lotus pedestal. Her right hand is in *kaṭyavalambita* on the hip, and the left in *sūcī* by her chest, points at Naṭarāja. Nandi stands behind (Plate 18); musicians sit on either side of Apasmāra.

Plate 23	Naṭarāja	
Period 1	Type A.III (SK)	8 arms
Deccani region	Jumbulingesvara	Pattadakal (Ka)

The upper right hand holds an axe entwined by a snake and the left hand holds an unidentifiable object. The main left arm is in *gajahasta* on the same side as the foot in *kuñcita*. The main right hand is badly weathered but it is probably in *saṃdaṃsa*. The lowermost right hand is in *muṣṭi*, and rests at the waist, and the lowermost left hand, also in *muṣṭi*, rests on the thigh. The other right hand holds a *ḍamaru*, and the left encircles Devī's shoulders. Nandi is to the right of Śiva.

Plate 24	Naṭarāja	
Period 1	Type A.V	4 arms
Deccani region	Virupakṣa temple	Pattadakal (Ka)

The two main arms have their hands in *muṣṭi* and hold a snake overhead which dangles downwards, its erect hood resting beneath Śiva's right arm. The other right hand holds a staff of similar design to that held by Naṭarāja of Type A.I from the same temple. The other left hand in *dola* (*NŚ*) encircles Pārvatī's shoulders. A snake is tied around Naṭarāja's thighs (see also Plates 19 and 26); its erect hood, close to the thigh, emphasizes Śiva's phallic nature, an iconographic feature also common in non-dancing Bhikṣāṭana *mūrtis* from the southern region (Plate 64b). Pārvatī displays *sūcī hasta* in the right hand and *dola* in the left; the same *hastas* seen in the Pārvatī standing beside Naṭarāja on the Papanatha temple (Plate 21). Nandi stands on Śiva's right and musicians are on both sides.

Plate 25	Naṭarāja	
Period 1	Type B	4 arms
Deccani region	Virupaksa temple	Pattadakal (Ka)

Naṭarāja dances on Apasmāra with the left arm in *gajahasta*, the opposite side to the leg that is raised. The upper right hand holds a *ḍamaru*, the lower (damaged), was probably held in *patāka/saṃdaṃśa* beside the shoulder. The lower left arm holds a staff with a representation of Nandi on it (*nandi dhvaja*) similar to that seen in another Naṭarāja from the same temple, and in the Cave temple at Tirupparamkunram.[40]

Plate 26	Naṭarāja	
Period 1	Type A.III (TK)	8 arms
Deccani region	Virupaksa temple	Pattadakal (Ka)

Naṭarāja dances on the back of a kneeling Apasmāra. The hands on the left from top to bottom are in *saṃdaṃśa hasta* at crown level, holding a pot of fire, hanging in *dola hasta* (*NŚ*) and the lowermost hand in *kartarīmukha hasta* is against the left thigh. The uppermost right arm holds a drum, the main right hand is broken, but was probably in *haṃsāsya* or *saṃdaṃśa hasta* as the index finger and thumb are joined; another in *kaṭakāmukha hasta* holds on to a snake which twines around the girdle. This is an unusual feature. The lowermost right hand holds an unidentifiable object. The third eye is vertical.

The Pallava Naṭarāja in Avanibhajana's Cave at Siyamangalam [41], of Type C.I, from the first period, southern region, also holds the same type of pot containing fire. The pot disappears in later images, particularly of Type C.I, where the fire is usually supported by the hand in *ardhacandra hasta*.

Plate 26

Plate 27	Naṭarāja	
Period 1	Type E	8 arms
Deccani region	Virupaksa temple	Pattadakal (Ka)

This is one of a relatively small number of Naṭarāja images depicted in Type E; the others being from the same period, southern region (Plates 32 and 34). In all cases the position of the main pair of arms, one in *gajahasta*, and the other held straight upwards, appears to be identical. The similarity between all three images of Type E is very striking.

The image is badly damaged but one right hand holds a trident while another rests on the thigh in *kartarīmukha*. One left hand holds a *nandi dhvaja*, an attribute seen in the hand of another Naṭarāja image from this temple (Plate 25) as well as in the Cave temple at Tirupparamkunram (TN).[42]

Plate 28	Naṭarāja	
Period 1	Type B	10 arms (?)
Deccani region	Kailasa temple	Ellora (Ma)

The main hand is in *muṣṭi/saṃdaṃśa* and the main left arm is in *gajahasta*, on the opposite side to the raised leg. The uppermost right hand holds a *ḍamaru*, the next an unidentifiable object, and the next a club. The uppermost left arm is thrown upwards, the next in *muṣṭi hasta* holds the tail of a snake, which dangles downwards, and the next two hands are broken. A drummer sits on the left and Devī on the right.

Plate 29	Naṭarāja	
Period 1	Type A.III (SAg)	8 arms
Deccani region	Svarga temple	Alampur (AP)

Naṭarāja is placed in a *kūḍu*, the most popular position for him in this region. The right main arm is in *gajahasta* while the main left hand is in *saṃdaṃśa*. One right hand holds a snake while another in *mayūra hasta* rests on his right knee. One left hand holds an axe and the one next to it is in *tripatāka hasta*.

Plate 30	Naṭarāja	
Period 1	Type A.III (SAg)	8 arms
Deccani region	Brahmesvara temple	Alampur (AP)

This image is on the ceiling and has at one time been painted over. The main right arm is in *gajahasta* and the main left hand in *saṃdaṃśa* as for the previous example (Plate 29). One of the right hands holds a trident, another rests on his thigh. The positions of the left hands are unclear except for the lowermost which rests in *ardhapatāka* on Naṭarāja's left thigh.

Plate 31	Naṭarāja	
Period 1	Type A.III (TAg)	4 arms
Deccani region	Alampur Museum	Ālampur (AP)

Naṭarāja dances in this ceiling slab surrounded by the guardians of the quarters. The main right arm is in *gajahasta*, and the left hand is in *saṃdaṃśa*. One right hand holds a trident. There is a halo behind his crown, indicating that this is an early piece.

Plate 32	Naṭarāja	
Period 1	Type E	10 arms
Southern region	Muktesvara temple	Kancipuram (TN)

The main arms are in *patāka/ardhacandra* and *gajahasta*. One left hand is in *vismaya*, one holds a drum, and another rests on Naṭarāja's thigh. The attributes in the right hand are unclear. To the right of Naṭarāja, Bhikṣāṭana is depicted and to the left, Gajāsurasaṃhāramūrti, two important aspects of Śiva that are discussed in Chapter VI.

Plate 33	Naṭarāja	
Period 1	Type A.V	10 arms
Southern region	Muktesvara temple	Kancipuram

The main hands are in *saṃdaṃśa* and *gajahasta*. One right hand holds a snake but the other attributes are not distinguishable. Naṭarāja has a moustache, a Gupta feature. The flying figures carry fly whisks. The small dwarf beneath Naṭarāja's feet is standing and not in the prone position typical of most images of Naṭarāja. A small rounded figure imitates Śiva's dance. Usually this figure is emaciated. The nearby drummer is reminiscent of the Naṭarāja outside Cave I at Badami (Plate 18) and the Muktesvara compound image from Bhubaneswar (Plate 13a). Devī stands nearby but Naṭarāja does not touch her as in eastern and Deccani images from this period.

Plate 34	Naṭarāja	
Period 1	Type E	10 arms (?)
Southern region	Kailasanatha temple	Kancipuram (TN)

This image is the best preserved Naṭarāja of Type E on the Kailasanatha temple. All of them have the main right arm in *gajahasta*, palm facing forwards, and the main left arm held straight upwards, holding the hand over the head so that the palm faces downwards. This position of the left arm is also seen in a Type D image from the third period, southern region, at Cidambaram on the Naṭarāja temple (Plate 117).

The uppermost right hand holds (possibly) a bunch of grass, the next a *ḍamaru*, and the lowermost rests on the knee in *kartarīmukha hasta*. The uppermost left hand holds an unidentifiable object, the next, in *ardhacandra*, is held by the shoulder as is the lower in *saṃdaṃśa*.

Plate 35	Naṭarāja	
Period 1	Type D	8 arms
Southern region	Kailasanatha temple	Kancipuram (TN)

The two main hands are: right held in *ardhapatāka*, and the left in *kartarīmukha hasta*; these are also depicted in the Type E image on the same temple (Plate 34). The *kartarīmukha hasta* is unusual for Naṭarāja images but it is also depicted in the Naṭarāja from the Deccani region, first period, outside Cave I (Plate 18).

One right hand in *patāka* helps to push the right leg back. This image has been extensively restored and some of the attributes and *hastas* may not be the original ones.

Plates 36a	Naṭarāja	
Period 2	Type A.III (SK)	8 arms
Eastern region	Muktesvara temple	Bhubaneswar (Or)

Each side of the tower of this temple has a Naṭarāja dancing and all are slightly different. Three are illustrated here, of which two have eight arms. All three examples have the snake held overhead and are ithyphallic, with Nandi between the legs looking upwards. Devī is not present here as she is in one other example (Plate 36c).

Plate 36b	Naṭarāja	
Period 2	Type A.III (SAg)	6 arms
Eastern region	Muktesvara temple	Bhubaneswar (Or)

While there are only six arms here the snake is held overhead as in the other examples. The right main arm is in *gajahasta* while the left hand is probably in *mayūra hasta*. One right hand holds a drum. The breasts on this image are developed but there can be no doubt that this is Śiva as the image is ithyphallic.

Plate 36c	Naṭarāja	
Period 2	Type A.III (SAg)	8 arms
Eastern region	Muktesvara temple	Bhubaneswar (Or)

The two uppermost hands in *muṣṭi* hold a snake overhead with hood erect. One right hand holds the *ḍamaru*, and another an unidentifiable object. One of the left hands in *kaṭakāmukha* (*NŚ*) holds a trident, and another in *sarpaśīrṣa* touches Devī under the chin. The main right arm is bent at the elbow so that the hand rests by the shoulder and the left arm is in *gajahasta*, ending with the left hand in *mayūra*, palm facing forward. The left foot in *agratalasañcara* is on the same side as the arm in *gajahasta*. Naṭarāja is ithyphallic.

Plate 37	Naṭarāja	
Period 2	feet broken	arm (?)
Eastern region	Khiching temple	Khiching (Or)

This image is badly damaged but it has been included because it is another example of second period Orissan Naṭarāja that is ithyphallic, and Nandi is looking upwards, which emphasizes this feature. Only the drum in the upper right hand remains. The face still shows the full cheeks and lips so characteristic of earlier sculptures from the same region.

Plate 38	Naṭarāja	
Period 2	Type A.III (TAg)	12 arms
Eastern region	Karachi museum	Be

The uppermost hands are interlocked in *karkaṭa* while the next two support a snake. A tiny figure holding its hands in *añjali* emerges from the hood of the snake. One right hand holds a trident, another a dagger, and the lowermost hands in *muṣṭi* hold a string of severed heads. The main right arm is in *gajahasta* and is broken; it is on the same side as the foot in *agratalasañcara*. Yamunā stands on a crocodile on Naṭarāja's left, and Devī on her lion on his right. Naṭarāja dances on Nandi who looks upwards. The image is ithyphallic. A tiny figure of Type A.I dances below with the right arm outstretched horizontally, while the left hand holds a *khaṭvāṅga*. Bands of musicians on either side and a skeleton figure dances below.

Plate 39	Naṭarāja	
Period 2	Type B	4 arms
Northern region	Sas temple	Nagda (Ra)

Śiva's left main arm is in *gajahasta*, and the right arm, bent at the elbow, holds *patāka hasta* beside his face. The other two images support the roof. Devi is on Śiva's left. This is part of a decorated window, a common feature in Orissan sculpture, from Period 1 (Plates 105, 106).

Plate 40
Period 2
Northern region

Naṭarāja
Type B

7 arms (?)
Arthuna (Ra)

Naṭarāja dances in a pose which appears to be a combination of Types B and C.II. This is because the body is twisted after assuming the Type B position. The snake is held behind the crown with one hand in *muṣṭi*, the other in *ardhapātāka*. The *khaṭvāṅga* in the left hand is the only attribute that can be clearly seen. A small Viṣṇu (identified by the discus in his left hand and club in his right hand) plays a drum and Nandi to his right also plays a drum.

Plate 41	Naṭarāja	
Period 2	Type B	8 arms
Northern region		Arthuna

As for most examples from the Gujara Pratihara period, the snake is held behind the crown. (Plate 43). In one right hand a trident is held, another is in *sūcī hasta*, and another held in front of the chest probably holds a half-skull. One left hand holds a *khaṭvāṅga* and another is in *patāka*. A tiny figure beneath Naṭarāja imitates his dance. Brahmā, identifiable by his three heads, plays a drum, whereas in Plate 40 Viṣṇu andNandi provide the percussion. All three, Viṣṇu, Nandi, and Brahmā, according to the texts, help keep the rhythm but it is more usual for Brahmā to play the cymbals (see Chapters I and II.

Plate 42	Naṭarāja	
Period 2	Type B	10 arms
Northern region	Sukhmahal compound	Bundi (Ra)

The snake is held overhead behind the crown with the hands in *muṣṭi*, figures facing forwards, and not high above the head, with the *muṣṭi* hands facing backwards, as in eastern images from Period 1 (Plates 13a, 17a). The only two weapons not damaged are the trident in the left hand and the shield in the right. The long garland that stretches to the ground is plain. Nandi is beside Naṭarāja and looks up at him but the image is not ithyphallic, the usual convention with Nandi looking upwards.

Plate 43 Naṭaraja
Period 2 Type A.III (SAg) 10 arms (?)
Northern region Gwalior museum (MPr)

The main left arm is bent and the hand is in *bastra*[43], while the main right hand is in *gajahasta* on the same side as the foot in *agratalasañcara*. The two uppermost hands hold a snake in *muṣṭi* while one on the right holds a *ḍamaru*, the other a trident, and another in *haṃsāsya* with the fingers pointing upwards is reminiscent of the much earlier image of Śiva from Samalaji.[44] A small figure between Naṭarāja's legs imitates the position of the hands, except that the left hand is in *patāka*, instead of *bastra*. This image has been identified as in the Gurjara Pratīhāra style.[45] Many of the Naṭarājas in this style have a tiny figure between the legs of the image, often imitating Naṭarāja's dance pose.

Plate 44 Naṭarāja
Period 2 Type B 10 arms
Northern region Gwalior museum (MPr)

The main right hand is in *alapadma* at shoulder level, while the left main arm is thrown upwards. The other right hands from top to bottom hold a trident, a bundle of sticks, and a snake. The fifth arm on the right is difficult to see but it rests on the thigh and hip. The other left hands hold a bow, a bell, and a *kapāla*. The broken object beside the bow indicates the presence of a fifth arm on the left side. A drummer and cymbal player lean outwards on either side of the image. This image is notable for the variety of its attributes and has been identified as belonging to the Paramāra style.[46]

Plate 45	Naṭarāja	
Period 2	Type B	10 arms
Northern region	Udayesvara temple	Udaipur (MPr)

The main right hand holds a *khaṭvāṅga*, and the main left hand is stretched straight downwards with the hand in *haṃsāsya*. Other hands on the right side hold, from top to bottom, a bell, a bundle of sticks, and a sword. On the left hand side only a *khaṭvāṅga* is identifiable. The figure is flanked by musicians leaning outwards. The torso is raised on the side opposite to the uplifted leg, as in the preceding image (Plate 44). There are numerous Naṭarāja images on this temple, some in *kūḍus*, as in this example, and others in niches. These images are in the Paramāra style.[47]

Plate 46	Naṭarāja	
Period 2	Type B	arms (?)
Northern region	Udayesvara temple	Udaipur (MP)

Although most of the arms and all the attributes have been destroyed, this image with the uplifted leg on the same side as the arm in *gajahasta* has been included because it, like all the Naṭarāja images on this temple, imparts a tremendous feeling for the dance. The attributes were no doubt similar to those in Plate 45. It is placed in a *kūḍu*, the most popular place for Paramāra images.

Plate 47	Naṭarāja	
Period 2	Type A.III (SAg)	10 arms
Northern region		Lakhamandal (UP)

Of the two main arms, the left is in *patāka* and the right in *gajahasta*. The right arm in *gajahasta* is on the same side as the foot in *agratalasañcara*. The uppermost hands are bent backwards at the wrists so that the palms point upwards and rest by the head. Early images of **Naṭarāja** from Orissa often hold the uppermost pair of hands framing the face, or near the head, in a similar fashion, but in the Orissan examples the palms face backwards. The next pair of arms hold the snake overhead, which is also typical of Orissan and Deccani Naṭarājas as well as of Siva dancing in his aspect as Vīṇādhara from the eastern region (see Chapter VI). One right hand holds the *ḍamaru*, and the lowermost right hand touches a seated female figure under her chin (see also Orissan and Paṭtadakal Naṭarājas from the first period). The lowermost left hand rests on the thigh in *kaṭyavalambita*, and another left hand holds a club trident. A large garland hangs down to the knees of the image.

Plate 48	Naṭarāja	
Period 2	Type A.III (TK)	4 arms
Northern region	Balesvara temple	Jageswar (UP)

The two main arms are in *patāka* and *gajahasta*; this latter *hasta* is on the same side as the foot in *kuñcita*. The other hands are both in *muṣṭi*, the left holding a snake, and the right a trident. The composition of this Naṭarāja figure is similar to the image on the ceiling of the Papanatha temple, Pattadakal (Plate 22), from the first period. Skanda is in the upper left-hand corner, Gaṇeśa in the upper right, and both are seated. An orchestra plays on either side of Naṭarāja. All the figures display some Gupta characteristic: the tight curls on the wig of the drummer, the tied locks of Naṭarāja, the flautist, and the female figures. These are all anachronistic features which often survived in the hills after their disappearance from the plains.[48] The loin cloth worn by Naṭarāja is of the same design as the one worn by the Bhikṣāṭana figure from Sahi of Type A.V*, Period 2; now in the British Museum, London. Both these images come from the NW Himalaya.

Plate 49	Naṭarāja	
Period 2	Type B	8 arms
Southern region	Brahmapurisvara temple	Pullamangai (TN)

The main right hand is in *ardhacandra*, the main left is in *gajahasta*, twisted at the wrist so that the palm faces outward. The arm in *gajahasta* is on the opposite side to the uplifted leg. The uppermost right hand holds a *ḍamaru*, the next an axe, and the next an unidentifiable *hasta*. The uppermost left hand is in *ardhacandra* and supports a flame, possibly inside a vessel. (Another Naṭarāja image from the same temple holds a vessel of fire.) The next left hand in *muṣṭi*, holds a snake, and the next, also in *muṣṭi*, supports a trident. A drummer sits on Śiva's left.

Plate 50	Naṭarāja	
Period 2	Type B	4 arms
Southern region	Kuranganatha temple	Srinivasanallur (TN)

The main hands are: right in *ardhacandra* by the shoulder, with the left thrown upwards. This is the same combination as for Naṭarāja from the Brahmapurisvara temple at Pullamangai of Type A. The lowermost left hand holds a trident, and the upper right a bell with a handle shaped like a thunderbolt. Nandi peers from the upper right corner and a drummer plays beside Śiva's left foot.

Plate 51	Naṭarāja	
Period 2	Type C.I	4 arms
Southern region	Brhadisvara temple	Tanjore (TN)

This example is clearly a copy in stone of the bronze Naṭarājas from this period. The main arms in *gajahasta* and *patāka* are distinct while the other two hands probably hold fire and the drum. Some of the painting remains on the back wall.

Plate 52	Naṭarāja	
Period 2	Type C.I	4 arms
Southern region	**Karunasvami temple**	Tanjore (TN)

This Naṭarāja is much heavier in appearance than the example from the Brhadisvara temple (Plate 51) but the main arms are the same: *gajahasta* and *patāka* and the drum is held in the right hand and the fire in the left hand, both conventions for bronzes of this period. The hair flowing outwards from his crown has been sculpted to look like the snakes Śiva wears in his matted locks. The skull in the centre of the crown is also reminiscent of bronze Naṭarājas. This representation of Naṭarāja is possibly the most interesting one from this period as it includes the *bhakta* Kāraikkālammaiyār dancing to Naṭarāja's left while an orchestra accompanies him on the right. Apasmāra does not have an arched back but kneels beneath Śiva's foot.

Plate 53	Naṭarāja	
Period 3	Type B	8 arms
Deccani region	Hoysaḷeśvara tempie	Halebīd (Ka)

The main right arm is in *dola* and the main left hand in *śukacancu* rests by the left knee. The right arms hold a rosary, *khaṭvāṅga* and sword, while the left hands hold a drum, shield, and a half-skull.

Plate 54	Naṭarāja	
Period 3	Type B	8 arms
Deccani region	Hoysalesvara temple	Halebid

The main left arm is in *gajahasta* while the main right hand in *patāka* has a rosary between the thumb and index finger. The other right hands hold trident, and thunder bolt, which is also held by Paramāra images of the second period (Plate 44). The left hands hold a drum, shield and a half-skull.

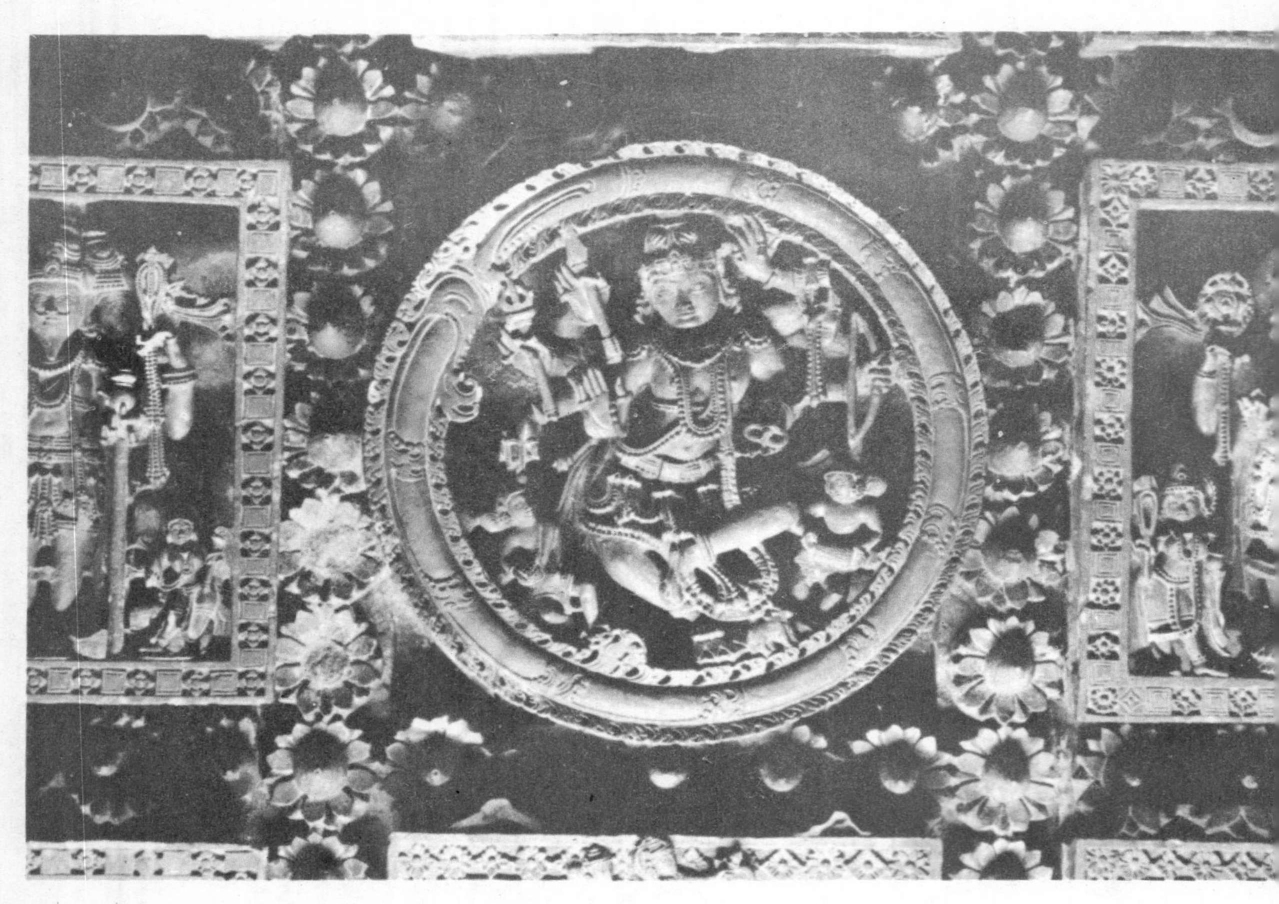

Plate 55	Naṭarāja	
Period 3	Type B	8 arms
Deccani region	Hoysalesvara temple	Halebid (Ka)

The ceiling of this temple is covered in carvings and this is one of numerous depictions of Naṭarāja. The main right hand holds a rosary, the main left hand is uplifted in *alapadma* (*vismaya*). The other right hands hold an arrow, trident and drum, while the left hands hold a bow, drum, and trident.

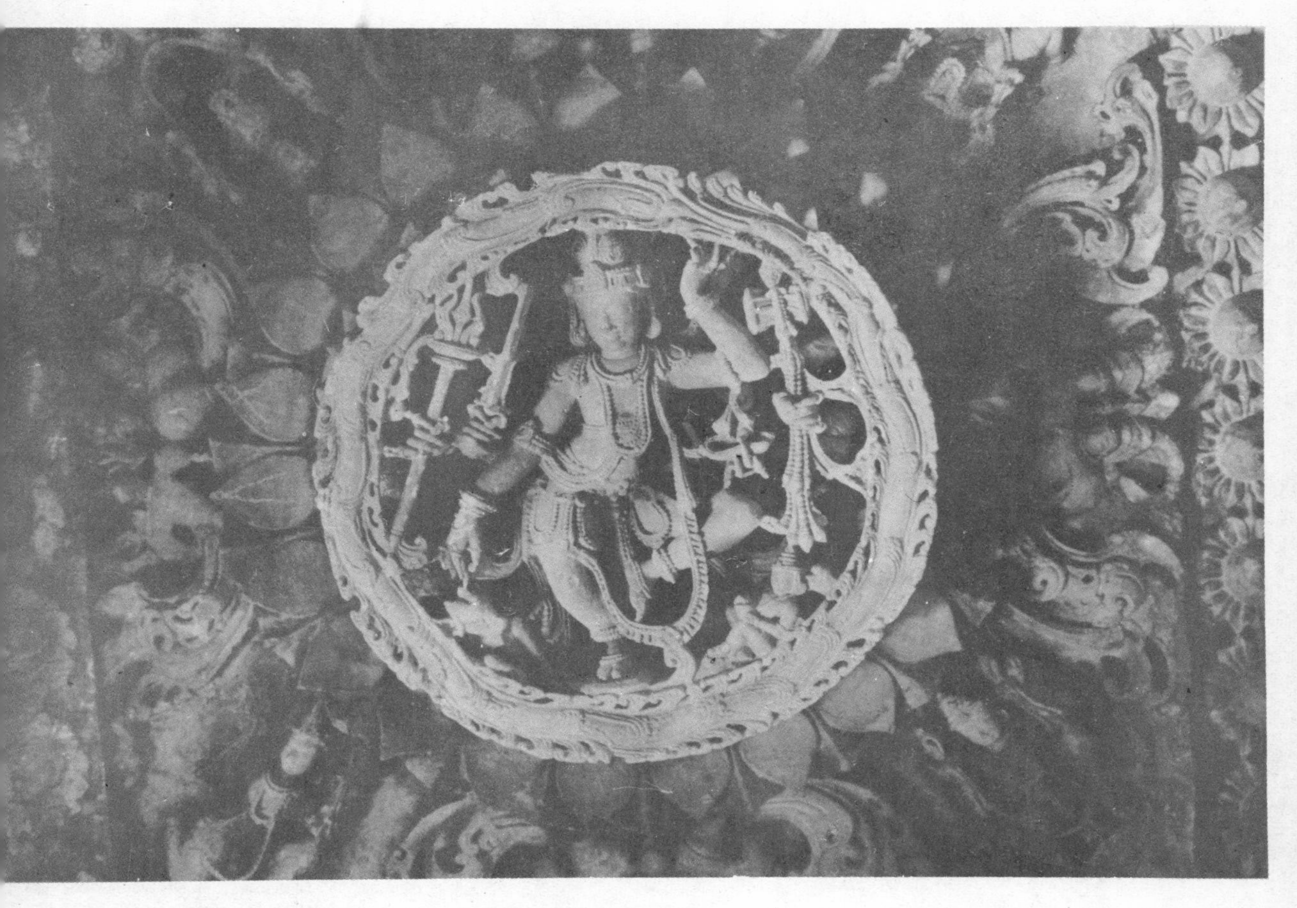

Plate 56	Naṭarāja	
Period 3	Type B	8 arms
Deccani region	Hoysalesvara temple	Halebid (Ka)

This Naṭarāja is also on the ceiling of the temple. The main right arm is in *dola*, the main left hand is in *alapadma* (*vismaya*) which is held in the same position as for the other example. The sword and trident are held in the right hands while the drum and a half-skull are held in the left hands.

Plate 57	Naṭarāja	
Period 3	Type B	10 arms
Deccani region	Delhi museum	Ka

The main right hand is in *patāka* with a rosary held between the index finger and the thumb. The main left hand holds a lemon. Śiva holds a *khaṭvāṅga* and *ḍamaru* in his right hands and in his left hands a trident, shield, bow and snake. Nandi reclines behind.

Plate 58	Naṭarāja	
Period 3	Type B	4 arms
Southern region	Naṭarāja temple	Cidambaram (TN)

This is a rather static figure as there is no deflection of the hips. The back right hand holds a *ḍamaru*, the back left a flaming torch. The main right hand is in *ardhacandra*, and the main left in *gajahasta*. The leg that is raised is on the same side as the arm in *gajahasta*, unlike the other southern example, from the second period (Plate 49). This image is one of the main niche figures on the eastern *gopura*.

Plate 59	Naṭarāja	
Period 3	Type D	2 arms (?)
Southern region	Naṭarāja temple (Gopura)	Cidambaram (TN)

There are numerous depictions of Naṭarāja in this pose on the *gopuras* of the Naṭarāja temple. Only two hands can be clearly seen and these are in the usual positions for images in this pose.

Plate 60	Naṭarāja	
Period 3	Type D	4 arms
Southern region	Airavatesvara temple	Darasuram (TN)

The main arms are in the usual position for Type D images: the right in *patāka* by the chest and the left stretched overhead. One right hand holds a drum. Apasmāra is beneath Śiva's feet. A *gaṇa* dances in Type B on one side and a drummer is on the other. This is one of many dance carvings on pillars of the porch and in this temple, dance formed a regular part of daily worship.

CHAPTER V

Components of the Naṭarāja Image

The function of attributes and other subsidiary elements in iconography is to refer to different mythological events or particular tasks that a god may perform. It follows from this that to multiply the number of references, the number of symbols held must be increased. In dance, hand signs are used to indicate the various attributes of Śiva. For example, the half-skull begging bowl (*kapāla*) is shown with the *śarpasirsa* hand position (Plates 64a and b) and the sword with *ardhapātaka* (Plates 64c and d). Some attributes, such as the skull resting atop a staff (*khaṭvāṅga*) are considered too complicated to be shown. Others such as the ring of flames (*tiruvāśi*) which often surrounds bronze images of Type C.I Naṭarājas are very rarely shown. In general, the dances current today depict a smaller variety of attributes than those in sculpture.

Sculpture depicts the actual attributes while dancers can only suggest them. While some multi-armed images hold a wide variety of attributes, others display hand signs; yet despite the number of hand positions described in the *NŚ* and the number of arms available on many of the images, the actual range of those employed is relatively small. The use of a limited number of hand positions is also characteristic of the pure dance (*nṛtta*) portions of both Bharata Nāṭyam and Oḍissi. In fact the *AD* lists only thirteen single hand gestures out of a possible twenty-eight that are to be used in pure dance[1] (Plates 9a–jj). These twenty-eight are used in the narrative portions of the dance and in different combinations; thus there are numerous possible variations.

In considering the development of the Naṭarāja image we must first look at Śiva's most famous form, of Type C.I, in which he has four arms, one in *gajahasta*, one in *abhaya*, one holding a *ḍamaru*, and another in *ardhacandra* holding a flame. It is this pose that is assumed in the Bharata Nāṭyam tradition when Naṭarāja is depicted, the arms being held to imitate either the front pair (*gajahasta* and *abhaya*) or the rear pair (*śukacancu* and *ardhacandra*) (Plates 61a–d).

The combination of one arm in *gajahasta* and the other bent so that the hand rests near the shoulder, is seen in some Gupta and first-period images of Naṭarāja, and continues throughout all periods and regions. The hand sign used for the hand near the shoulder in later images is *patāka/ardhacandra*, while in the earlier ones it may also be in *saṃdaṃśa*. The other two hands usually hold the flame and the *ḍamaru*, but these are not depicted with the same frequency in all periods and regions.

Although many more images exist than those discussed here, the variety of hand signs identifiable in Naṭarāja figures in all periods and regions is limited, and practically all the variations are depicted in the first period. The most common positions for the main arms for images from the first period are given below. Images with more than one pair of arms often include two or more of these combinations:

> One arm in *gajahasta* and the other in *patāka/ardhacandara/saṃdaṃśa*; One arm in *dola* (*NŚ*) or thrown upwards, and bent at the elbow so the hand rests by the shoulder.

Less common combinations are:

> One arm in *gajahasta*, the other in *haṃsāsya* by the shoulder; One arm in *gajahasta*, the other in *alapadma* by the head.

The use of the *saṃdaṃśa hasta* for one of the main hands in combination with *gajahasta*, appears in the first period in the Deccani (Plates 18, 23, 25, 29 and 30), eastern (Plate 15), and southern (Plate 33), regions. It continues until the second period. For the arm in *gajahasta* the hand may be held in *patāka*, palm facing outward (Plate 22), as in earlier images, or downwards (Plates 15, 16, 17a, 23 and 25). Images from the third period from the northern and eastern regions often have

Plate 61

The four arms normally depicted in Type C.I bronzes of Naṭarāja have their counterparts in three different combinations of hand positions in Bharata Nāṭyam.

Plate 61a

The left hand is in *gajahasta*, the right in *ardhacandra/patāka*. The back right hand in *śukacancu* holds the drum (*ḍamaru*,) the back left hand in *ardhacandra* supports the flame. Except for the use of *ardhacandra hasta* supporting the fire, there is no difference between the hand signs used in Bharata Nāṭyam and those commonly seen in Coḷa and later bronzes from south India. Kivalur, 11th *c.* Tanjore Art Gallery. See Plate 1b for full figure.

61b

Plate 61b

The right arm is in *gajahasta*, and the left in *patāka/abhaya*, symbolizing protection

Plate 61c

The left hand is in *alapadma*, symbolizing holding the fire, and the right is in *śukacancu* symbolizing holding the drum

Plate 61d

The left arm is in *gajahasta* as in Plate 61a but the right in *śukacancu* holds the *ḍamaru* as in Plate 61c

61c

61d

this hand on the end of the *gajahasta* in *mayūra hasta*. One main hand in *haṃsāsya*, the other in *gajahasta*, is a combination found in some first period images from the eastern region (Plates 13a, b, 14) while one arm in *gajahasta*, the other in *ùlapadma* at the level of the head is seen in first and second period images from the same region. Many Naṭarāja images have their subsidiary arms resting on the hip, and on the thigh (Plates 13a, 15, 16, 17a, 18, 20 and 21). That the hands rest in these particular positions could indicate a relationship with the hand positions used in the *tribhaṅga* position seen in the Oḍissi dance style, where the feet are of Type A.I (Plate 8d). Several Naṭarāja images of the first period from the eastern and Deccani regions, and some of the second period from the northern region have these combinations. However, these hand positions are not found in third period images of Naṭarāja.

Among common single hand gestures, sculptures with one arm thrown upwards are seen from the first period in Deccani images (Plates 18, 21, 27 and 28) and in the second period southern (Plate 50) and northern regions (Plates 44). Southern images continue to depict this arm position until the third period.

One or both hands at head level so that the palm faces inwards is found in the eastern (Plates 15, 16, 17a) images of Naṭarāja from the first period. Representations of *karaṇas* from the second and third periods often show the same hand position, a pose not seen in the basic steps (*adavus*) of Bharata Nāṭyam today.[2]

Haṃsāsya hasta in one of the main hands of Naṭarāja appears in the first period for images of the Deccani region (Plate 19) and in images from the eastern region (Plates 13a, b, and 14). Other images from the northern and eastern regions have their subsidiary hands in *haṃsāsya*. *Haṃsāsya hasta* is commonly used in both the *nṛtta* and *nāṭya* portions of Oḍissi and Bharata Nāṭyam. First period images from the Deccani region may have the main arm in *dola* (*NŚ*), but more often, *dola hasta* is represented by one of the subsidiary hands (Plates 18, 19). This *hasta* is used in the Bharata Nāṭyam and Oḍissi dance styles in both the *nṛtta* and *nāṭya* portions.

Most of the Type A images have the same arm in *gajahasta* as the foot in *kuñcita* or *agratalasañcara*. There are, however, some exceptions. Usually Type B images with one arm in *gajahasta* have this *hasta* on the side opposite to the uplifted leg. Most images of Type C have the same arm in *gajahasta* as the leg lifted up and across the body. There are, however, some exceptions here too, in particular the bronze in worship in the Madurai temple, for which there is a peculiar mythical explanation for the opposite leg being raised.[3]

Attributes carried by Naṭarāja and other dancing figures of Śiva are divided here into three categories on the basis of frequency. The three most common, comprising the first category, are: the snake, the trident, and the *ḍamaru*. Practically all images of Śiva carry at least one of these attributes and it is these that most often identify the image.

The *ḍamaru* is held by images from all periods in the Deccani and eastern regions, while in the southern region it is less common in the first period but increases in popularity, so that by the third period, particularly in Type C.I images, it is one of the most common attributes. The *ḍamaru* is shown in the Bharata Nāṭyam dance style, being suggested in poses and in movement when Naṭarāja's dance is portrayed (Plates 61a-d).

The origin of the other two most common attributes, the trident and the snake, is linked to Śiva's dance, as recorded in the *Cidaṁbaram Māhātmya*. Along with a tiger and Apasmāra, they emerge from the sacrificial fire prepared by the misguided sages (see Chapter IV). Because sculptures of Siva with these attributes pre-date the existing text of the *Cidambaram Māhātamya*, it seems likely that their inclusion results from a desire to rationalize features derived from an earlier mythology. Most Bharata Nāṭyam recitals include at least a fleeting reference to the *Cidaṃbaram Māhātmya* story (see Plates 62a-e).

The *triśula* is perhaps Śiva's most popular weapon in iconography—it appears in Naṭarāja images from all four regions in the first two periods. It is first seen in the eastern and Deccani regions, later spreading to other regions. The trident is also held by some *karaṇa* and dancing figures, as well as other aspects of Śiva, such as Vīṇādhara, and Bhairava, when depicted in dancing postures (Chapter VI). In southern images from the third period it is less frequent. One of the hand signs described in the *Abhinayadarpaṇa* is *triśula* and this is employed in Bharata Nāṭyam when depicting Śiva but usually only when the *Cidaṁbaram Māhātmya* is being portrayed (Plates 62a–e). It is more commonly used to symbolize the spear of Kārttikeya, Śiva's son. When describing Śiva, the same gesture, with the hand held before the forehead, is used to allude to Śiva's third eye (Plate 65c), and it seems possible that the association of Śiva with the three-pronged weapon in iconography may ultimately derive from an allusion to the 'third eye of enlightenment'.

The snake in particular has been associated with Śiva in all aspects from the earliest times and is one of the commonest attributes of Naṭarāja. It may be held in either hand or in both, in which case it is usually raised overhead. The snake held overhead in both hands appears in the eastern (Plates 13a, b, 17a) and Deccani (Plates 18, 19, 24) Naṭarājas from the first period and continues to be common in the eastern region until the third period. Some northern images have this feature(Plates 40–3, 47), but only one southern example, on the Kailasantha temple, Kancipuram, from the earliest period, holds the snake overhead, and in this case a small figure emerges from the hood with its hands held in *añjali*, a feature also seen in eastern images of the second period.

In Deccani images, the snake is usually present, held overhead in both hands, or to the side in one hand (Plates 18, 19, 24, 29). There are also examples of the snake held in one hand from all the other regions (Plates 15, 16, 20, 33, 43, 44).

Śiva may hold a snake in southern sculptures but in Bharata Nāṭyam the snakes are not held but worn as Śiva's ornaments: in his hair, as bracelets on the arms, around the wrist, ankles, neck or as his sacred thread. When the Bharata Nāṭyam dancer adopts the Type C.I pose to symbolize Śiva's cosmic dance, it is usually preceded or followed by a description of these snakes (Plates 63a–f).

The snake held overhead is an important attribute of Naṭarāja not only in sculpture but also in his depiction in the Oḍissi dance style (Plate 63a). The pose adopted in the dance when holding the snake overhead is of Type B, despite the fact that all the examples in sculpture from the eastern region are of Type A. The Orissan text, the *Śilpa Prakāśa*, however, illustrates an image of Naṭarāja, holding a snake overhead of Type A[4] and hence it is possible that the dance maintains a sculptural tradition which is no longer evident in existing icons.

The second category comprises somewhat less common attributes, which are found in most regions at one time but are not universally associated with Naṭarāja. These are: the axe, the skull, the fire, the rosary, the *khaṭvāṅga* and an erect phallus.

The axe does not appear in many images of Naṭarāja, but is found in images from the first and second period in the Deccani region, and the first period in the eastern region. In the southern region, the first period image of Type C.I at Siyamangalam holds an axe, but otherwise it does not appear in this area until the third period. Depictions of Śiva in Bharata Nāṭyam sometimes use the *ardhapatāka* hand position (as defined in the *Abhinayadarpaṇa*), to symbolize the axe (Plates 64c, d).

The vessel with fire is held by an image from the southern region from Siyamangalam, but fire as an attribute is generally not common in Type A images from the southern region until the end of the second period, after which several stone sculptures and most southern bronzes of Type C.I are depicted holding fire. Three Deccani images of the first period hold a similar type of vessel containing fire to that held by the Siyamangalam Naṭarāja, but otherwise fire is not included in Naṭarāja images beyond south India. In Bharata Nāṭyam fire held in the left hand is symbolized by *alapadma hasta* (Plates 61a–d).

In the Deccani region, the skull used as a begging bowl appears as an attribute of Naṭarāja in only one example from the first period, but it is common in all periods in images from the eastern region. Two second period Naṭarājas from the northern region also hold the skull. The depiction of this attribute in Bharata Nāṭyam is performed by displaying the *śarpasirṣa* hand position and it is only included in items describing Śiva in his form as a wandering beggar (Plates 64a, d) (see Chapter VI). This provides an example of the way in which sculpture as a static representation can simultaneously include references to various aspects of Śiva's mythology, whereas in the dance, when dif-

Plate 62

Some incidents from the *Cidaṃbaram Māhātmya* as presented in Bharata Nāṭyam (including representations of the trident, malignant dwarf and tiger).

Plate 62a

The right hand in *triśula* symbolizes the trident which emerged from the sacrificial fire. The left hand in *muṣṭi* holds on to the end of the trident.

Plate 62b

The dwarf Muyalagan, or Apasmāra, is depicted in a position of submission with both hands in *patāka* beside the shoulders.

62a

62b

Plate 62c

Both hands held in *urnanabha* can represent the claws of the tiger

Plate 62d

The last gesture is immediatly followed by both hands again in *urnanabha* but the palms are downwards and used to make ripping gestures representing Śiva tearing the skin off the tiger.

Plate 62e

The tiger skin is then tied around Śiva's waist, using both hands in *catura*.

Plate 63

Gestures used to represent Śiva's serpents in Oḍissi and Bharata Nāṭyam

Plate 63a

In the Oḍissi dance style the snake held overhead is symbolized by both hands either in *muṣṭi*, or in *śukacancu* as shown here. The palms are uppermost. The manner in which the snake is held overhead is very similar to that seen in sculptures from the eastern and Deccani regions. (See Plates 13a, 17a, 18, 19 and 24).

Plate 63b

Bronze Naṭarājas usually have many snakes and cobras with erect heads. In this example Naṭarāja has snakes in his matted hair, in his crown, as bracelets, and as ornaments for his upper arms and body. This is also graphically depicted in Bharata Naṭyam. Naṭarāja, Kilayur, 14th c., Tanjore Art Gallery.

Plate 63c

The erect hood of the cobra is depicted by both hands in *Sarpaśirṣa ḥasta* moving downwards from above the head to the centre of the body.

Plate 63d

End of the movement depicting the hooded cobra.

Plate 63e

The outline of the upper arm ornaments and bracelets made of serpents is depicted with one hand in *Sarpaśirṣa hasta*.

Plate 63f

The arms held sideways with the hands in *Sarpaśirṣa hasta* symbolize snakes in Śiva's matted locks. (See Plates 64g, h. for Śiva's matted locks in Bharata Nāṭyam)

ferent attributes are presented sequentially, Śiva's different manifestations appear as separate entities.

In the first period, the rosary is found exclusively amongst images of Naṭarāja and Ardhanārīśvara (Chapter VI) from the eastern region, with only one possible exception from the Deccani region. By the third period, however, several Naṭarāja figures from the Deccani region hold a rosary.

The *khaṭvāṅga* is practically confined to third period images of the Deccani region (Plates 53–7) and northern region from the second period (Plates 40, 41, 45). The *Śilpa Prākāśa* includes a *khaṭvāṅga* in its illustration for Naṭāmbara II but I do not know of any example of it in Orissa.[5] This attribute is apparently too complicated to be shown successfully in dance.

Only eastern region images of Śiva dancing are depicted as ithyphallic; these include stone and bronze images. The images are of the first to third periods, and include several representations of Naṭarāja and dancing Vīṇādharas. In the dance no attempt is made to refer directly to Śiva's ithyphallic nature, but the most common gestural reference to Siva is the *śikhara* hand sign, which represents the *liṅga*, and hence refers directly to his sexuality (Plates 10a, b).

In the third, least common, category are a number of attributes not often seen in images of Śiva: the garland held overhead, the scarf held overhead, the lotus, the noose, the bell, the dagger, the sword, the shield, the water-pot, the deer and the *nandi dhvaja* (staff surmounted by Nandi). Many of these are found in northern and eastern images of the second period, and Deccani images of the third. Unlike multi-armed images of the first period, which often do not carry attributes, the later images usually have an attribute in each hand, hence the increased variety of symbols (Plates 64c, d, i, j).

Most of these attributes are not associated with any particular region or period. Among other exceptions is the scarf, which is held by several images from the eastern and Deccani regions. Although the scarf is not frequently depicted as an attribute of Naṭarāja, it is shown in sculptures of dancers from the eastern region of the earliest period (see Chapter VII).

The water-pot is an attribute also seen in images of Vīṇādhara of the second period from the eastern region (see Chapter VI), and is similar to those carried by wandering mendicants today.

The deer is confined to the southern region. Its significance is sometimes explained as symbolizing the unpredictability of the mind but it must also be related to Śiva's manifestation as Paśupati, Lord of the animals. In Bharata Nāṭyam the deer is symbolized by *simhamukha hasta*, frequently in combination with *ardhapatāka* symbolizing the axe. This combination of axe and deer is frequent in south Indian bronzes of the Cōḷa period (Plates 64c, d).

The *nandi dhvaja*, though of infrequent occurrence, is an example of an attribute that is found in certain images from both the southern and Deccani regions in the first and second periods. The flag-pole in Śaivite temples is often close to the reclining Nandi which faces the shrine, while in Pahārī miniatures the flag of Śiva normally carries a picture of Nandi. Dancers indicate this attribute as a flag using the *ardhapatāka* hand sign (Plates 64i–j).

Minor images associated with Śiva dancing

Among minor images associated with Śiva dancing, Apasmāra, the small dwarf, is normally depicted lying beneath his feet. The practice of placing major iconographic pieces on the back of minor figures is an ancient one. Deformed creatures, intended as sculptural representations of spirits but resembling Apasmāra in general form, are depicted supporting *Yakṣas/Yakṣīs* and female figures on railing pillars of Buddhist monuments[6] from the second century B.C. V. S. Agrawala explains the presence of a figure beneath the feet of several Hindu deities thus: 'Each Deva is conceived of on the plane of manifestation in the hero-pattern (*eka-vīra*). It means that in order to demonstrate its effective existence, he must have his counterpart in the form of an *Asura*... The *Asura* is intolerant of the *Deva*. He strives to invade and penetrate into the sphere of the *Deva*. The *Deva* as hero resists and retaliates and his onslaught ends in prostration of the *Asura*.'[7]

The Gudimallam *liṅga*,[8] one of the earliest representations of Śiva, shows him standing in *sama pāda* on a fantastic creature with pointed ears.

Plate 64

Further attributes of Śiva in Bharata Nāṭyam

Plate 64a

One hand in *Sarpaśirṣa* symbolizes the begging bowl formed from a half skull (*kapāla*). This usually indicates Śiva's form as Bhikṣātana. See Chapter VI.

Plate 64b

Bhikṣātana in bronze, Tiruvenkadu, 11th c. Tanjore Art Gallery.

Plate 64c

The left hand in *ardhapatāka* represents the axe, the right hand in *simhamukha* represents the deer. These attributes are shown when describing Śiva.

Plate 64d

Both the deer and the axe are supported by *tripatāka hasta*. This bronze of Śiva is accompanied by Parvatī sitting on his left (not shown), Melayúr, 13–14 th c. Tanjore Art Gallery

Plate 64e

The left hand in *ardhacandra* placed beside the head represents the crescent moon worn by Śiva. The right hand in *śikhara* beside the mouth accompanied by a slight smile shows Śiva's beatific expression.

Plate 64f

Head of bronze Naṭarāja, Kivalur, 11th c., Tanjore Art Gallery. See also Plate 1b for the full image.

Plate 64g

The hands with fingers outstretched shake and move down and outwards representing Śiva's matted locks.

Plate 64h

Bronze Naṭarāja, Kilayur, 14 th c. Tanjore Art Gallery.

Plate 64i

To symbolize a flag with Nandi (the bull and Śiva's mount) imprinted on it (*nandi dhvaja*), the dancer first holds one hand in *simhamukha* to represent the bull. The *nandi dhvaja* flies above all Śiva temples in south India. The gesture indicates that Śiva resides in the particular temple mentioned in the song.

Plate 64j

The left hand in *tripatāka* symbolizes a *gopura*, the gateway to a temple. The right hand in *ardhapatāka* represents Śiva's standard flying. The juxtaposition of these two *mudrās* indicates that Śiva's flag bears a picture of Nandi. In this case the *mudrās* used in dance in no way represent the depictions in sculpture or painting. See also Chapter IV, Plate 10b for the depiction in Bharata Nāṭyam of Śiva riding on Nandi.

Later images of Śiva such as one from the southern region on the Dharmarajaratha at Mahabalipuram,[9] and from the Deccani region at Pattadakal (Plates 20–2, 25–6) personify the creature on which Śiva stands. The textual reference to Apasmāra, however, is considerably later than its depiction in iconography,[10] and not until the southern legend associated with the Cidambaram temple is the dwarf actually named Mūyaḷagan and considered to be evil personified[11] and the symbol of forgetfulness.[12] In this myth, Śiva as Naṭarāja dances on Apasmāra's back and breaks it,[13] which fits the standard description of Apasmāra writhing on his stomach, his body usually lying parallel to Naṭarāja's shoulders with the head on the right side.[14] There are examples, however, where Apasmāra faces left[15] and he is also shown kneeling[16] or supporting Śiva with his shoulders, hands and head[17] or head alone.[18] While Apasmāra is an important feature of the Cidambaram myth, particularly in images of Type C, he is also found in southern Naṭarāja images of Types A, B, C, and D, and in some Deccani images of Types A and B. He is never found in Naṭarājas of Type E, and is not usually found in images from the eastern and northern regions.

Various *āgamas* specify that Apasmāra should be present when Śiva dances in certain modes,[19] but in the discussion of *karaṇas* the *NŚ* does not mention Apasmāra.

Forms of Śiva such as Sukhāsanamūrti (Umāmaheśvaramūrti),[20] Tripurāntakamūrti,[21] Bhairava,[22] Andhakāsuravadha,[23] Dakṣināmūrti[24] and Gaṅgadharamūrti[25] sometimes include Apasmāra under one or both of Śiva's feet.

In the illustrations included here, Apasmāra is present only in images of the first period from the Deccani region (Plates 20–2, 25–6) and of the third period from the southern region (Plates 59, 60). As far as stone sculptures are concerned, Apasmāra is by no means universally included in Naṭarājas of the southern region,[26] and in stone he appears most frequently in first period images of the Deccani region. Perhaps because Apasmāra is frequently present in later bronzes from the southern region, many authors have considered it a characteristic of that region, despite the fact that he is often absent from earlier bronzes. In Bharata Nāṭyam, Apasmāra is depicted rather literally with the dancer arching her back and looking over one shoulder (Plate 62b).

Nandi

Śiva's vehicle (*vāhana*) is Nandi, the bull, and he is depicted seated or dancing upon it. The *MP* states that Śiva should dance on Nandi[27]—the philosophical implications of Śiva's relationship with the bull[28] have been discussed by Sivaramamurti.

Iconographic representations of Śiva dancing on Nandi are found in Bengal[29] (Plate 38), Orissa,[30] Assam[31] and Nepal,[32] from the second and third periods. The Amrtagatesvara temple at Melakkadambur[33] in south India has a bronze image of Śiva dancing on the bull, but this is actually a Pala sculpture from Bengal, removed later to the south.

Nandi is present in stone images from the earliest period from the southern (Plate 35), eastern (Plates 15–17a), and Deccani (Plates 18, 22–4) regions. There is a unique sculpture of the first period from the southern region, of Nandi dancing in Type A.V.*, while Naṭarāja is shown dancing in Type D (Plate 35). Images from the latter part of the second and from the third period in the eastern region (chiefly Bengal) dance on Nandi (Plate 38). Most images from the eastern region which include Nandi are ithyphallic, and show Nāndi looking up. One southern (Plate 50) and one northern (Plate 42) image from the second/third periods includes Nandi.

In some stone sculptures and paintings which have been identified as 'Śiva's evening dance', Nandi plays the drum.[34] Bharata Nāṭyam always includes Nandi as the drummer when the orchestra for Śiva's dance is described.

Devi

Devi appears in Deccani region images from the earliest period, and also in the Gupta Naṭarāja image from Sirpur. In the southern representations Devī is not depicted as often, nor is she incorporated into the image through one of Naṭarāja's arms touching her, as in eastern and Deccani images of the first period (Plates 15–17a, 20–4). In the few examples from the northern region, Devī is sometimes present, often playing a lute (Plate 47, 48). In Bharata Nāṭyam it is rare for

Devī's presence to be alluded to when Naṭarāja's dance is described.

Gaṇeśa

In the eastern region, Gaṇeśa is present in only one early Naṭarāja image (Plate 13a) and does not appear thereafter. This is also true of the Deccani region, where several first period images have Gaṇeśa present (Plates 18–20), but later images do not. Only one northern image incorporates Gaṇeśa (Plate 48). In dance, Gaṇeśa is usually invoked prior to a recital but he is not normally included in the description of Śiva's dance.

Kārttikeya (Murugan, Skanda)

Kārttikeya riding his peacock does not appear as often as Gaṇeśa. He is present in a first-period image of Vīṇādhara from the eastern region (see Chapter VI) and a second-period Naṭarāja image from the northern region (Plate 48). Otherwise he is shown only as a small child whom Devī holds either in her arms or by his hand. Like Gaṇeśa, Kārttikeya is rarely included in items which describe Śiva's dance, but unlike Gaṇeśa there are numerous Bharata Nāṭyam songs which describe his amorous exploits.

Musicians

Musicians accompanying Naṭarāja are found in some representations from all regions and in all periods, and in different aspects of the dancing Śiva (Chapter VI). In the dance it is usually the celestial orchestra—Nandi and Viṣṇu playing drums, Brahmā playing the cymbals, and Sarasvatī the *viṇā*, which are described.

Bhṛṅgi

Bhṛṅgi, the emaciated sage, dances in those myths that are associated with his devotion to Śiva.[35] In images of the dancing Śiva of the first period in the Deccani region, Bhṛṅgi is sometimes shown dancing beside or between Śiva's legs. Second period northern images from the Gurjara Pratīhāra school also have this feature (Plates 41, 43). Bhṛṅgi is not often seen in eastern images but is represented in three sculptures from the region bordering the Deccani area: the Gupta image from Sirpur,[36] as well as two images of the second period from Somesvara[37] and Mukhalingam[38] (Plates 17a, b). Some images from the eastern region in second period Bengal have Bhṛṅgi dancing nearby. In the later second and third periods, Bhṛṅgi is sometimes depicted with three legs,[39] a feature associated with one of the Ardhanārīśvara myths. Bṛṅgi is rarely included in dance.[40]

Dikpālas

The eight guardians of the quarters (*dikpālas*), Indra, Agni, Yama, Nirṛti, Varuṇa, Vāyu, Kubera and Īśāna, feature in several descriptions of Śiva's dance. The *bhakta* Kāraikkāl Ammaiyār (6th c.) writes: 'When Thy crossed hands with bracelets move, the very cardinal points shiver.'[41]

The *MP* has the following prayer: 'May the lotus feet of Bhava, who shook the *diggajas* at the time of His dance, disperse all obstacles.'[42]
The poet Yogeśvara writes:

> Guardians of the quarters, move aside:
> Clouds quit the sky! . . .
> Remove your heaven, Brahmā;
> my Śambhu must have room to dance.[43]

The *NŚ* recommends that the guardians of the quarters be placated by the dancer walking round the stage before the performance begins.[44] Oḍissi and Kuchipudi dance recitals follow the precepts whereby the dancer with hands in *añjali* or *puṣpāñjali* goes to the eight quarters of the stage to rid it of evil spirits before beginning the recital.

Because of this association of the *dikpālas* with the dance in general and Naṭarāja in particular, it is natural that they should be featured in the iconography, At least one second period image from Tirupparamkunram in the southern region includes some of the *dikpālas*,[45] while Naṭarājas of the earliest period from the Deccani region are frequently accompanied by at least a few. The Naṭarāja image in the Ramesvara Cave at Ellora has four *dikpālas* over his left shoulder: Indra, Brahmā, Nirṛti and Agni; the remainder are above his head.[46] Other instances where *dikpālas* are present when Śiva dances, are at Elephanta,[47] Cave 14 at Ellora,[48] and at Aihole.[49] The most highly developed concept of the eight *dikpālas* surrounding a dancing Śiva is featured in eastern Cālūkyan and Hoysaḷa ceilings from the first and third periods (Plates 31, 55). They are also present when Śiva is illustrated dancing as

Gajāsurasamhāramūrti[50] At Amrtapura in the Deccani region (Karnataka). (This aspect of Śiva is discussed in the next chapter).

The presence of *dikpālas* indicates the cosmic nature of Śiva's dance, demonstrating that space itself moves as Śiva dances.[51] Some invocatory items in Bharata Nāṭyam may include obeisance to the *dikpālas* either in association with Śiva's dance or as part of the prayer. *Natanam Adinar*, a dance item in which Śiva's dance is described, represents the trembling of the eight quarters. While most Oḍissi invocatory items ask for the *dikpālas*' blessings, the main prayer is usually addressed to Gaṇeśa, Devī or the ten incarnations of Viṣṇu.

CHAPTER VI

Other Dancing Images of Śiva

Myths are created, not to mirror reality, but to convey the teaching of certain principles or to arouse a spiritual state in the person to whom they are related. One of the functions of myths is to impart traditional values, but they can also arouse strong religious fervour. They can be transmitted through many different media; in words, either spoken or sung, in drama, in dance, in paintings or in sculpture.

The shape and attributes of an image are not arbitrary but have evolved and been passed on, first orally, and later in a written form.[1] However, all images, including dancing images, do not always adhere to the iconographic texts and mnemonic verses (*dhyāna ślokas*) available to us.[2] An excellent example is provided in the *Śilpa Prakāśa*, a text which applies to Orissan sculpture, where the *dhyānas* for images do not include the wide variety of Naṭarājas or other aspects of dancing Śiva from this region depicted in sculpture. The relevant texts may simply have been lost, but it is also possible that individual sculptors have not adhered to the prescribed texts but instead have chosen to interpret the mythology according to their own inspiration.

There is a close association between dance in mythology, iconography, and live dance, but despite this, sources for iconographic representations of Śiva cannot always be found in mythology. In addition, some aspects of Śiva for which dance forms a part of the myth are never represented dancing either in sculpture or in live dance. The treatment of myths in live dance offers greater flexibility than is available to the sculptor; while myths may be interpreted literally, following the words of the song, additional subsidiary stories may also be introduced by a fleeting pose or hand gesture in the improvised portions of the dance. The latter are generally not predetermined but spring from the dancer's knowledge and mood during the performance. This is the poetry of the dance, performed when the same line is sung over and over again—a line which only suggests the almost infinite varieties possible. It is here that the dancer's knowledge of myths and command of the numerous combinations of hand positions is revealed. Some of these possibilities have been given in Chapter V and others will be included here. In this chapter, I shall examine and compare several aspects of Śiva's dancing forms, from the point of view of mythology, iconography, and the manner in which they are shown in dance. To show the range of different aspects of Śiva which may be depicted in dance poses I have included illustrations of Tripurāntaka, Ardhanārīśvara, Kālārimūrti, Gajāsurasaṃhāramūrti, Bhikṣāṭana, Vīrabhadra, Bhairava, and Viṇādhara, all of whom are occasionally depicted dancing. Although Bhikṣāṭana and Vīrabhadra are only rarely shown in dancing poses, they have been included because the mythology associated with them includes Śiva's dance and they both appear in live dance. Each aspect is usually represented in several of the eight dance poses included in Type A, and to a lesser extent in poses of Types B and C.II, but Type C.I and D are absent. Examples are so numerous that no attempt will be made to discuss all the relevant dancing images; instead attention will be concentrated on a few representative examples which were listed in Chapter IV under the period and region to which they belong.

In the living dance tradition of Bharata Nāṭyam, some but not all of Śiva's aspects other than Naṭarāja which are depicted in sculpture, are shown by the dancer in the *nāṭya* portions of the dance. Of these eight manifestations of Śiva, only four are depicted or alluded to with some frequency in Bharata Nāṭyam: Ardhanārīśvara, Kālārimūrti, Gajāsurasaṃhāramūrti, Tripurāntaka, and Bhikṣāṭana. The representation in dance of four of these is illustrated: Ardhanārīśvara (Plates 68 a-c), Kālārimūrti (Plates 71a-b), Tripurāntaka (Plates 66a-c) and Gajāsurasaṃhāramūrti (Plates 78 a-c), Ardhanārīśvara being the most popular. That is not to say that there is insufficient vocabulary to portray all eight manifestations of Śiva, but simply that I have not seen them frequently incorporated in the dance.

Among the manifestations of Śiva portrayed in dance, Naṭarāja can be identified on the basis of a single pose even with minor variations in the position of the hands, and the same applies to Kālārimūrti, Gajāsurasaṃhāramūrti, and Ardhanārīśvara. The latter, however, is usually portrayed in a more complex manner involving a number of gestures which culminate in the pose. Other manifestations are illustrated in the dance in a less symbolic manner and their identification depends more heavily on the context and the accompanying song. For instance, firing an arrow from a bow symbolizes Tripurāntaka in the context of a Śaivite piece, if it is shown in conjunction with the appropriate symbolism for the triple cities. It may also refer to the destruction of the god Kāma (desire) by Śiva's third eye if depiction of the bow is preceded by the mood of spring and the arrows are shown as flowers (Plates 66 a-c). In a Vaiṣṇavite piece, however, the bow forms the symbolic signature for the Rama *avatār* and assuming a pose holding a bow is sufficient to identify this characterization. The context is similarly important in the interpretation of iconography; where specific attributes such as the snake or *ḍamaru* allow an image to be definitely identified as Śiva, the accompanying non-specific attributes can then be given specific interpretations, the bow in this context referring to Tripurāntaka.

Tripurāntaka (The destroyer of the three cities)

Tripurāntaka is Śiva in his aspect as destroyer of the three cities of the demons. The myth of Tripurāntaka-Śiva in the Sanskritic tradition is probably an extension of Indra's feat in the *Ṛg Veda,* where he dances after the destruction of ninety cities:

> Thou Indra, the dancer, with delight (in battle) thou hast destroyed ninety cities; dancer (in battle) thou hast destroyed them with thy thunderbolt.[3]

In the *Mahābhārata,* it is Śiva, not Indra, who destroys the triple cities. There is no mention of a dance of victory,[4] but the account of the origin of dance in the *NŚ* centres on the Tripurāntaka story, when Indra, king of the gods, says to Brahmā:

> We want an object of diversion, which must be audible as well as visible. As the (existing) of [*sic*] *Vedas* are not to be listened to by those born as *Śūdras*; be pleased to create another *Veda* which will belong equally to all colour groups (*varṇa*).[5]

Brahma creates the *Nāṭya Veda* and also two dramas (*nāṭya*): the *Amṛta-Manthana*[6] (churning of the ocean) and the *Tripuṛadāha* (the burning of Tripura), to be presented at the festival of Indra. After seeing the Tripurāntaka drama, Śiva remembers the dance when he performed this feat and requests his disciple, Taṇḍu, to teach dance to Bharata, who subsequently composes the *NŚ*.[7] Thus the inspiration of the Tripurāntaka episode led to dance becoming an accompaniment to drama and the two have remained inseparable to the present day.

I have never seen this story enacted in Oḍissi, but in Bharata Naṭyām this exploit may be alluded to in any item which describes Śiva (Plates 66 a-c). It also forms the subject of one of the dance dramas in the repertoire of Yakṣagāna, the semi-classical style from Karnataka.[8]

The second verse of the invocatory prayer (*nāndī*) of the *Mudrārākṣasa* recalls Śiva's dance as Tripurāntaka:

> May Our Lord Śiva's cautious dance of yore,
> That celebrated Tripura's defeat
> When he most mercifully spared the world,
> And held the power of his thudding feet,
> Which threatened earth with burial, in check
> And kept the gestures of his flinging hands,
> Which would have burst out of the world in bounds,
> And lest it light upon an aim and burn,
> Did not allow his third dread eye to gaze,
> Once more protect you from vicissitudes![9]

This dance of Śiva is also known in the Tamil tradition, and is described thus in the *Cilappatikāram:*

> The *Koḍukoṭṭi,* danced by Śiva, Umā keeping time on one side, on the burial ground where Bārati (*Kāḷi*), danced with faultless rhythm and

Plate 65	Tripurāntaka (?)	
Period 2	Type C.II	4 arms
Southern region	Muvar temple	Kodumbalur (TN)

Śiva holds a bow in his main left hand and his uppermost right hand is lifted and bent behind, ready to remove an arrow from a quiver, suggesting that this could be a representation of Tripurāntaka. The other left hand is in *saṃdaṃśa* with the palm facing outwards, while the other right hand holds an axe. Śiva looks downwards to his left.

The legs, in Type C.II, strongly suggest the posture for Gajāsurasaṃhāramūrti, as most of these images from the second period onwards, from the southern region, are of this type. In fact this is the only non-Gajāsurasaṃhāramūrti image of Type C.II known to me. Because Śiva's main attribute is the bow, however, and because he is not holding an elephant hide behind him, as he does in an image of Gajāsurasaṃhāramūrti from the same temple, I have identified this image as Tripurāntaka dancing. It is a very unusual depiction and forms the only example of Tripurāntaka dancing, other than in *ālīḍha,* known to me.

Plate 66
Presentation of the Tripurānṭaka story in Bharata Nāṭyaṁ

Plate 66a

One hand held in *alapadma* (city), the other in *triśula* (three), symbolize the three cities of the demons.

Plate 66b

Śiva discharges a single arrow to cause the destruction of the triple cities.

The left in *śikhara* represents the bow, the right in *kaṭakāmūkha* draws back the arrow.

Plate 66c

When Kāma attempts to arouse Śiva he is burnt to death by the fiery gaze of Siva's third eye.

The right hand in *hamsāsya* moving out from the forehead represents the flames from Siva's third eye.

avoiding using time-measures, when the big fire-tipped arrow obeyed His command to burn the three cities (of the Asuras) at the request of the Devas.[10]

Tamil *bhaktas* such as Sundarar (A.D. 710–35). found inspiration for devotional poetry in this dance:

> When you destroyed the three cities, you directed two of your three survivors to be your doorkeepers and you graciously let the third one play on the drum while you danced on the cremation ground to the joy of your consort.[11]

The popularity of the Tripurāntaka story continued in the south, and according to Raghavan it appears in the *Vaṭāraṇya Māhatmya,* the local legend associated with the shrine of Tiruvalangadu.[12]

Stone sculptures of Tripurāntaka are frequently represented in *ālīḍha sthāna,* a standing posture in which one knee is bent and extended and the other is straight.[13] Some scholars such as Sivaramamurti interpret Tripurāntaka in this pose to be dancing.[14]

Ālīḍha is certainly a pose used in Bharata Nāṭyam in pure dance (*nṛtta*) (Plate 66f) as well as descriptive dance (*nāṭya*), and the *NŚ* prescribes *ālīḍha* and *pratyālīḍha* (its mirror image) as the poses for the beginning and end of the movement in which an arrow is drawn back and then released[15] (Plate 66d). However, just because *ālīḍha* is frequently used in dance, it does not necessarily follow that all images in *ālīḍha* are dancing.[16] The criterion for deciding whether or not a pose can be considered as portraying dance must be whether the dance, in a particular sculptural representation, is the god's main activity. When Śiva is in *ālīḍha sthāna* in his chariot and is primarily engaged in battle, for instance, he cannot be considered to be dancing. We may therefore conclude that although *ālīḍha* can be used as a dance pose,[17a] not all iconographic representations in *ālīḍha* are of dance (Plates 66 d,e). Only one illustration of Tripurāntaka, possibly dancing in Type C.II, is discussed; this is shown in Plate 65.

Ālīḍha

Ālīḍha is given in the *NŚ* as the pose to be assumed in dance and drama when depicting all acts relating to heroic and furious sentiments.[17b] The *Raghuvaṃśa* gives *ālīḍha* as the warrior pose assumed by Śiva as Tripurāntaka,[17c] while the *Agni Purāṇa* discusses *ālīḍha* under the science of archery (*dhanur veda*), but does not specifically mention Tripurāntaka.[17d] Vatsyayan states that *ālīḍha* is used in both dance and sculpture when the firing of arrows from a bow is portrayed.[17e] When dance is presented as an offering to please Śiva the *Śiva Purāṇa* recommends *ālīḍha.*[17f]

In the descriptions of *ālīḍha* there is some confusion as to which knee should be bent and when the pose should be called *pratyālīḍha.*[17g] This, however, does not concern our discussion. What is of interest is that this position of the legs, with either knee bent, is used in Bharata Nāṭyam,[17h] in both the *nṛtta* portions (Plates 66d,e,f).

The *ālīḍha* pose in Bharata Nāṭyam and sculpture.

Plate 66e

Firing an arrow in sculpture.

Plate 66d

Depicting firing an arrow in the *nāṭya* portion of Bharata Nāṭyam. The left hand is in *śikhara* and the right in *śukatuṇḍa hasta.*

Plate 66f

Ālīḍha used in the *nṛtta* portion of Bharata Nāṭyam. The same *śikhara hasta* which symbolizes the bow in Plate 66d is used again. The *ālīḍha* pose here is purely decorative and the *śikhara hasta* in this context has no symbolic significance.

Ardhanārīśvara (The Lord that is half woman)

The relationship between Śiva and his wife Pārvatī forms a very important element in the mythology of Śiva,[18] and in his Ardhanārīśvara form, Śiva displays half male and half female attributes, showing that his body is merged with that of his consort. There are many myths associated with Śiva in this form, but none of them specifically mentions dance.[19] The *MP* does not mention a dancing form when it outlines the technical requirements for Ardhanārīśvara,[20] but the *Mālavikāgnimitra* states that Śiva's Ardhanāriśvara aspect embraces the dance: 'Rudra has divided it (dance), into two parts in his own body blended with that of Umā.'[21] The two parts are *tāṇḍava* (vigorous) and *lāsya* (tender).[22] *Tāṇḍava* was the first dance created by Śiva, and *lāsya* was created when Pārvatī imitated his movement.[23] Śiva instructing Pārvatī in the techniques of *lāsya* has been eulogized in poetry by Yogeśvara (A.D.8–900)

> Pretty eyebrows put your arm like this
> and take your pose so,
> Stretch not too high, but bend your toes
> See? Just look at me.'
> Thus Śambhu teaches Pārvatī
> with voice-drum sweet as thunder
> May what he adds for rhythm of her dance
> the clapping of his hands, protect you.[24]

In dance Śiva is associated with the *tāṇḍava* or masculine elements and Pārvatī with the *lāsya* or feminine. Śiva's representation as Ardhanārīśvara can be considered the most literal expression of the interplay of the male (*puruṣa*) and female (*śakti*) elements in the cosmic cycle. For the two aspects of Indian classical dance, the vigorous and the gentle, to be represented in one image we must look to the dancing Ardhanārīśvara form, where the left, or Pārvatī, side is intended to represent *lāsya,* and the right or Śiva side, *tāṇḍava.* Dancing images of that type are not usually found in Tamil Nadu, although the Tamil text, the *Cilappatikāram*, mentions Śiva dancing as Ardhanāriśvara.[25] The same situation seems to apply in Bengal where no image of Śiva, dancing as Ardhanārīśvara is known to me, although the twelfth century inscription from Nauhati invokes the blessing of Ardhanārīśvara in dancing form.[26] However, the depiction of Ardhanārīśvara dancing is important in the living dance traditions from these two areas. In Plate 67 there is an example of a dancer performing in the Seraikella Chhau style as Ardhanārīśvara. Even the costume has half of Śiva's attributes, such as the tiger skin, and half of Pārvatī's, the sari. This semi-classical dance style is from the eastern region and the annual spring festival in which this dance style plays an important part, is dedicated to Ardhanārīśvara.[27] Ardhanārīśvara is also depicted in the Yakṣagāna dance drama tradition from the Deccani region.[28]

The dance of Ardhanārīśvara is also performed in the Kuchipudi style from the southern region (Andhra Pradesh). The body is divided by a handkerchief attached to the middle of the head, covering half the face. When the dancer performs *lāsya,* as exemplified by Pārvatī, the female half of the face is uncovered and for the *tāṇḍava* or vigorous dance, the Śiva half of the face is exposed. The costume is also divided, so that the right side is in masculine dress and the left feminine. These two dance styles, Kuchipudi and Chhau, may be considered dance dramas and as such they often employ costumes rather than rely on the symbolic gestures used in Bharata Nāṭyam to suggest the Ardhanārīśvara form (Plates 68 a-c).

There are relatively few Ardhanārīśvara sculptures in dance poses compared to those in static postures. In southern India, Coḷa images of Ardhạnārīśvara are numerous, but they are not depicted dancing. Ardhanārīśvara represented dancing appears commonly only in Orissa (eastern region), the images dating from the first period (Plates 69–70). In these images both Nandi, Śiva's vehicle, and Pārvatī's mount, the lion, appear below the sculpture. The feminine aspect of the Parvatī side is emphasized by a mirror and by the addition of a longer garment.[29] Elsewhere, there is a northern representation of Ardhanārīśvara dancing from Nepal, in which the figure dances on the reclining animals.[30]

Plate 67
Ardhanārīśvara **Eastern region** **Dancer in Seraikella Chhau tradition**

The costume is clearly Ardhanārīśvara, with a sari and feminine jewellery on the left and a tiger skin on the right. The right hand held in *kapittha* above the head symbolizes the river Gaṅgā and the left in *alapadma,* moving at the wrist. symbolizes shaking the *ḍamaru*.

Plate 68

Ardhanārīśvara, as depicted in the Bharata Nāṭyam dance tradition.

68a

68c

68b

Plate 68a

The dancer makes a gesture dividing the body from top to bottom with the left hand in *mṛgaśīrṣa hasta*.

Plate 68b

The left hand opens from *mukula* to *alapadma* under the left breast, symbolizing Pārvatī. The phallic nature of Śiva is suggested by the right hand in *śikhara hasta* encircling the left (still in *alapadma*).

Plate 68c

In an alternative representation, Śiva is again suggested by *śikhara* but the left hand in *kaṭakāmukha* is used for Pārvatī. The right encircles the left to suggest that Śiva unites Pārvatī in his own body. *Kaṭakāmukha hasta* is frequently seen in bronzes of Pārvatī and this *hasta* is convenient for holding a lotus.

Plate 69	Ardhanārīśvara	
Period 1	Type A.III (SK)	? arms
Eastern region	Satrughnesvara temple	Bhubaneswar (Or)

This is probably the earliest depiction of Ardhanārīśvara dancing. The Śiva half holds a trident between the thumb and forefinger of one hand and supports a rosary, in *haṃsāsya,* in another. Nandi is on the Śiva side and looks up at him; an indication that the image was probably ithyphallic. The left, or Pārvatī side, holds a mirror in *haṃsāsya hasta* and her vehicle, the lion, stands beside her. The costume is longer on the Pārvatī side, suggesting a skirt. Śiva wears breeches. Since the costume approximates that worn by dancers in the Seraikella Chhau tradition it is worth comparing them (Plate 67).

An erect snake emerges from the earring on the Śiva side; the other side is broken. Even the face can be considered to display two aspects; the fuller lips on the Śiva side contrasting with a slight smile on the more delicate lips of Pārvatī.

Plate 70 Ardhanārīśvara
Period 1 Feet broken 8 arms
Eastern region Parasuramesvara temple Bhubaneswar (Or)

Except that the feet of the Ardhanārīśvara on the Satrughnesvara temple (Plate 69) are intact, these two images are very similar. Since the feet of this image are missing, I am unable to classify it, but there is no doubt that this image is dancing because of the movement depicted in the torso. The right knee is strongly bent, but the left only slightly. The image is eight armed, and warrants discussion because it is early, and many of the *hastas* and implements it holds appear in later images. The top left hand holds a mirror in *haṃsāsya* (see also Plate 69), the next in *ardhapatāka* holds an object, possibly palm-leaf scriptures, the next hangs loosely at the side in *dola hasta* (*NŚ*), and the last is in *patāka hasta*. On the right the uppermost hand in *kartarīmukha* holds an unidentifiable object. The lowermost hand holds a rosary, as in Plates 13a and 69. Another hand rests on the knee, and the main hand in *haṃsāsya* is held beside the chest. The combination of *dola* (*NŚ*) and *haṃsāsya* for the two main hands is also seen in the Naṭarāja images from the Cave Temple at Aihole, from the same period (Plate 19). The earring on the Pārvatī side is smaller than that on the Śiva side from which the head of a snake (?) emerges (see also Plate 69). The image is probably ithyphallic.

Kālārimūrti (Śiva in the form of the enemy of time)

Śiva as the victor over Kāla (time) or Yama (the lord of death), is represented by Indian sculptors in various ways, one of which is in the act of performing a triumphal dance, although no dancing form is mentioned in either the mythology of Kālārimūrti[31] or the *āgamic* instructions for preparing the image.[32] The myth is located in the village of Tirukkadaiyur, in the southern region. Mārkaṇḍeya, a young devotee of Śiva, was doomed to die on his sixteenth birthday. When Yama, the god of death, arrived to take him, the boy clung to the *liṅga* that he was worshipping, and hence Yama's noose encircled the *liṅga* as well as his victim. Angered by this sacrilege, Śiva emerged from the *liṅga* and slew Yama with his trident.

The iconographic representations of Kālārimūrti have probably three variations. The first is associated with the Mārkaṇḍeya myth when Śiva, the supreme godhead, exercises his omnipotence by superseding the laws of *karma*,[33] emerging from the *liṅga* as Kālārimūrti to slay Yama (often kicking him in the chest),[34] while the second shows Śiva, victorious over Kāla, dancing on his prostrate body,[35] and the third combines both aspects: Śiva dances on Kāla's chest while Mārkaṇḍeya stands nearby.[36] Only the last two types depict dance.

I cannot provide interpretations for the multitude of myths that surround Śiva,[37] but here is an example of the different levels on which they can be approached. On one level, this myth illustrates Śiva's power to intervene on behalf of a devoted follower, and assume a destructive aspect, killing Yama; but in a wider context, when Śiva dances it demonstrates his power over death, and shows that he alone is the master of time. This aspect finds its expression in the concept of Śiva as Kālārimūrti, the victor over time (*kāla*), who is the partner of death:

'Being the master of and one with Maya [cosmic illusion] I [Śiva] become united with Kāla [time eternal] and create the universe and also draw it together [i.e. destroy it]... saying this [Śiva] started dancing.'[38]

In expressing Śiva's supremacy over time, the myth of Kālārimūrti endows him with the same absolute powers as are embodied in the idea of his '*ānandatāṇḍava*' dance (Śiva's dance of creation and destruction). Both forms can therefore be considered to have cosmic significance, a possibility overlooked by most previous writers. The association of Śiva, Kāla, and dance, explains why images of Kālārimūrti are frequently depicted dancing.

Śiva's dance not only destroys death, but may also re-establish it. The story is related in the *Vāyu Purāṇa*, where Śiva dances on Gaya, the *asura* with the power to grant immortality.

> The town [Gaya in Bihar] received its name from the *asura* Gaya who was so holy that all who touched or even saw him were assured of a place in heaven. Yama god of the underworld complained that this state of affairs was beginning to empty hell, so Viṣṇu instructed Brahmā to perform a sacrifice on Gaya's body. The *asura* when approached readily agreed and lay down on the ground so that his body might serve as an altar. The gods performed the sacrifice and then proceeded to transfix the demon to the ground so that he might never move from there again. But the *asura* still moved even though the elephant god Gaṇeśa sat on his neck and Vāyu the wind god held down his feet and Yama placed a stone on his head and sat upon it. Then Śiva danced on his back the mystic *tāṇḍava* dance and Gaya lay still, but once the dance was over he stirred again until Viṣṇu added his weight.[39]

I do not know of any sculptural representations of this myth.

In Bharata Nāṭyam, Kālārimūrti is depicted frequently during the enaction of, or allusion to, the Mārkaṇḍeya myth. This is because the Mārkaṇḍeya story is popular in south India. Many songs accompanying the dance describe it in detail and others make passing reference to it. Even if the poetry does not specifically refer to Śiva as Kālārimūrti, it is one of his manifestations that frequently appears in the improvised portions of the Śaivite repertoire. In dance, Yama is very rarely depicted, despite the fact that the *A.D.*

gives explicit directions for his representations: 'Yama is to hold *paśa* (noose) with his left hand and *sūcī* with the right one.'[40]

Six illustrations of dancing Kālārimūrtis are given here. The three images from the southern region of the first and second periods are of Type B and all have four arms (Plates 72-4). The three images from the Deccani region, third period, are of Types A. III and B and are many armed (Plates 75-7). All of the southern images have *sūcī hasta* in the right hand, the same *hasta* given in the *AD* for depicting Yama in live dance. In two of the illustrations Śiva dances on the stomach of Yama, in two on the side, and in two on the back.

71a

Plate 71
Kālāri mūrti as depicted in Bharata Nāṭyam

Plate 71a
The hands in *muṣṭi* symbolize holding the trident. The feet are in Type C.II, the same position for Gajāsurasaṃhāramūrti in dance (Plate 78c), and usually adopted in southern images of Gajāsurasaṃhāmūrti, although in these the arms are held upwards, supporting the skin of the elephant (Plates 84–6). The example of Tripurāntaka in sculpture is also in Type C.II (Plate 65). The downward thrust is accompained by a fierce expression.

71b

Plate 71b
The trident is removed from Kāla's body and the dancer looks at Kāla.

Plate 72	Kālārimūrti	
Period 1	Type B	4 arms
Southern region	Kailasanatha temple	Kancipuram

Śiva holds a noose in his main right hand and a trident in his other right hand. The main left hand is in *sūcī* pointing upwards (unlike in Plates 73-4 and Gajāsurasaṃhāramūrti images when it points downwards (Plates 84-6) and the other left hand is in *alapadma*. Naṭarāja images from this same temple also often have one hand in *alapadma*. Kāla kneels beneath his left foot and is nearly as large as Śiva.

Plate 73	Kālārimūrti	
Period 2	Type B	4 arms
Southern region	Śiva temple	Gangaikondacolapuram (TN)

The two arms on the right hold an axe and a trident, the two on the left are in *sūcī hasta* pointing down at Kāla (see also Plate 74), and one in *alapadma* supporting a deer. Both Kāla and Śiva have fangs. Kāla is kneeling facing downwards, with his body twisted, half turned so that he looks up at Śiva.

Plate 74	Kālārimūrti	
Period 2	Type B	4 arms
Southern region	Muvar temple	Kodumbalur (TN)

The main right hand holds the noose overhead and the main left hand in *sūcī hasta* points down at Kāla. The other right hand holds a club while the other left is in *kartarīmukha hasta*. Fangs and an angry expression give the image a terrifying aspect. Kāla kneels below but turns to look at Śiva. The image is unusual for Type B in having the uplifted foot also turned outwards in *tryaśra*.

Plate 75	Kālārimūrti	
Period 3	Type A.III (SK)	8 arms
Deccani region	Kesava temple	Belur (Ka)

The uppermost right hand of the image is in *kaṭakāmukha* and holds a trident, the next in *muṣṭi* holds a sword, and the next holds on to a small flat object. The uppermost left hand holds a *ḍamaru*, the next a snake, and the next a *kapāla*. The main right hand is in *ardhacandra*, with a rosary draped across it. The left arm is in *gajahasta* on the same side as the foot in *kuñcita*. Śiva dances on the stomach and chest of Kāla, and the identification of the image as Kālārimūrti rests on this fact.

Plate 76	Kālārimūrti	
Period 3	Type B	8 arms
Deccani region	Hoysalesvara temple	Halebid

Śiva's main right hand holds the handle of a broken sword, the main left hand holds a shield. The uppermost right hand holds a trident which points down at his victim, while another right hand holds a club. The uppermost left hand holds a drum and the others an elongated half skull and severed head, the latter alluding to his aspect as Bhairava and making this image syncretic Kālārimūrti/Bhairava. Because of the kneeling Kāla below Śiva's left foot, I have classified this image as Kālārimūrti.

Plate 77	Kālārimūrti	
Period 3	Type B	8 arms (?)
Deccani region	Kesava temple	Belur (Ka)

The main left hand holds a shield, the main right a dagger. The uppermost left hand bolds a *ḍamaru*, the next a bow, and the lowermost a severed head. Kālārimūrti dances on the chest of a corpse holding the severed head in his hands. A long decorative garland extends to below his knees. The presence of a penis which is not erect is unusual for images of Śiva. The third eye is vertical. The fangs give this image a terrifying aspect, a feature which is also found in representations of Bhairava (see Plates 88, 89) and Gajāsurasamhāramūrti (Plates 80, 84–6). The image is flanked by small skeleton figures.

Gajāsurasaṃhāramūrti (The destroyer of the elephant demon)

Śiva as Gajāsurasaṃhāramūrti conquers a monster in elephant form by compelling it to dance to death. Śiva then performs a victory dance wearing its hide.[41]

Śiva dancing in this form is well known in classical literature. Kālidāsa in his *Meghadūta* describes it thus: 'Śiva himself started his dance against a background of elephant hide.'[42] The poet Satananda writes: 'Kāla (Śiva) makes fast the elephant-skin cloak while Kālarātri puts in his hand the skull. May Śambhu's servants as the dance begins with separate tasks thus busied purify you.'[43] The *MP* in its section on iconography requires that: 'The image of Lord Śiva in his dancing posture should be made with ten arms wearing the hide of an elephant.'[44]

In the actual images, however, 'wearing' has been loosely interpreted and the elephant hide extends behind like a large cape.

In the Bharata Nāṭyam tradition, Śiva ripping the hide of the elephant and then tying it about his shoulders is frequently shown (Plates 78 a-c). The exploit is also commonly alluded to merely by adopting the final pose—a flourish often included in the improvised portions.

All the three images illustrated from the Deccani region are of Type B, from the first and third periods (Plates 79-81). The one example from the eastern region is in *ālīḍha* and is from the first period (Plate 82). The four examples from the southern region are from all three periods and are of Type C.II, the same pose used to depict Gajāsurasaṃhāramūrti in Bharata Nāṭyam (Plates 78a-c). The head of the elephant is held to one side or danced upon in Deccani images from the first period (Plate 79).[45] This is also the case for southern images from the first two periods (Plate 83). By the third period, in Deccani and southern images, Śiva is only depicted dancing on the head of the elephant(Plates 80, 81, 84-6). One example from the northern region of Type A from the second period depicts the elephant's head to one side.[46] While the position of the elephant's head varies and the feet may be of Types A, B or C.II, these do not affect the position of the arms which are, in all cases, outstretched, holding the skin as a cape behind the figure.

Gajāsurasaṃhāramūrti images may also be syncretic both when Śiva is shown dancing and when he is not. Sivaramamurti refers to an image dancing in his dual aspect of Gajāsurasaṃhāramūrti/Tripurāntaka,[47] and an image of Śiva as Gajāsurasaṃhāramūrti/Bhairava from the Madhukesvara temple, Mukhalingam in the eastern region first period is illustrated (Plate 82).

Plate 78
Gajāsurasaṃhāramūrti as depicted in Bharata Nātyam.

78a

78b

78c

Plate 78a

The left hand in *mṛgaśīrṣa hasta* indicates the elephant demon, Gajāsura.

Plate 78b

Siva drapes the elephant hide around his shoulders. The hands are held in *kapittha hasta.*

Plate 78c

A more dramatic pose symbolizes Śiva holding the hide of Gajāsura behind him. This pose of Type C.II is identical with that seen in Cōḷa depictions of Gajāsurasaṃhāramūrti (Plates 84–6).

Plate 79	Gajāsurasaṃhāramūrti	
Period 1	Type B	4 arms
Deccani region	Virupaksa temple	Pattadakal

Two arms hold the elephant's skin overhead and one right hand rests in *dola hasta* against the edge of the skin. The other left hand rests on the thigh. The uplifted left foot rests in *agratalasañcara* on the head of the elephant.

Plate 80	Gajāsurasaṃhāramūrti	
Period 3	Type B	8 arms
Deccani region	Hoysalesvara temple	Halebid (Ka)

Śiva's uppermost arms support the elephant's hide and hind feet. The right main arm is in *dola (NŚ)* and the left main arm is in *gajahasta.* One right hand holds a trident while in the left hands he holds a drum, half-skull and severed head. Śiva's expression is one of fierce calm with the skulls in the crown, the fangs and the bulging eyes evoking fierceness and the full face and complete poise of the body projecting his control over the situation. The orchestra perched above the left foot of the elephant leaves no doubt that Gajāsurasaṃhāramūrti is dancing. Nandi reclines on the left foot of the elephant in most Hoysala representations of Gajāsurasaṃhāramurti but not in the southern representations (see Plate 81).

Plate 81	Gajāsurasaṃhāramūrti	
Period 3	Type B	16 arms
Deccani region	Kesava temple	Belur

Śiva holds an axe in his main right hand and a bell in his main left hand. The other attributes in his right hands are: an elephant goad, thunder bolt, drum, and club. In his left hands he holds a half skull, clappers, snake, thunder bolt and *khaṭvāṅga*. The two uppermost arms support the elephant hide and hind legs. Nandi and three skeletons are on his left; four-headed Brahmā plays a drum as does another musician.

Plate 82	Gajāsurasaṃhāramūrti	
Period 1	Ālīḍha	6 arms
Eastern region	Madhukesvara temple	Mukhalingam (AP)

This image is clearly syncretic, combining aspects of both Gajāsurasaṃhāmūrti and Bhairava. The prominence of the elephant hide held aloft with both hands in *patāka* places it with the Gajāsurasaṃhāramūrti images. One left hand holds a half-skull into which pours the blood of the victim impaled on his trident. The image is ithyphallic and Nandi between his legs looks upwards, a convention for most Naṭarāja images from the eastern region (Plates 15–17a). A skeleton crouches by Śiva's left leg while the goddess moves away to the left.

Plate 83	Gajāsurasaṃhāramūrti	
Period 1	Type B/C. II	10 arms
Southern region	Kailasanatha temple	Kancipuram (TN)

The uppermost arms hold the elephant hide above Śiva's head while the left toe presses against the head of the elephant. Period 2 images from the southern region depict the elephant's head to the side of Śiva, while Period 3 images revert to Śiva dancing on its head (Plates 85,86). One right hand holds a trident, another an axe. The uppermost left hand is in *alapadma,* a *hasta* also seen in images of Naṭarāja and Kālārimūrti (Plate 72) from this same period and region.

Plate 84	Gajāsurasaṃhāramūrti	
Period 2	Type C.II	4 arms
Southern region	Muvar temple	Kodumbalur (TN)

Gajāntaka holds an elephant hide behind him with his two uppermost arms. In his right hand he holds an elephant tusk, and his left hand is in *sūcī,* pointing downwards. This *hastą* is also seen in the same position in images of Kālārimūrti. The elephant head is not in evidence but the position of the hands and body, and the presence of the tusk strongly suggest that this image is Gajāsurasaṃhāramūrti.

Śiva has fangs and an elaborate hair-style. Devī is on the right moving away in fear.

Plate 85	Gajāsurasaṃhāramūrti	
Period 3	Type C.II	6 arms (?)
Southern region	Naṭarāja temple (Gopura)	Cidambaram (TN)

Śiva dances on the elephant's head and Devī recoils in fear on his left. Three of the hands are in *sūcī*: one right hand is at the level of his crown, the lower right hand points upwards, and the lower left points downwards at the elephant's head. The example from Darasuram also had Śiva's left hand pointing downwards to draw attention to his victim (Plate 86).

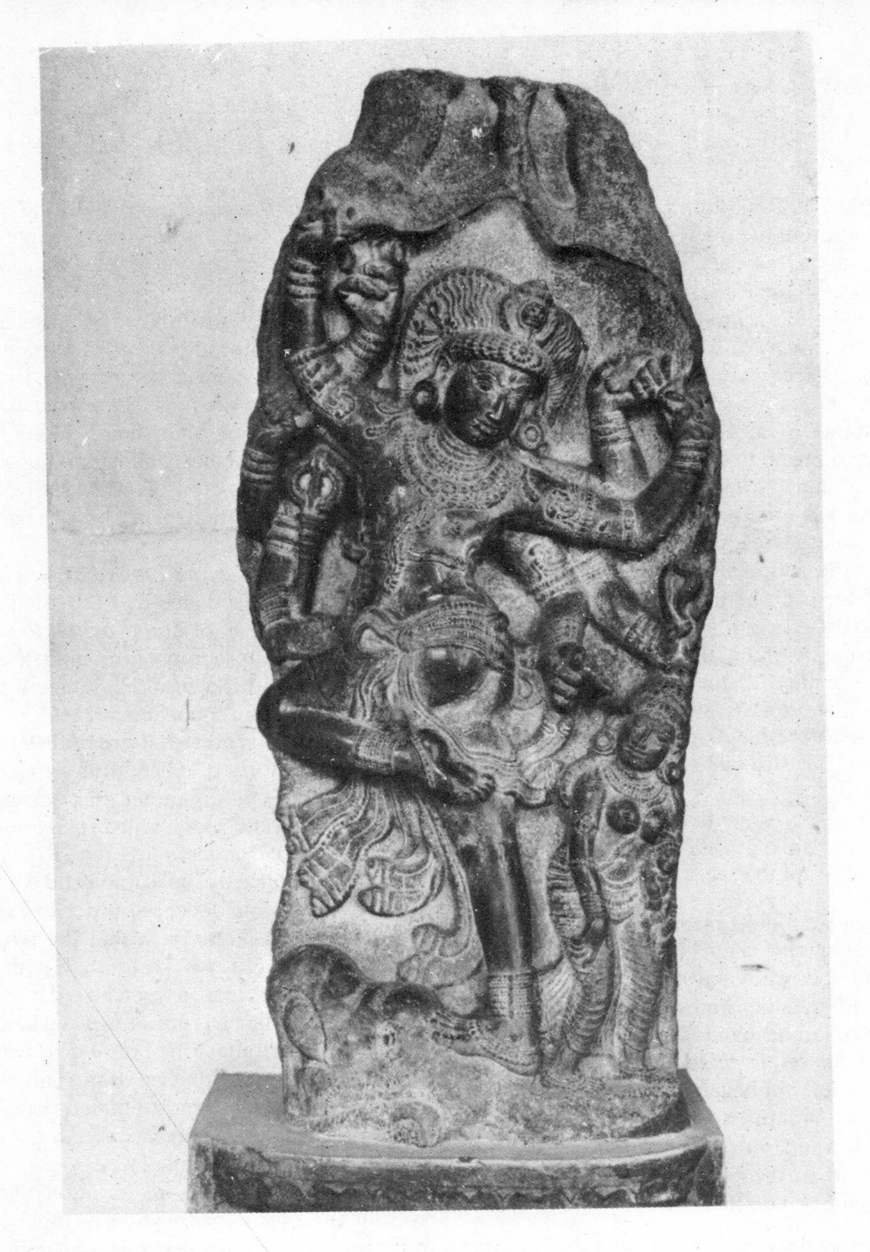

Plate 86	Gajāsurasaṃhāramūrti	
Period 3	Type C.II	8 arms
Southern region	Airavatesvara temple	Darasuram, now in **Tanjore Art Gallery (TN)**

Śiva stretches the elephant hide behind him and dances on its head. In one right hand he holds a drum, in another a trident. In one left hand he holds a pestle, in another a snake and the lowermost in *sūcī hasta* points down at the elephant. The crown has a skull in the centre and his matted locks which make up the crown are made to look like snakes. The knit eyebrows, bulging eyes and fangs combine to give his face a fierce expression. Devī is on his left and moving away, but appears to be satisfied that he has everything under control.

Bhikṣāṭana (The wandering mendicant)

In his form as Bhikṣāṭana, Śiva is a wandering beggar, and there are numerous myths associated with him in this aspect. Some of these are important for us in that they mention both erotic and cosmic dance. Bhikṣāṭana's erotic dance is described in the *Siva Purāṇa* when he performs before Mena, Pārvatī's mother, in an attempt to charm her and win the hand of her daughter. 'In the meantime, Śiva, favourably disposed to His disciples and prone to divine sports, assumed the guise of a dancer and approached Menakā.[48] Mena who was greatly delighted took gems and jewels in gold vessels in order to give [them] to him.[49] But the dancer did not accept the gifts. He requested for [sic] the hand of Pārvatī and began to sing and dance again.'[50]

Unfortunately Mena, though attracted by Śiva's dance, is horrified at the prospect of a dancing beggar as a son-in-law and refuses his requests. Despite parental objections Śiva eventually marries Pārvatī, but strained relations with his wife's family persist.

In the Pine Forest myth as related in the *Liṅga Purāṇa,* it is Bhikṣāṭana's erotic dance that attracts the wives of the sages.

> Śiva then wandered into the Pine Forest, and the wives of the sages there fell in love[51] with him and followed him everywhere. Śiva was naked, ithyphallic, and dancing, and begging with a skull in his hand. The sages became furious and cursed his *liṅga* to fall to the ground. The *liṅga* fell but began to cause a terrible conflagration; Brahmā and Viṣṇu tried in vain to find the top and bottom of it, and peace was only restored when the sages agreed to worship the *liṅga* together with their wives.[52]

In both accounts, as in most representations in painting and sculpture of this aspect, Śiva is the erotically seductive mendicant, not the emaciated, ascetic type (Plate 87).

The south Indian version of the myth, recorded in the *Kōyilpurāṇam,*[53] provides yet another variant and has become the most important and widely known of all the myths associated with Śiva's dance.

The story begins with Śiva disguised as a mendicant approaching the wives of certain sages in the Tillai forest near Cidambaram. The women are so overcome with lust when confronted with his handsome form that their jealous husbands send a tiger, snake and finally a malignant dwarf (Apasmāra) to destroy their rival. Śiva subdues each in turn, finally dancing on the back of the dwarf.[54]

While in the *Siva* and *Liṅga Purāṇas* it was the eroticism of Śiva's dance that attracted his audience, in the case of the *Kōyilpurāṇam* Śiva's beauty alone aroused uncontrollable desire in the sages' wives and the resulting dance was one of victory rather than seduction.

Iconographic representations of the erotic mendicant, in the form of a beautiful young man, not dancing, who is plump rather than emaciated, are numerous in south India. One explanation for this is that the chroniclers of the *Kōyilpurāṇam* ignored the dance of Bhikṣāṭana and connected it with Śiva's cosmic dance, in order to explain the iconography of Naṭarāja within the structure of the pre-existing myth associated with Cidambaram.[55] For this reason when he is depicted dancing in south India he is not shown as a beggar[56] but has cosmic attributes: the fire of destruction, and the *ḍamaru* symbolizing creation. This is the mythical origin of Śiva's most familiar dancing pose, variously called: *ānanda tāṇḍava, nādānta, bhujaṅgatrāsita* (see Table 1).

In the Bharata Nāṭyam tradition there is no specific pose for depicting Śiva as the mendicant, but several mimetic gestures are combined in dance to portray this form[57] (Plates 64 a, b).

The iconographic representations of Bhikṣāṭana dancing are very rare, and I know of only one image that could be identified as such (Plate 87).

Plate 87	Bhikṣāṭana (?)	
Period 2	Type A.III(SAg)	2 arms
Eastern region	Muktesvara temple	Bhubaneswar (Or)

From the position of the body there can be no doubt that this emaciated figure is dancing. The left arm is in *dola (NŚ),* and the right holds a mirror/rattle. The drummers on either side of him dance, the one on the left in Type A.I, the one on the right in Type A.III. Although no attributes are shown, this figure may represent Śiva as Bhikṣāṭana.

Bhairava (The terrifying one)

Bhairava is Śiva in his terrifying aspect, and is traditionally regarded as a demon who dances in the cremation ground. The *Cilappatikāram* calls this dance *koḍukoṭṭi.* [58] According to the *Kūrma Purāṇa*, Bhairava performs his dance at Banaras, where he has been sent by Viṣṇu to do penance for killing Brahmā.[59] The myth describes him dancing while carrying the body of Viṣvaksena (Viṣṇu's doorkeeper whom he had killed in anger after being refused admittance to Viṣṇu). Although the dance is not described it seems to be a joyful one, unlike his Bhairava or terrifying form:

> Being praised hither and thither by *Pramathas,* the great ascetic (Śiva) was dancing with the body (of Viṣvaksena) placed in his hands ... the soul of endless *Yoga,* danced again and again.[60]

In examples of dancing Bhairava in sculpture, however, the body of Viṣvaksena is not shown, and it is more likely that the artists intended to depict any dance of Bhairava's in the burning ground, rather than this specific incident. This is supported by the fact that images of Bhairava frequently show the head surrounded by a halo of flames (Plate 89). Dance is Bhairava's medium for expressing his mercurial nature, impelled by excessive joy or anger. In fact, his eccentricity is emphasized by his association with non-conformist activities such as dance.

The concept of Śiva as a wild irresponsible figure riding on his bull, frequenting the burning ghats, dancing with goblin attendants and decorating himself with skulls seems to be stronger in the north Indian tradition than in the south. His fearsome aspect finds expression in sculptures such as the syncretic representation from Mukhalingam in *ālīdḥa* (Plate 82) which combines features of Śiva killing the demons Gajāsura and Andhakāsura. The whole composition is dominated by the horizontal thrust of the trident, drawing the eye to the right and emphasizing the one-sided nature of the deity portrayed. This contrasts strongly with the finely-balanced composition of the *ānanda tāṇḍava* image where creation counterpoises destruction and the eye is led to the centre.

The apparently anti-social side of Śiva's character is highlighted in a number of Bharata Nāṭyam *padams* known as *nindu stutis,* in which Śiva's mythological actions are referred to with false insults.

In many pieces his aspects as Bhairava and Bhikṣāṭana are intertwined, creating a picture of a mad beggar. Two Tamil *padams*, *Peyandi* and *Ettai Kondu,* bring out the distress felt by Pārvatī's mother at her daughter's attachment to Śiva, and describes him in unflattering terms. Although I know of no Oḍissi dance items which include Bhairava, this deity plays a central part in the yearly Chhau dance festivals at Mayurbañj in Orissa.[61] The mythology of Bhairava is strongly connected with dance, yet there are only a limited number of representations of Bhairava in dance poses.[62] Two examples of Bhairava dancing are illustrated: one from the eastern region and one from the southern region (Plates 88, 89). Both are from the third period, of Type A.III, and have flames emerging from their crowns, three heads, and four arms. Both images have fangs and present a frightening appearance, and hence illustrate the terrifying dance of destruction which forms part of Śiva's cosmic dance.

Plate 88	Bhairava	
Period 3	Type A.III (TAg)	4 arms
Eastern region	**Sūrya temple**	Konarak (Or)

Several dancing Bhairavas and musicians decorate the *jagamohan* of the Surya temple. This particular Bhairava holds a trident in one right hand in *kaṭakāmukha (NŚ),* while another right hand in *sarpaśīrṣa* supports a *kapāla.* The upper left hand holds a drum. The three heads of the image all have fangs and crowns surmounted by rising flames. Snakes are used for decorations around his ankles and as his sacred thread. The figure dances on a boat. This image is closely similar to the Bhairava from the Airavatesvara temple at Darasuram (Plate 89), having in common, three heads, a crown of flames, and the same foot and body positions.

Plate 89	Bhairava	
Period 3	Type A.III (SAg)	4 arms
Southern region	Airavaṭesvara temple	Darasuram (TN)

The upper right hand holds a trident pointing downwards, as does the Kālārimūrti from the Hoysalesvara temple (Plate 76). The lower right hand holds a sword. The upper left hand holds a club and the lower left an unidentifiable object. The image has three faces, all with a third eye, moustache, and fangs. Snakes decorate the upper arms, ankles and waist, and form the sacred thread.

Vīrabhadra (The hero, a title used mainly in connection with the myth of the destruction of Dakṣa's sacrifice)[63]

In addition to the two aspects of Bhikṣāṭana, as an emaciated yogi and as a beautiful sensual mendicant, a third aspect can be distinguished in both the *purāṇic* and folk traditions. This is the grotesque, semi-comical character of Śiva as a demented outcaste, wandering from place to place singing and dancing and wearing rags. It is Śiva as the non-conformist, the iconoclast, who thus precipitates the course of events leading to his manifestation as Virabhadra.

Good illustrations of Śiva dancing energetically are to be found among the Pahārī hill paintings;[64] and Śiva the madman, intoxicated with cannabis and dancing from place to place, is still a popular theme in the miracle plays of Mathura, and the dance-drams of the Mayurbhañj Chhau and Kuchipudi traditions. I know of no pose or song, however, that describes Vīrabhadra in the Bharata Nāṭyam style.

Śiva's unhappy relationship with his parents-in-law, which was mentioned in connection with the Bhikṣāṭana myth, crops up again when his father-in-law, Dakṣa, refuses to invite him to a great sacrifice that he is preparing. Dakṣa never fully accepted the mendicant Śiva and continues to object to his anti-social behaviour, mentioning his dance as a particular source of annoyance:

> Śiva always wanders about dancing and singing and doing other despicable things. This makes me ashamed, and besides he does not even have a proper house. Because of this, and being embarrassed before society, I have not invited him to my sacrifice, but afterwards I will bring him here and honour him privately.[65]

This reference to Śiva being socially unacceptable leaves no doubt as to the low status given to dancers.

Dakṣa's rejection of Śiva resulted in Śiva assuming his Vīrabhadra form,[66] and two dances are known to have been performed at this time. The first, Śiva's dance of victory after he destroyed Dakṣa's sacrifice, is recorded in the *NŚ*.[67] The second is Śiva's dance of grief after Satī has committed suicide through shame that her father had insulted her husband. Śiva, overcome, 'took up her body and danced in grief, troubling the world with his dance'.[68]

A bronze sculpture (possibly unique), from Trivandrum illustrates Śiva's dance of grief in his Vīrabhadra aspect.[69] A tiny figure of Devī is thrown over Śiva's left shoulder. The image is of Type B.

One of the right hands holds a discus which is a particularly important attribute, because it was with this weapon that the gods eventually dismembered Satī in order to stop Śiva's destructive dance.[70] Bits of Satī's body were scattered in various places throughout India: 'Where the *yoni* fell [Kamarupa in Assam] Śiva took the form of a *liṅga* and peace was re-established in the universe.'[71]

Although the depiction of Śiva with Satī on his shoulders is rare in iconography, the episode is shown in the Chhau dance tradition from the Jalda area of Bengal,[72] and also, in the Yakṣagāna dance drama from Karnataka, the destruction of Dakṣa's sacrifice is portrayed.[73] Dakṣayagya is a favourite item in Kathakali. Here Śiva as Vīrabhadra is one of the terrifying 'red-beard' characters, the make-up being similar to that used for major villains, emphasizing the destructive nature of the manifestation. In the Kathakali version, Satī does not commit suicide but adopting her equally horrifying aspect as Bhadrakālī, assists Vīrabhadra in destruction of the sacrifice.

Vīṇādhara Dakṣiṇāmūrti (holding the lute)

Vīṇādhara is the gracious form of Śiva holding a lute (*vīṇā*). Although no specific myth containing dance may be associated with the aspect of Vīṇādhara, the connections between dance and music in the Indian tradition are sufficiently intimate to account for the occurrence of Vīṇādhara images in dancing poses. Dakṣiṇāmūrti Śiva may also be depicted providing the rhythm essential to dance by beating the drum, but for this he is usually seated, a posture which will not be dealt with here.[74] Since Śiva is the chief repository of dance and music which is revealed through the *NŚ*[75] it seems logical to depict Dakṣiṇāmūrti dancing to his own music. Images of Vīṇādhara not in a dance pose are found in the southern, eastern and northern regions where he may be depicted holding the instrument seated,[76] seated on Nandi,[77] standing in Type A,[78] or along with the seven mothers.[79]

The *MP* gives directions for the latter: 'The image of Bhagavan Vīreśvara should be placed in front of the images of the Mātrikās [seven mothers], it should be on a bull, having plaited hair, holding a *vīṇā,* and trident, in a standing posture.'[80]

Most extant images however depict Vīṇādhara dancing alone. These are found in the northern and eastern regions. In addition, there are numerous illustrations of Vīṇādhara dancing on the bull, but only from the eastern region, and when he dances in the company of the seven mothers these images are found only in the northern region. The foot positions found among images of Vīṇādharas dancing alone are of Types A.I–III. The most frequent position for the *vīṇā* is to be held across the body with two hands, one of which is usually in *ardhapatāka.* There are also examples in sculpture of the *vīṇā* being held in one hand to the side of the body.[81]

Two of the earliest examples of dancing Vīṇādharas come from Orissa (eastern region), but despite the fact that they pre-date the *Śilpa Prakāśa,* this text does not include instructions for the preparation of them. The Vīṇādhara from Asanpat (Plate 90) differs from other Orissan sculptures in style and is probably the earliest piece extant. Another early dancing Vīṇādhara from the eastern region, in Orissa at Bhubaneswar, is from the Satrugnesvara temple (Plate 91). The occurrence of dancing Vīṇādhara and Ardhanārīśvara (Plates 69, 70) images on the earliest temples at Bhubaneswar suggests that at this period, *c.* the sixth-seventh century, dance formed a very important motif in Orissan Śaivite iconography.

A dancing Vīṇādhara from the second period, also from the eastern region (Assam), on the Kamakhya temple is not illustrated here. It is four armed and all but the right hand which supports the *vīṇā*[82] are broken. The figure is dancing on Apasmāra, a feature uncommon for the northern region and for Vīṇādhara images. Another unusual feature, the matted locks flowing only to the right side, suggests to Sivaramamurti that this Vīṇādhara image has some of the attributes of Ardhanārīśvara. The belt is very similar to those worn by Oḍissi dancers today (Plate 96a).

Dancing Vīnādharas from the northern region are nemerous, particularly from the Gurjara Pratīhāra dynasty. A striking example is located in the Museum of Indian Art, West Berlin,[83] from the second period of Type A.III (SAg). It shares certain iconographic features with Naṭarājas from different regions and periods: the halo behind the head is reminiscent of the first period dancing Śiva outside Cave I at Badami (Plate 18), and the damaged shawl in the upper left hand recalls the image of Naṭarāja from Elephanta,[84] also from the first period. A small figure with its right leg obscured by Śiva's right foot and its left knee raised, pushes Śiva's knees apart. This small figure is seen in earlier images such as the Gupta Naṭarāja at Sirpur,[85] as well as images from Ellora[86] and in other Gurjara Pratīhāra images (Plate 43) but in most cases its pose imitates that of Śiva.

Another example from the northern region, in the Jhalawar museum[87] of Type A.III (TAg), is unusual in holding the *vīṇā* in one hand to one side of the body. The main hands are in the classic *gajahasta/patāka* combination typical of Naṭarāja, and this appears therefore to be a syncretic image. Dancing Vīṇādharas are also found in Cambodia and in Vietnam.[88]

There are four illustrations of Vīṇādhara dancing alone: two from the first period, eastern region (Plates 90, 91), one from the second period, northern region (Plate 92), and one from the third period Deccani region (Plate 93). The northern and eastern images are of Type A; the Deccani image is of Type B.

Vīṇādhara dancing on the bull

In Bengal, all Vīṇādhara images known to me are depicted dancing on Nandi, but they are alone, and not in the company of the seven mothers as required by the *MP.*[89] Nandi is usually shown with his head tilted upwards, possibly to emphasize Śiva's ithyphallic nature.[90] Only one illustration of Vīṇādhara dancing on the bull is given here; a Type A image from Bengal of the third period (Plate 94).

Vīṇādhara dancing with the Seven Mothers

The *Liṅga Purāṇa* describes Śiva's dance with the seven mothers thus:

After quaffing the nectar-like dance of Śiva up to the throat [i.e. after enjoying the dance of Śiva very much] Parameśvarī danced in the midst of the ghosts happily along with the Yoginīs.[91]

Most representations of Śiva dancing with the seven mothers, however, hold the *vīṇā*, a requirement of the *MP*, but this text does not stipulate that he should also be in a dancing posture.[92] No doubt the descriptions in these two texts account for the occurrence of Śiva in both his dancing and non-dancing forms, when he is represented with the seven mothers.[93] One example of Vīṇādhara dancing with the seven mothers is illustrated in Plate 95.

Plate 90	Vīṇādhara	
Period 1	Type A. III (TK)	8 arms
Eastern region	Asanpat	State Museum, Bhubanesvar (Or)

The two main hands hold the *vīṇā,* allowing the neck of the instrument to pass between the thumb and index finger. Of the other two left hands, one supports the trident, while the other in *patāka,* palm facing outward, touches the chin of Nandi, standing on Śiva's left and looking upwards. As the image is ithyphallic the usual convention is to have Nandi looking upwards and between Śiva's legs (Plates 15, 16, 17a). The remaining hands are in *muṣṭi* holding an unidentifiable object, and *kaṭakāmukha (NŚ)* holding a rosary. A devotee holds his hands in *añjali* on Śiva's right.

Plate 91	Vīṇādhara	
Period 1	Type A.II (KK)	10 arms (?)
Eastern region	Satrughnesvara temple	Bhubaneswar (Or)

The *vīṇā* and several of the arms are badly mutilated. This image was probably ten armed as there is evidence of five arms on the right side. The two arms overhead hold a snake in *muṣṭi*, one right hand rests on the thigh in *kaṭyavalambita*, while another in *haṃsāsya* holds a rosary, palm pointing towards the body, not facing outwards as in other early images such as the dancing Ardhanārīśvara image from this same temple (Plate 69). The *vīṇā* is badly damaged, but one right hand rests on the end of it. The left hands are mainly broken but one in *muṣṭi* clasps the trident (one of the weapons prescribed by the *Matsya Purāṇa* for Vīṇādhara, see above). There is evidence of another left hand resting on the thigh. The image is ithyphallic and the bull stands behind Śiva's left leg. Skanda playfully bestrides a peacock on Śiva's right.

Plate 92	Vīṇādhara	
Period 2	Type A.III(SAg)	8 arms
Northern region	Nilakanthesvara temple	Nilakantha (Ra)

The two main arms support the *vīṇā*, the left in *haṃsāsya*. The uppermost right hand holds the *ḍamaru*, and the hand below it a staff. The uppermost left arm is crooked around the *khaṭvāṅga* held in *muṣṭi* by the arm below. The lowermost hands both hang downwards poised above the heads of a drummer on the left, and a devotee on the right. The right side of the body is raised on the same side as the foot in *agratalasañcara*. Between the legs of Vīṇādhara the head and shoulders of a small figure can be seen. Śiva's matted locks piled up in a crown resemble those seen in the images from the Gwalior museum of Naṭarāja (Plates 43, 44). A garland is draped around Vīṇādhara and hangs below his knees.

Plate 93
Period 3
Deccani region

Vīṇādhara
Type B
Hoysalesvara temple

8 arms
Halebid

The *vīṇā* is held across Śiva's chest. His upper left hand holds a noose. The other attributes are unclear or damaged. Two female figures fan him with fly whisks while a peacock approaches him from the left.

Plate 94	Vīṇādhara	
Period 2	Type A.III(SAg)	12 arms
Eastern region	Dacca Museum	Natghar (Be)

The uppermost hands are interlocked in *karkata hasta,* as in the Bengali Naṭarāja image from the same period (Plate 38). The next pair of hands hold a snake, from the head of which emerges a small human figure with hands in *añjali.* This same feature is also illustrated in a Naṭarāja of Type B, from the Kailasanatha temple at Kancipuram. The lowermost left hand supports a water-pot. The two main arms support the *vīṇā.* This is another example of Śiva dancing on Nandi who looks upwards. The image is ithyphallic and a garland hangs to the level of the thighs. For another Vīṇādhara also from Natghar see SRM p. 300.174.

Plate 95	Vīṇādhara dancing with the Mātṛkās and Gaṇeśa	
Period 3	Type A.III(TK)	2 arms
Northern region	Mathura museum	Find place unknown

Vīṇādhara dances at the left hand end of the panel, the Mātṛkās are in the middle and Gaṇeśa is at the other end. Vīṇādhara supports the *vīṇā* with both hands in *ardhapatāka,* the left higher up on the neck of the instrument. Gaṇeśa holds a tooth in his right hand and sweets in his left. A long garland encircles Vīṇādhara and hangs below his knees. Each image has a halo behind its crown.

Plate 96

The *vīṇā* in Oḍissi dance

In sculpture Śiva as Vīṇādhara carries a *vīṇā*, but in dance, in particular the Oḍssi dance style, the *vīṇā* is restricted to Devī.

Plate 96a

The *vīṇā* is shown by the right hand in *sūcī* inicating the neck of the instrument, and the left in *kapittha* indicating the head of it.

Plate 96b

The right hand in *śukacancu* indicates plucking the sympathetic strings and the left in *mṛgaśīrṣa* presses against the frets. This example closely resembles depictions of Vīṇādhara in sculpture (see Plates 92–5).

Conclusions

It may be appreciated from the foregoing discussion that Siva's dance extends to many of his iconographic representations, and is not limited to his Naṭarāja form. While six of these eight aspects are often represented in sculpture in dancing poses, the available evidence on Bhikṣāṭana and Vīrabhadra show very few. Except for Śiva as Vīṇādhara, all the seven aspects of Śiva discussed in this chapter are depicted in the living dance traditions, some more often than others, and it is curious that the importance of dance in the mythology of a particular aspect seems to have no correlation with the frequency of its depiction either in the living dance tradition or in sculpture. Tripurāntaka, Vīrabhadra, Bhiksāṭana and Bhaírava, four aspects with at least one myth in which dance is mentioned, are however rarely depicted in dancing sculpture, and only infrequently in Bharata Nāṭyam. In contrast, the Ardhanārịśvara aspect has no specific myth in which a dance is mentioned, yet there are several images of Ardhanārīśvara dancing, particularly from the eastern region, where Ardhanārīśvara is not only the deity to whom the Seraikella Chhau dance festival is dedicated, but is also depicted in a literal fashion with a costume of half male and half female garments. In the southern dance styles of Bharata Nāṭyam and Kuchipudi, Ardhanārīśvara is frequently depicted, but no sculptural representations in dancing postures come from this region. Like the Ardhanārīśvara form, Śiva Vīnādhara does not have dance directly associated with its mythology. Of the eight manifestations of Śiva discussed here, only Vīnādhara is not usually depicted in Bharata Nāṭyam. This is not surprising, since I know of no dancing Vīnādharas in sculpture from the southern region, but only from the eastern, northern, and Deccani regions.

The Gajāsurasamhāramūrti form has dance associated with its mythology and the depictions of this form in sculpture are shown dancing; these come mainly from the Deccani and southern regions. It is the southern style, Bharata Nāṭyam, that describes Śiva in this form. Kālārimūrti is a southern image that may be depicted in sculpture in a dancing pose as the victor over Kāla (Time). In the Bharata Nāṭyam dance style the same pose is assumed and is enough to suggest this aspect of the myth. But as in sculpture, when Śiva kills Yama, all the main characters in the myth (such as that of Mārkaṇḍeya) may also be represented in the dance.

Śiva the dancer may perform various types of dance in his many aspects; the same dance may be common to more than one aspect. As Tripurāntaka, Vīrabhadra and Gajāsurasaṃhāramụrti, he performs the dance of victory, while the Ardhanārīśvara image in dance posture represents the two qualities of dance: *tāṇḍava* and *lāsya*, as well as suggests the erotic dance of creation. Bhikṣāṭana's erotic dance is performed for Mena, Pārvatī's mother, in an attempt to win her daughter's hand in marriage. In his form as Bhairava, Śiva's dance is joyful when he learns that he will be absolved of the crime of chopping off one of Brahmā's heads. Śiva reveals his mercurial nature through his dance, particularly as Bhairava: one moment ecstatic and inebriated, the next, the embodiment of anger as he dances the dance of destruction. Śiva's dance of grief as Vīrabhadra is also destructive. As Kālārimūrti, his dance symbolizes both his destructive nature and his mastery over time. Śiva is the creator of both music and dance; as Vīṇādhara he plays the *vīṇā,* and dances to his own music.

The unpredictable correlation between mythology, dance traditions and sculpture in the frequency with which dance is associated with Śiva's different manifestations, suggests that neither dancers nor sculptors have allowed themselves to be confined by rigid rules in their attempts to interpret the mythology. Because dance is such an integral part of the mythology and worship of Śiva, it is evident that it has inspired sculptors from time to time to incorporate it into the iconography of diverse manifestations and that the tradition evolved, at least in part, separately from the practice of dance.

Decorative Dancing Figures

There are more dancing figures in Indian iconography than in the art of other world religions. While these dancers are found depicted on buildings intended for religious purposes and many of the early images resemble either wholly or in part those at present being worshipped, it does not necessarily follow that the dancers are performing a religious dance. Just as the epigraphical and literary references to dance do not always differentiate between secular and religious types, so too there is a similar ambiguity in early representations of dance in painting and sculpture.

Some of the earliest sculptures in the Indian subcontinent from the Indus valley civilizations of Harappa and Mohenjo-daro are of dancers: a stone statuette from Harappa (3000–2000 B.C.)[1] and a bronze dancing figurine from Mohenjo-daro (2500–1500 B.C.).[2] We can only speculate as to their purpose. The Harappa torso was identified by Marshall as a prototype of the Naṭarāja image, perhaps because later south Indian bronzes of the dancing Śiva with one leg raised and lifted across the body employed this same twisted torso.[3] However, there are no distinguishing features to signify that this is Śiva, or indeed that either the Harappa torso or Mohenjo-daro dancing girl[4] have any religious significance.

I had suggested earlier that it was pointless to try to differentiate between dance as part of divine worship and as secular entertainment performed by courtesans for kings. The dance scene depicted in the painting in Cave X at Ajanta which Yazdani entitled: 'The Arrival of a Rājā with his Retinue to Worship the Bodhi Tree', was identified as religious,[5] possibly because the main theme of the picture is worship. This interpretation is not necessarily correct, however, because the dancers are an independent compositional element grouped around the king, and not the tree; hence the appearance of dancing girls in the king's retinue may simply indicate their presence at court. The earliest Brahmanical records give ample evidence of dance in both secular and religious contexts[6] but while the Pali canon forbids monks and pious laymen (*daśaśīla upāsaka*) to see dancing, it forms a popular motif in Buddhist monuments.[7] Hence the true role of dance in early Buddhist worship remains obscure.

Some writers however do try to differentiate between secular and religious dance. Although E.V. Havell also describes the male dancer in the painting in the Bagh Cave No. 4 as religious, once again there seems no reason to dismiss the possible secular nature of the occasion.[8] In fact, unless a dancing image is of a particular deity, or the dance is unequivocally part of divine worship, it is very difficult to assign a role to the dance.

Because dance permeated many aspects of life in India, it was natural that it should be frequently depicted and such representations were no doubt influenced by the living dance tradition of that time. For this reason, the Mohenjo-daro dancing girl is particularly important because the position of the hands in a clenched fist position (*muṣṭi*), one hand placed on the hip, the other on the thigh, is still shown today for the *tribhaṅga* position in the Oḍissi dance style (Plates 8d,e). This very early depiction of these hand positions is not an isolated example. A Kuṣāna terracotta figurine of a female dancer from Bhita (Uttar Pradesh)[9] and many first period images of Naṭarāja from the Deccani and eastern regions also show them (Plates 13a, 14, 17a, 18, 20).

In Table 2 five broad types of dance pose are defined. In the earliest depictions of dancers, dated no later than the third century A.D. we find only two Types, A and C. In Chapter IV these two types are also shown by the earliest extant Naṭarāja dated fifth and sixth century A.D. Most of these early dancing figurines do not have both knees bent. The dancing figurine from Bhita has the left leg straight while the feet are of Type A.I*; the feet of the dancing girl from Mohenjo-daro are destroyed but, while both knees are bent, they point forwards, not sideways, which is the usual convention for later images.

The illustrations of dance at Sanchi, Nagarjunakonda, and Amaravati are numerous. Two dancing girls in reliefs from Amaravati (second century A.D.)[10] illustrate the same twisted trunk as the Harappa torso. In one example a leg is lifted and swung across the body as in Type C. I; the leg in contact with the ground is bent. The hands are in the same positions as those of the dancers from Cave X at Ajanta, whose feet have been destroyed: one thrown upwards, the other in *patāka,* a common combination for Naṭarāja images (see Chapter IV).

In another example from Amaravati,[11] the pose is similar except that the leg which is brought across the body is not held up but rests on the ground in *añcita,* Type A. IV. The hands are different: both may be in *kaṭakāmukha* (*NŚ*), the right by the shoulder, and the left at the side. Both hands hold the ends of a scarf which goes round the figure. A Naṭarāja image (Plate 13a) and representations of dancers from the first period in the eastern region, are also depicted holding a scarf (Plates 103, 105).

A male dancer from Amaravati (third century A.D.)[12] has the same foot position as the last example. The right arm extends upwards, and the left is in *patāka* by the shoulder, the combination seen in the dancers from Cave X at Ajanta. Images of Naṭarāja from the first period, Deccani region (Plate 21), and from the second period in the southern region (Plate 50) display the same combinations in the main arms.

Several dancing figures with one leg straight, the other bent, and varying foot positions, are on the Prasenajit pillar at Bharhut.[13] Two of the dancers are of Type A.III. The central female dancers have the left hand thrown upwards, bent back at the wrist, in *patāka,* palm facing forward, while the right hand in *patāka* is beside the right shoulder. The small male dancer also holds his right hand in *patāka,* slightly higher than his shoulder, but his left is held in *haṃsāsya,* close to his mouth, both palms facing outwards.

The dancer on the lintel outside the Rani Gumpha (cave) at Udayagiri dated second century A.D.[14] has the left leg straight but the feet are of Type A.III*. The right hand is in *patāka* beside the shoulder and the left hand stretched horizontally to the left, the direction from which she is moving. The musicians on her left play a flute, a stringed bow-type instrument, and two elongated drums.

These are only a few examples of the numerous early sculptures of dancers of Type A. While there are isolated examples of dancers with both knees bent,[15] this is not common for images of Type A until Gupta and later times. Several examples from the first period (550–800 A.D.) from the Deccani and eastern regions will be discussed in which both knees are bent (Plates 101, 103, 104–107). However, bent knees are not universal by this time and there are numerous exceptions (Plate 102).

Several themes emerge from this cursory description of depictions of dance dated no later than the third century A.D. The first is the preference for showing dancers with one arm extended upwards and the other in *patāka.* Those images that are not depicted in this way show only a very limited variety of other possibilities, and all of these can be seen in later Naṭarājas and other dancing figures. The second is the very early appearance of the twisted torso to allow the leg to be lifted across the body, which, except for the isolated examples such as the Gupta Naṭarāja at Bhumara (Uttar Pradesh) (fifth–sixth century A.D.)[16] and at Siyamangalam (Tamil Nadu) (seventh century A.D.)[17] does not become popular in the iconography of Naṭarāja until the time of the Cōḻas. The majority of the images have one leg straight, a feature that does not carry over into early images of Naṭarāja. It is important to examine early representations of dancing figures to assess the variety of poses available for sculptors to work with in creating images of Naṭarāja. In this respect it is sometimes interesting to notice the preponderance of Type A figures among both dancers and Naṭarājas from the earliest times to the first period.

Among sculptures of dancing figures, from the earliest period, and from the Gupta period in particular, the most complete range of dance poses (Types A–E) is illustrated by the *gaṇas* (see Table 4). Sculptures of *gaṇas* in all five types of dance poses predate, or at the latest are contemporaneous with, the earliest Naṭarāja images. These dwarfish figures are a common motif in sculpture, and appear in the literature as Śiva's companions. In some sculptures they are depicted in close proximity to images of Naṭarāja (Plates 29, 35) while in others or alone they may form decorative friezes on their own (Plates 97–100). It is possible that these, though considerably earlier in date and from a different region, may have had a similar function to that of the *karaṇa* carvings on the *gopuras* and the *vimāna* of later temples, namely to express the full range and diversity of Śiva's dance. The sculptural representations of *gaṇas* at Ajanta and Badami display a greater range of poses than do first period Naṭarāja images from the same region, which are of Types A and B (see Chapter IV). Illustrations of *gaṇas* are shown from the Deccani (Badami and Ajanta), and northern (Deogarh) regions.

Chapter V shows that several of the earliest representations of Naṭarāja of Type A have the hands in *patāka, haṃsāsya, saṃdaṃśa*, and *gajahasta*. Examples of these are: from the eastern region, in the Mukteśvara compound (Plates 13a, b,) and on the Parasuramesvara temple (Plate 14); and from the Deccani region, outside Cave I at Badami (Plate 18). The images from the Muktesvara compound and the Parasuramesvara temple place the arm in *gajahasta* over the wrist of the hand in *haṃsāsya*.

Dancers from this early period display the same *hasta* combinations. One example from the Deccani region, at Deogarh (Plate 101) has the right hand in *gajahasta* thrown over the wrist of the left which is in either *saṃdaṃśa* or *patāka hasta*. A dancer from the southern region of the second period on the Brahmapurisvara temple at Pullamangai (Plate 110) has her arms in the same position, while another dancer from this temple illustrates the *ardhacandra gajahasta* combination that is more common in Naṭarājas of that period (Plate 111). Another combination for the hands shared by both dancing figures and Naṭarāja images is one hand thrown back at head level, and the other in *gajahasta*. A Naṭarāja image from the Gupta period illustrates this (Plate 12).

The dancer at Śiva's wedding from the Bharatesvara temple, first period, eastern region (Plate 103) holds one hand in *alapadma*, with the hand thrown backwards at head level and the other hand is in *dola hasta*. Deccani Naṭarāja images from the third period (Plate 56) also have this same combination.

The sculpture of a dancer from Aurangabad (Plate 107) rests one hand on the hip in a loose *muṣṭi*, and the other on the thigh in *kartarīmukha*. Both these hand positions are depicted in a Naṭarāja image from the same region and period, outside Cave I at Badami (Plate 18), although the *kartarīmukha hasta* in the latter image is partly damaged.

A sculpture of a dancing girl from Deogarh (Plate 102) stands with one arm resting on the thigh in *kaṭyavalambita*, a position assumed in Ardhanārīśvara images from the eastern region of the same period; one example is on the Parasuramesvara temple (Plate 70), the other on the Satrughnesvara temple (Plate 69). The other hand of the female dancer from Deogarh rests in *alapadma* by her chest; a position which is not found in Naṭarāja images of this period.

Representations of dancers and of all aspects of Śiva dancing of Type A from the first two periods are shown in *tribhaṅga* with the torso raised on the same side as the foot, slightly in front in *tryaśra* (Type A. I), *kuñcita*, or *agratalasañcara* (Type A. III). The majority of dancers from the first two periods are of Type A, with a few of Types B and E. The only Naṭarāja images of Type E are from the first period. While several pre-Gupta dancing figures (see above) and a Gupta Naṭarāja from Nachna Kuthara (see Chapter IV), are of Type C, dancing figures of this type do not appear in the first period. By the end of the second period, however, Type C re-emerges in the southern Naṭarāja figures (see Chapter IV), but is still relatively uncommon in decorative dancing figures (except for the sculptural representations of *karaṇas*). Type D, like Type C, is depicted in representations of *gaṇas* and some Naṭarājas from the first period (see Table 4), but almost disappears until the latter part of the second and third periods. Decorative dancing figures in this pose are not represented until the third period and then only rarely, and usually in *karaṇa* figures.

By the third period, sculptural representations of the one hundred and eight *karaṇas* described in the *NŚ* were common in the southern region; therefore this period is rich in the depiction of a wide variety of dance poses. Many of these poses and hand positions are related to the depictions of earlier Naṭarāja images from all four regions. The early images of Naṭarāja are multi-armed, but rather than holding attributes they depict a variety of *hastas* that are repeated in later images of dancers. By the first period, most of the *hastas* depicted in images of dancing Siva were established as the possible *hastas* for decorative dancing figures. These included: *patāka, haṃsāsya, alapadma, dola (NŚ), kartarīmukha, mayūra, ardhacandra, gajahasta, muṣṭi, kaṭakāmukha,* and *saṃdaṃśa. Sūcī, karkota,* and *tripatāka* were added later. In south India in the third period while sculptures of dancers illustrate a great diversity of *hastas,* the depictions of Naṭarāja are largely confined to Type C.I and the range of *hastas* displayed becomes more restricted: one main arm in *gajahasta,* the other bent and resting by the shoulder in *abhaya hasta,* and the other two hands holding the fire in *ardhacandra* and the drum in *śukacuncu.* In multi-armed images from the third period from the Deccani region (Plates 53–7), each arm usually holds a different weapon. The feet of Naṭarāja images from the third period are of Types A, B, C and D; the last three types are the most common.

Despite the diverse positions of the hands represented in *karaṇa* figures, amongst decorative dancing figures the most common positions of the hands seen in the earlier dancing figures keep recurring; one arm usually in *gajahasta, dola,* or thrown upwards, combined with the other in *alapadma* at head level, *patāka, saṃdaṃśa,* or *haṃsāsya.* Dancers not intended as *karaṇa* figures show these hand and arm positions almost exclusively. Like early Naṭarāja images they are seen with almost equal frequency in Types A and B. Types C and D are also represented in decorative dancing figures of the third period but their depiction is largely confined to *karaṇa* figures. Type E (as in the first two periods) is usually restricted to flying figures and celestial musicians.

Conclusions

The greatest variety of poses for Naṭarāja is found in the first period. Among the dancing figures, only the *gaṇas* of the first period display this same diversity. By the end of the second period and during the third period, as the Naṭarāja image begins to show less imagination, the variety of dancing figures increases. These dancing figures were intended to represent the full range of possible dance poses and most of them are related to images of Naṭarāja. Three of the series of *karaṇas* show female dancers: Cidambaram (Plates 2, 114–19), Tiruvannamalai (Plates 4, 121): Vrddhacalam (Plate 3); and two show male dancers: Tanjore[18] and Kumbakonam (Plate 120). Some of the latter are possibly intended to represent Śiva himself.[19]

Of the current classical dance styles, the Oḍissi style is the closest to the *karaṇa* figures as well as to the early carvings from all over India. To what extent there was a continuous interaction between dancers and teachers of dance, and the carvings of dancers, is a matter of conjecture. But it seems likely that at certain centres (especially the Surya temple at Konarak) the sculptured dance forms had a strong influence on maintaining the form of the Oḍissi tradition. It is abundantly clear from the carvings of dancers, and those of Naṭarāja, that the overall concept of Indian dance has remained essentially similar from at least the Gupta period, and it is difficult to believe that this remarkable continuity has not been aided by the numerous durable illustrations of the art on the many temples of India as well as the written instructions in texts.

The similarity of images of Naṭarāja to those of dancing figures, particularly *karaṇa* images, is striking. A general comparison of dancing figures with the range of sculptures showing depictions of Naṭarāja indicates that the latter group includes in its repertoire the full range of dance poses included in the former. Many of these movements, as they can be deduced from sculptured dancing figures, are no longer found in the current repertoire of Indian classical dance, while others have remained constant, and some new ones have been introduced, a testimony that this has been a living and therefore evolving tradition.

The essential principles of the dance include the same guidelines that are observed by the sculptors: bent knees, shoulders parallel to the back wall and intricate hand gestures. Some sculptures display anatomically impossible positions, but despite this there remains a close interrelationship between dance practice and its sculptural representation.

This connection between the living dance tradition and sculptures of dancers and Naṭarāja is wholly in keeping with the idea of Śiva as the creator of dance and of his dance encompassing every form of dance movement.

Plate 97	*Gaṇa*	
Period 1 (Gupta)	Type B	2 arms
Northern region	Dasavatara temple	Deogarh (MPr)

The right arm is bent at the elbow and thrown upwards to head level, with the palm facing backwards. The left arm is in *gajahasta,* palm facing outwards and is on the same side as the uplifted leg. In the earliest Type B Naṭarāja from the southern region, outside the Mugalarajapuram Cave (Table 4) the arm in *gajahasta* is on the same side as the uplifted leg and this is seen for dancers as well as *gaṇas*.

A scarf encircles the upper arms of this *gaṇa* as it does in images of dancers from the first period, eastern region (Plates 103, 105) as well as images of Naṭarāja from the first period from the eastern region (Plate 13a). The hair style is Gupta.

Plate 98	*Gaṇa*	
Period 1	Type C. I	2 arms
Deccani region		Ajanta (Mah)

The right hand is thrown up to head level. The left foot raised up and across the body accompanies the left arm in *gajahasta,* as it does for nearly all images of Naṭarāja of this type. The hand of the arm in *gajahasta* is twisted so the palm faces outward. The left foot is in *kuñcita.* A scarf encircles the *gaṇa*'s arms. The necklace (torque) and curled hair are Gupta characteristics. Apart from the Naṭarāja at Bhumara (see beginning of this chapter) this pose is not seen in northern representations of Naṭarāja.

Plate 99	*Gaṇa*	
Period 1	Type A.III(SK)	2 arms
	Type C.I	
	Type E	
Deccani region	Cave II	Badami (Ka)

The central *gaṇa* has the right hand thrown upwards to head level (see also Plate 98) and the left hand rests on the knee. These hand positions are depicted in Naṭarāja images, but not always together.

The *gaṇa* on the left in Type C.I has one hand in *gajahasta* and one in *saṃdaṃśa,* two hand positions frequently depicted in images of Naṭarāja, particularly in the first two periods (see conclusions to this chapter).

The *gaṇa* on the right is of Type E. The left hand is thrown upwards to head level while the other arm balances a pot on its elbow.

Plate 100	*Gaṇas*	
Period 1	Type A.III(TK)	4 arms
	Type D	2 arms
Deccani region	Cave I	Badami (Ka)

The *gaṇa* in the centre is of Type D, a pose seen in Naṭarāja images from the southern region (Plates 35, 58–60) from the first period onwards, and southern depictions of dancers from the third period (Plates 115, 117). The left hand thrown upwards, palm facing inwards and the right in *gajahasta* resembles the *gaṇa* from Deogarh (Plate 97).

The *gaṇa* on the right of Type A.III(TK) has four arms, an unusual feature for *gaṇas*, and it is therefore possible that this represents Naṭarāja. The two uppermost arms hold something overhead and the two lowermost are in the position for *tribhaṅga* (see also first period Naṭarāja images from Orissa) (Plates 13a–16).

Plate 101	Dancer (female)	
Period 1 (Gupta)	Type A.III(TK)	2 arms
Northern region	National Museum, Delhi	Deogarh (MP)

The left hand of the dancer is unclear and is in either *saṃdaṃśa* or *patāka,* with the right arm in *gajahasta* thrown over the wrist of the left arm. The position of the hands, feet and body are very similar to those of two of the earliest Naṭarājas from the eastern region at Bhubaneswar (Plates 13a, 14). The dancer's skirt recalls the Kuṣāṇa skirt worn by both men and women[20] except that it ends at the knee. She wears tight trousers beneath the skirt. This circular hair style is also seen on an early Naṭarāja image from Bhumara (see Chapter IV, Gupta period). The full face is characteristically Gupta.

Plate 102	Dancer (female)	
Period 1 (Gupta)	Type A.I*	2 arms
Northern region	National museum, Delhi	Deogarh (MP)

The central dancer stands with her right leg straight and the weight of her right foot thrusts her right hip outwards. The right hand in *alapadma* rests by her chest. The left hand rests on the thigh in *kaṭyavalambita,* a *hasta* seen in Naṭarāja images particularly when they are standing in *tribhaṅga.* The dancer wears a costume similar to that seen in Plate 101. She is surrounded by an all female percussion orchestra, playing sticks, cymbals, and drums.

Plate 103	Dancer (female)	
Period 1	Type A.III(SAg)	2 arms
Eastern region	Bharatesvara temple	Bhubaneswar(Or)

The dancer is second from left. Her left hand is thrown upwards in *alapadma,* palm facing inwards, and her right hand holds on to a scarf. Male dancers (Plate 105) and images of Naṭarāja (Plate 13a) from this same region and period also hold a scarf. Her torso is raised on the same side as the foot in *kuñcita.* This has been identified by Panigrahi as Śiva's marriage procession.[21] Śiva on the far right rides a bull.

Plate 104

Plate 104	Dancer (male)	
Period 1	Type A.I.	2 arms
Eastern region	Parasuramesvara temple	Bhubaneswar (Or)

A dancing figure on the far right holds his right hand in *śukacuncu*, and the left in *gajahasta*. The arm in *gajahasta* is not thrown over the wrist of the other hands as it is for an image of Naṭarāja from the same temple (Plate 14), and for the dancer from Deogarh (Plate 101). Like Plate 103, Panigrahi has identified this panel as depicting dancing at the wedding of Śiva and Pārvatī.[22] For reference to dance on this occasion see Chapter 1.

Plate 105	Dancers (male)	
Period 1	Type A.V	2 arms
	Type A.III(SK)	2 arms
Eastern region	Parasuramesvara temple	Bhubaneswar (Or)

The dancers on the upper right and left are both of Type A.V, but the one on the left has the body twisted, and both hands are in *ardhapatāka*, the right touching the back of the thigh, and the left raised and bent back horizontally so that the hand rests on the shoulder. The back view is seldom represented in sculptures of this period, although by the third period, Śiva as Bhairava is depicted with a twisted body position.[23] (See also Plate 40 for a northern image of Naṭrāja, with a twisted body position from the second period).

The dancer on the right holds a scarf with both hands as does the Naṭarāja from the same period and region in the Muktesvara compound (Plate 13a). The left hand rests on the hip, also a favourite position for the hands of Naṭarājas from the eastern and Deccani regions from the first and second periods.

The central dancer is of Type A.III(SK) and has the right arm uplifted to head level, hand in *saṃdaṃśa*, holding a scarf, while the left arm hangs downwards.

Plate 105

Plate 106	Dancers (male)	
Period 1	Type A.III(TK,TAg)	2 arms
Eastern region	Parasuramesvara temple	Bhubaneswar (Or)

The middle dancer of the upper panel is of Type A.III (TK) and has the right hand in *patāka* or *haṃsāsya* with the left in *gajahasta* thrown over it. Early representations of Naṭarāja from the same region from this temple (Plate 14) and from the Muktesvara compound (Plate 13a) have similar hand positions.

The middle dancer of the lower panel is of Type A.III (TAg) and has the same combination of hands as the upper dancer except that the left hand in *gajahasta* is held below the right wrist instead of resting above it. Hence we can be certain that these two positions occur contemporaneously in Orissa in both the sculptural representations of dance scenes and of Naṭarāja (Plates 13a, 14-16).

Another interesting grill window now on the Kapilesvara temple[24] but considered to be of similar date to Plates 105, 106, illustrates three dancers, all of Type A; the first on the left is in Type A.V, and the other two are of Type A.III. The dancer on the left has the right arm thrown up to head level, and the other hand rests on the hip in *kaṭyavalambita.* The central dancer has the right hand at head level and the left in *gajahasta,* very similar to the pose adopted in Oḍissi dance when representing an elephant (except that the arms are reversed), and also worth comparing with the depiction of the *karihasta karaṇa* on the east *gopura* of the Naṭarāja temple at Cidambaram (Plate 5c). The dancer on the right has the right hand in *saṃdaṃśa,* and the left in *gajahasta* (see lower panel here).

Plate 106

Plate 107	Dancer (female)	
Period 1	Type A.III(SAg)	2 arms
Deccani region	Cave VII	Aurangabad (Ma)

This dancer from a Buddhist cave holds her left hand in *kartarīmukha hasta* against the thigh and her right hand in a loose *muṣṭi* rests on the hip. The hand positions are the same as for two of the lower hands of the Naṭarāja from the same region and period outside Cave I at Badami (Plate 18).

With the exception of the *naṭṭuvan*, who beats the time for her dance, the musicians are female.

Plate 108	Dancer (female)	
Period 2	Type B	2 arms
Eastern region	Muktesvara temple	Bhubaneswar (Or)

The main left arm is in *gajahasta* with the palm facing outward, and the main left hand is held by the shoulder in *kaṭakāmukha.* This dancer is typical of Type B decorative dancing figures, the leg raised being on the same side as the arm in *gajahasta.* Although Naṭarājas from the eastern region are only found in Type A, dancers of Type B are fairly frequent.

Plate 109	Dancer (female)	
Period 2	Type A.V	2 arms
Southern region	Kuranganatha temple	Srinivasanallur(TN)

The dancer has the right arm in *doḷa(NŚ),* the left in *ardhacandra* resting by the shoulder. The drummer on the right has the feet in Type A.IV, a pose not frequently depicted.

Plate 110	Dancer (female)	
Period 2	Type A.V	2 arms
Southern region	Brahmapurisvara temple	Pullamangai (TN)

The right hand is in *saṃdaṃśa,* the left in *gajahasta,* palm facing outward and thrown over the wrist of the other hand. This combination with one arm thrown over the wrist of the other appears in the first period both for dancers from the northern region from Deogarh (Plate 101), and for Naṭarāja images from the eastern region from Bhubaneswar (Plates 13a, 14).

Plate 111	Dancer (female)	
Period 2	Type A.V	2 arms
Southern region	Brahmapurisvara temple	Pullamangai (TN)

The hand positions, the right in *ardhacandra* beside the bust and the left in *gajahasta*, are common both for decorative dancing figures and Naṭarāja images. *Ardhacandra hasta* is frequently seen in bronze Naṭarājas of Type C.I but less commonly in stone sculptures where *patāka* is used instead. The arm in *gajahasta* is twisted so that the palm faces outward (see also Plate 22) a feature seen in several stone Naṭarāja images but not usually in bronzes.

Plate 112	Dancer (male)	
Period 2	Type A.III(TAg)	2 arms
Northern region	Nilakanthesvara temple	Nilakantha(Ra)

The right arm is in *gajahasta* with the hand in *mayūra hasta.* This is similar to an image of Naṭarāja from the same period, but the eastern region on the Muktesvara temple at Bhubaneswar (Plate 36c). The other arm is bent at the wrist so that the hand rests by the shoulder in *ardhapatāka.* The arm in *gajahasta* is on the same side as the foot in *agratalasañcara,* the usual convention followed by images of Naṭarāja as well as the representation of Naṭarāja in the Oḍissi dance style (Plate 1c).

 Representations of dancing figures from the third period (A.D. 1100 to about 1450):

While both *gaṇa* figures and images of Naṭarāja illustrate all five types of dance posture by the first period, it is not until the end of the second and during the third period that dancers show this same diversity. There are thirteen illustrations from the third period which are related to an image of Naṭarāja and/or earlier representations of dancing figures.

Plate 113 See facing page for caption.

Plate 114

Plate 114	Dancer (female)	
Period 3	Type C.II	2 arms
Southern region	Naṭarāja temple	Cidambaram (TN)

The dancer has the left arm extended horizontally, the hand in *haṃsāsya*. The right arm crosses the body in *gajahasta* and holds a stick. The position of the legs in Type C.II is usually reserved for depictions of Śiva dancing as Gajāsurasaṃhāramurti from the southern region (see Plates 85, 86), and for the illustration of the *bhujaṅgatrāsiṭa karaṇa* on the same temple (Plate 116). Note that the depiction of the *bhujaṅgatrāsita karaṇa* at Tanjore on the Brhadisvara temple shows the feet of Type C.I.[25]

A decorative dancing figure from the same period but the northern region is also of Type C.II* (Plate 124).

Plate 113	Dancer (female)	
Period 3	Type A.I.	2 arms
Deccani region	Hoysalesvara temple	Halebid (Ka)

The dancer has the right arm uplifted and the hand held with the palm facing inwards. Images of Naṭarāja from the eastern region adopt the same position for the hands. One example is from the Vaital Deul temple from the first period (Plate 15).

The left hand of the dancer is held in *sarpaśīrṣa* below the bust. The *sarpaśīrṣa hasta* held in this position in the Oḍissi tradition suggests a full breast and may be done with both hands.

Although this piece originates from an area in which Bharata Nāṭyam is now performed (at least in the cities of Mysore and Bangalore), the position of the body suggests a very different style of dance from that seen today.

Plate 115	Dancer (female)	
Period 3	Type D	2 arms
Southern region	Naṭarāja temple	Cidambaram (TN)

The left arm is in *gajahasta,* the right in *haṃsāsya.* The right leg is lifted straight upwards. The representation of this pose is usually restricted to images of Śiva, as according to Tamil mythology Śiva employed this pose in a dance contest with Pārvatī who was too modest to imitate. This pose is never used by women in Indian classical dance today. Naṭarāja in this same pose and from the same temple is shown in Plate 59, although the *gajahasta* is absent, and instead the arm is extended straight upwards. This female dancer is on the base of the fifty-six pillared hall.

Plate 116	*Karaṇa* figure (female)	
Period 3	Type C.II	2 arms
Southern region	Naṭarāja temple	Cidambaram (TN)

The dancer has the right arm in *gajahasta*, the left in *patāka*. The right knee is lifted. This particular pose, Type C.II, has been described as illustrating the *bhujaṅgatrāsita karaṇa*.[26] Another dancer from the same temple (Plate 114) shares this pose which is usually restricted to representations of Gajāsura-saṃhāramūrti dancing from TN (Plates 85, 86).

Plate 117	*Karaṇa* figure (female)	
Period 3	Type D	2 arms
Southern region	Naṭarāja temple	Cidambaram (TN)

The right hand is in *patāka,* the left is held over the head and touches the right foot which is in contact with the forehead. The *karaṇa* has been labelled as *karaṇa* number fifty, *lalāṭa tilaka,* or placing the *tilaka* with the toe on the forehead. The Naṭarāja image from the same temple (Plate 59), also in this pose, has the right foot pointing upwards instead of touching the forehead (see also Plate 115), and the left arm raised over the head.

Plate 118	*Karaṇa* figure (female)	
Period 3	Type B	2 arms
Southern region	Naṭarāja temple	Cidambaram (TN)

The right arm is crooked around the uplifted leg, the right hand is in *haṃsāsya*. The left arm is thrown obliquely upwards with the hand in *haṃsāsya*. This position for the arms is depicted in a Naṭarāja image from the same region, second period, and of the same type at Srinivasanallur (Plate 50). This illustration is identical to the eighty-fourth *karaṇa* in the *TL*.[27]

Plate 119	*Karaṇa* figure (female)	
Period 3	Type A.I	2 arms
Southern region	Naṭarāja temple	Cidambaram (TN)

The dancer stands in *tribhaṅga,* the right hand rests on the hip, the left on the thigh. The left side is raised on the same side as the foot in front. This is a very good example of the *tribhaṅga* body position as seen in the Oḍissi dance style from the eastern region (see Plate 8d). The *tribhaṅga* body position is no longer found in the dance style typical of the area surrounding Cidambaram (Bharata Nāṭyam). The position of the hands in this *karaṇa* is frequently depicted by images of Naṭarāja (Plates 13a–17a). This image is on the east *gopura.*

Plate 120	*Karaṇa* figure (male)	
Period 3	Type B	2 arms
Southern region	Sarangapani temple	Kumbakonam (TN)

The left hand is extended upwards, the right in *dola (NŚ)* rests on the knee of the uplifted leg as it does for the earliest representation of Naṭarāja of Type B from the southern region at Mugalarajapuram (see beginning of this chapter).

Plate 121	*Karaṇa* figure (female)	
Period 3	Type C.I	2 arms
Southern region	Arunacalesvara temple	Tiruvannamalai (TN)

The dancer has the left arm extended obliquely upwards and the right in *dola* (*NŚ*) is on the same side as the leg raised across the body. The Naṭarāja at Siyamangalam, probably the earliest southern representation of Type C.I, also has the same arm in *dola* (*NŚ*).[28]

The *TL* assigns this pose to the *bhujaṅgāñcita karaṇa:* 'In this *karaṇa* the leg is in *bhujaṅga trāsita,* the right hand in *recita* and the left in *latā.*'[29]

Plate 122	Dancer and drummer (female)	
Period 3	Type A.III(TAg)	2 arms
Eastern region	Surya temple	Konarak(Or)

The dancer holds a staff in the right hand and the left arm is uplifted and bent so that the hand in *patāka* is close to the head. The torso is raised on the same side as the foot in *agratalasañcara*, so that the opposite hip protrudes. This shape of the torso is characteristic of the movement seen in Oḍissi dance.

The drummer is of Type A.I(TT). In Oḍissi, when beating a drum is depicted these same hand positions are used.

Plate 123	Dancer	
Period 3	Type A.III (TAg)	2 arms
Eastern region	Surya temple	Konarak (Or)

Both hands are in *patāka* with the palms facing outwards. The body is in a *tribhaṅga* position with the head on the same side as the protruding hip. The same pose is incorporated into *Batu Nṛtya*, one of the dance pieces of Oḍissi.

Plate 124	Dancers (female)	
Period 3	Types A.B.C.	2–4 arms
Northern region	Sringaracauri temple	Cittorgarh (Ra)

There are several dancers in this panel and from left to right they illustrate the following poses: Type A.I, Type B, Type A.V, Type C.II*, Type A.I, and Type A.V*.

The Śaivite affinities of the four-armed figures is indicated by the fact that one holds a trident and a *ḍamaru,* another a water-pot and a rosary.

Plate 125	Dancer	
Period 3	Type A.V	2 arms
Northern region	Jain temple	Mount Abu (Ra)

The hand beside the head is in *ardhapatāka;* the other hand rests by the chest. The *tribhaṅga* position of the body and the foot behind suggests that the toes of the foot behind will touch the ground as it is dragged to the front. In the dance from the eastern region, Oḍissi, this foot and leg movement is frequently used.

Appendix A

Dance Styles in India

This list refers only to those dance styles, both classical and folk, that are mentioned in this book, but many more exist. Although each dance style is restricted to a particular region, the styles often extend beyond state boundaries. Of the classical dance styles that I will be referring to, only Bharata Nāṭyam and Oḍissi were performed in temples, exclusively by women. These styles as performed today contain both pure dance (*nṛtta*) and mime (*nāṭya*) in almost equal proportions, whereas most other dance forms in India are predominantly dramatic in content and form part of a dance drama.

Bharata Nāṭyam

The classical dance style of Tamil Nadu and south Karnataka, particularly around Mysore city and Bangalore. Today it is the most popular dance style and is seen all over India. It contains both pure dance (*nṛtta*) and mime (*nāṭya*). It was formerly performed by a caste of female dancers called *devadāsīs* and constituted a regular part of daily ritual in the temples of south India. It was also performed on secular occasions in the courts of the southern states and during festivals. Many items regularly performed in this style are based on Śaivite mythology.

Chhau

There are three variations of this dance drama and two of them derive their name from the former princely state from which they originate. The dances are traditionally performed by men and masks are worn in two of the styles. Śiva as Ardhanārīśvara is worshipped as the presiding deity of the spring festival, the occasion on which dance competitions are held.

Mayurbanj: this is the only style in which a mask is not worn. It is clearly related to the classical dance style, Oḍissi, from coastal Orissa.

Purulia: a mask is worn in this style, which is the most vigorous of the three.

Seraikella: a mask is worn. The movements in this style are less vigorous and more refined than in the other two styles.

Kathakali

The dance style from the state of Kerala, originally done only by men and distinctive for its elaborate make-up. The beginning dance, *Todaiyam*, performed behind a curtain, is said by Bhavnani to represent the creative aspect of Śiva as Ardhanārīśvara.[1]

Kuchipudi

Performed in the village of Kuchipudi in Andhra Pradesh. This village was endowed by the Vijayanagar kings for the purpose of promoting this style of dance. Originally it was performed only by men, and it is mainly performed as a dance drama involving a number of artists, although solo items do exist.

Mohinī Āṭṭam

The female dance from Kerala resembling Bharata Nāṭyam but probably not performed as part of temple ritual. It is now virtually extinct in Kerala.

Oḍissi

The dance style of Orissa state formerly performed by *Maharis* (temple dancers), and *Gotipuas* (boy dancers) who travelled in troupes performing dance dramas throughout Orissa. Only one or two invocatory prayers and *Batu Nṛtya*, which includes various poses reminiscent of those illustrated in sculpture on the Surya temple at Konarak, include references to Śiva.

Yakṣagāna

A dance drama from south Kanara characterized by elaborate head-dresses. The Śaivaite themes in this dance style are numerous.[2]

For a detailed discussion of the styles of Indian lassical dance see: Bhavnani, E., *The Dance in India*, 2nd ed., Bombay, 1970; *Classical and Folk Dance of India*, Special Edition of *Mārg*, 1963; *Mohinī Āṭṭam*: Special Edition of *Mārg*, Vol. XXVI, No. 2, March 1973.

Appendix B

Regional Distribution of Images Illustrated

Regional divisions were chosen on stylistic grounds and limited to four so that a sufficient sample was available from each region.

Deccani region: includes Karnataka, Maharashtra, and part of Andhra Pradesh

Eastern region: includes Orissa, Bengal, Assam, Bihar and part of Andhra Pradesh and Madhya Pradesh

Northern region: includes Himachal Pradesh, Gujarat, Rajasthan, and Bihar, Uttar Pradesh and part of Madhya Pradesh

Southern region: includes Tamil Nadu, Kerala, and coastal Andhra Pradesh.

Appendix C

Chronology of the Images Illustrated

The images have been divided into four periods.

Gupta: images made in the classical Gupta style within the boundaries of the Gupta empire up to the sixth c. A.D.. (see Harle, J.C., *Gupta Sculpture*)

Period 1: 550 A.D. up to about 800 A.D.
Period 2: 800 A.D. up to about 1100 A.D.
Period 3: 1100 A.D. up to about 1450 A.D.

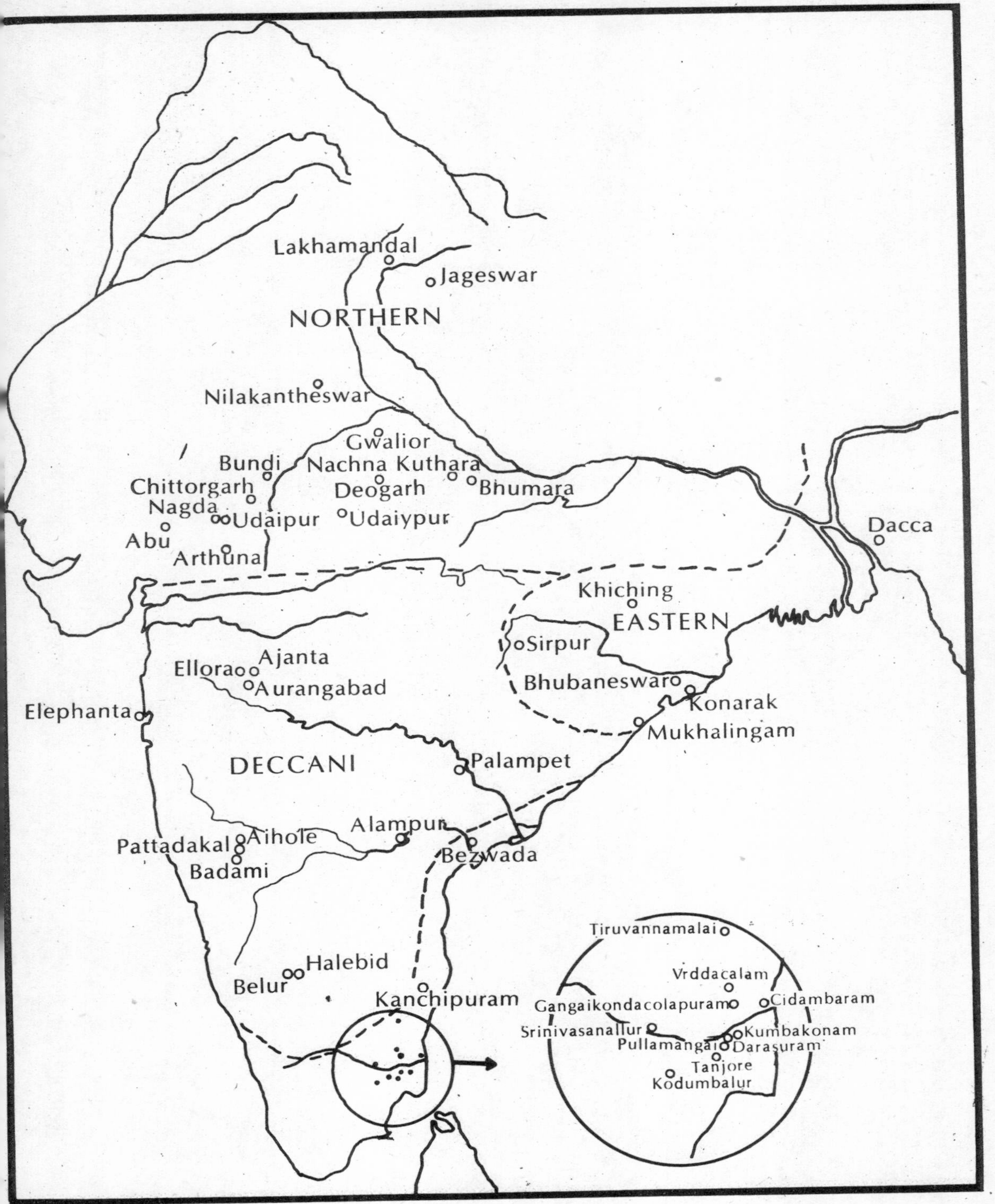

Regional Distribution of Images Illustrated

Glossary

In the case of Śiva's attributes, wherever there is an unequivocal English translation for the Sanskrit word, I have used the English word in the text for which the Sanskrit equivalent is given below. Where the idea in Sanskrit is not succinctly expressed by any one word in English, I have used the Sanskrit. This glossary records only those meanings of words that apply to this work.

abhaya: an iconographic term to describe a position of the hands which indicates fearlessness, a refuge; see Plate 9 c
abhinaya: 'to lead towards'; interpretation in the *nāṭya/nṛtya* sections of dance and drama of stories and emotional states
ādavallān: name of a particular dance pose of Śiva, derived from one of his names in Tamil; see Table 1
āgama: south Indian Sanskrit texts of which one part deals with iconography
agratalasañcara: a position of the feet; see Plate 7d
akṣamālā: rosary; attribute of Śiva
alapadma: a hand sign; see Plate 9a
alīḍha: a standing posture (*sthāna*) in the *NŚ*. One knee is bent and the other is straight; see Plates 66d-f
ānandatāṇḍava: a vigorous dance of Śiva expressing bliss; a particular dance pose of Śiva; see Chapter IV and Table 1.
añcita: literally, 'bent arched', a position of the foot; see Plate 7c. It is also an alternative name for the *alapadma hasta*; see Plate 9a
aṅgula: literally, 'finger, finger's breadth'; a measure used in iconography
añjali: literally, 'reverence salutation'; a position of both hands; see Plate 9b
aṅkuśa: elephant goad; one of Śiva's attributes
ardhamaṇḍalī or *maṇḍalī*: the basic position of Bharata Nāṭyam in which both feet are in *tryaśra* and both knees are bent. **See Plate 8f**
ardhapatāka: literally, 'half flag'; a hand sign; see Plate 9d
āsana: sitting posture
asura: evil spirit, demon
adavus: the basic dance steps in Bharata Nāṭyām
bāṇa: arrow, one of Śiva's attributes, also the name of a *hasta*; see Plate 9e
bengapattia: belt worn by Oḍissi dancers
bhakta: a devotee, a faithful worshipper
bhakti: having devotion
bhāva: feeling emotion, love
bhujaṅgāñcita: literally, 'bent like a serpent'; the 40th *karaṇa* in the *NŚ, VDP*; see Table 1
bhujaṅgalalita: literally, 'graceful like a serpent'; **āgamic name for one of Śiva's dance poses see Table 1**
bhujaṅga-naṭana: literally, 'dancing like a serpent': inconographic name for a hand sign; see Table 1
bhūmisparśa mudrā: literally, 'touching the earth'; iconographic name for a hand sign; see Plate 9 v
caṇḍatāṇḍava: *āgamic* name for a dance pose of Śiva; see Table 1
caitya:window; ornamental motif, resembling the window of a Buddhist rock-cut hall (sanctuary)
catura: literally, 'charming', name of a *karaṇa*, and one of the *karaṇas* selected by G. Rao for his classification of dancing images; name of a hand sign, see Plate 9f; *āgamic* name for a dance pose of Śiva; see Table 1
chandi: a Javanese temple
chowk: a basic position of the feet used in the Oḍissi dance style; see Plate 8c
cinmudrā vyākhyāṇamudrā sandarśanamudrā; iconographic names for a hand sign; seen Plate 9i
ḍamaru: one of Śiva's attributes; a drum shaped like an hour glass, played at both ends
daṇḍa: 'stick', a hand sign
darpaṇa: one of Śiva's and Pārvatī's attributes; particularly in the Ardhanārīśvara aspects
dhanus: bow; one of Śiva's attributes
dharma: way of life ascribed a Hindu by his status at birth
dhoti: garment consisting of a piece of cloth tiea around the waist
dhyāna śloka: mnemonic verse
dikpāla: regent or guardian of a quarter of the sky
dola/ḍolā: a hand sign; see Plate 9g
gajahasta: a hand sign, also called *latā, daṇḍa, kari hasta*; see Plate 9h
gadā: 'club'; attribute usually associated with Viṣṇu
gaṇa: one of Śiva's attendant dwarfs; see Chapter VII; also Table 4
gaurītāṇḍava: *āgamic* name for one of Śiva's dances
ghaṇṭa: bell; one of Śiva's attributes

gopura: temple gateway in south India
gumpha: cave
haṃsapakṣa: literally 'goose wing'—a hand sign; see Plate 9j
haṃsāsya: literally 'swan face'—a hand sign; see Plate 9i
hasta: 'hand' or hand sign, also called *mudrā*
kālitāṇḍava: *āgamic* name for one of Śiva's dances. According to the *Vaṭāraṇya Māhātmya* he performed this dance at Tiruvalangadu (TN), see Table 1
kamaṇḍalu: water pot or vessel with a tip; one of Śiva's attributes
kapāla: literally, skull: a bowl made out of a skull; one of Śiva's attributes
kapittha: a hand sign. See Plate 9k
karaṇa: the combined movements of hands and feet in dance as described in the *NŚ*. G. Rao based his classification of dancing Śivas on five *karaṇas*
kartarīmukha: literally, 'scissor face'; the name of a hand sign. See Plate 9m
karihasta: literally, 'elephant hand'; a position of the arm. See Plate 9h. Also called *gajahasta/daṇḍahasta/latā hasta*
karma: literally, 'deed'; acts of positive or negative moral value entailing reward or punishment in this or a future life
karkaṭa: literally, 'crab'; a position for two hands; see Plate 9l
kaṭakamukha khaṭakamukha: a hand sign; see Plate 9n
kaṭisama: name of *karaṇa* in the *NŚ* and one of Rao's categories in his classification; see Table 1
kaṭyavalambita: iconographic name of a hand sign; see Plate 9p
khaḍga: a sword, one of Śiva's attributes
khaṭakamukha kaṭakamukha: a hand sign; see Plates 9m, n
khaṭvāṅga: club with a human skull mounted on the handle; one of Śiva's attributes
kheṭaka: shield; one of Śiva's attributes
koyil kovil koil: Tamil word for a temple
kṣipta: literally, 'bent'; term used for the bent knee position in both dance and sculpture
kūḍu śukanāsa: decorative motif, a *caitya* window motif, horse-shoe-shaped decorative element on facade of monument
kuñcita: literally, 'curved, bent, contracted', a position of the foot. See Plate 7c
kuṭṭitam: literally, 'pounded, flattened'; movement of the foot in dance. One of A. Boner's categories for Naṭarāja images. The term *kuṭṭitam* comes from the *NŚ* and is synonymous with *nikuṭṭitam,* the term used in the *Nāṭya Veda Vivṛtti*. See Table 1
lalāṭa tilaka: 'a *tilaka* mark on the forehead'; name of a *karaṇa* in the *NŚ*. *Lalāṭa tilaka* was one of the five *karaṇas* selected by Rao for his classification of dancing Śivas. See Table 1
latā: literally, creeper'; name of a position of arm synonymous with *gaja, daṇḍa*, and *kari hasta*. See Plate 9h and Plate 9q
lalita: literally, 'amorous, graceful' name of a *karaṇa* in the *NŚ*. The *lalita karaṇa* was one of the five selected by Rao for his *karaṇa* classification of dancing Śivas. See Table 1
lalitāsana: literally, 'amorously seated'; a sitting posture
lāsya: literally, 'gentle, tender'; gentle dance representing the softer movements, usually performed by Pārvatī, the opposite of *tāṇḍava*. See Chapter VI, under Ardhanārīśvara.
liṅga: male organ or phallus; Śiva worshipped in the form of a stone or marble column which generally rises out of a *yoni* (the female organ)
main arm or hands: the foremost pair of arms or hands
maṇḍala: standing posture, of which three are discussed: *ālīḍha, pratyālīḍha*, and *sthānaka*; (see Plates 66d-f)
mayūra: literally, 'peacock'; position of the hands; see Plate 9r
mode: a term used to describe the various dances of Śiva given in *āgamic* texts
mṛga: deer; an attribute held by Śiva
mṛgaśirṣa: literally, 'deer's head'; name of a hand sign; see Plate 9s
mudrā: literally, 'sign or seal'; a position of the hands, synonymous with *hasta*
mukula: 'bud'; position of the hands; see Plate 9t
musala: pestle; one of Śiva's attributes
muṣṭi: literally, 'fist'; position of the hands; see Plate 9u
nādānta: the end result (*anta*) of *nāda* (the first sound). One of Coomaraswamy's categories for Śiva's dance. See Table 1
nandi: the blessing or benediction at the beginning of a Sanskrit drama
nandi-dhvaja: literally, 'Nandi flag'; a staff with an image of Nandi, Śiva's bull, on it
nāṭya: literally, 'mime'; the mimetic portion of dance; 'drama'
nikuṭṭitam: literally, 'pounded or flattened'; a movement of the feet synonymous with *kuṭṭitam*. Used by G. Rao in his description of the feet for the *catura karaṇa,* one of his categories for dancing Śivas

nṛtta: literally, pure dance; decorative dance without a particular story
nṛttamūrti: 'dancing image'
nṛtya: the mimetic portion of dance which also includes rhythmic passages; may also be a synonym for *nāṭya*
pāda: foot
paraśu: axe; one of Siva's attributes
pāśa: one of Śiva's attributes
patāka: literally, 'flag'; a hand sign; see plate 9v
puṣpapuṭa: literally, *puṣpa*—flower, *puṭa*—hollow, a hand sign; see Plate 9w
pustaka: palm leaf book; one of Śiva's attributes
pratyālīḍha: a position of the feet in both dance and sculpture, the reverse of the *alīḍha* posture. See Plates 66d–f
pūjā: worship
rasa: emotions as distilled through a work of art
recita: literally, 'thrown upwards'; name of a hand sign, see Plate 9x
ṛṣi: sage
sabhāpati: a dance pose of Śiva according to the *Karaṇagama*; see Table 1
sama: literally, equal, a position of the feet; see Plate 7a
saṃdaṃśa: literally, 'grasping pincers'; a hand sign; see Plate 9y
sandarśana/cinmudrā/vyākhyānamudrā: iconographic name of a hand sign; see Plate 9i
sandhyā: literally, 'twilight, evening'; one of Coomaraswamy's categories for Śiva's dance. Śiva's dance is described as *sandhyā* in several texts such as the *Śiva Pradoṣa Stotra*. See Table 1
sandhyātāṇḍava: name of a dance pose of Śiva according to the *Śilpasaṅgraha* and *Mayamata Āgamas*; see Table 1
saṃhāra tāṇḍava: wild and vigorous dance; name of a dance pose of Śiva, conceived as destroying the universe. See Table 1
sarpaśīrṣa: literally, 'serpent's head'; a hand sign; see Plate 9 aa
śikhara: literally, 'peak'; name of a hand sign; see Plate 9bb
siṃhakarṇa: literally, 'lion's ear'; iconographic name of hand sign; Plate 9dd
śloka: Sanskrit verse
sthāna/sthānaka: a standing posture
sthalamāhātmya(s): south Indian texts that record the regional history and legends of temples
sūcī: 'needle'; a hand sign; see Plate 9cc called '*tarjinī*' in icnography
śukacancu: the name of a hand sign used in Oḍissi dance and described in the *Abhinaya Candrika*. See Plate 9dd
śukanāsa/kūḍu: literally 'parrot's nose'; a term in architecture denoting part of the *sikhara* tower
śukatuṇḍa: literally, 'parrot's beak'; a hand sign; see Plate 9ee
svastika: literally, crossed; the name of a hand sign, Plate 9ff; also the name of a foot position, Plate 7f
talasaṃsphoṭita: the name of a *karaṇa* in the *NŚ*; one of the five used by Rao in his classification
tāmracūḍa: literally, 'red-crested' (cock); a hand sign; see Plate 9 gg
tāṇḍava: literally, 'vigorous wild dance of Śiva'; one of the categories used by Coomaraswamy in his classification
tapas: literally, 'heat'; religious austerity, penance, asceticism; Yogic practice
tarjinī: literally, 'threatening'; a hand sign used in iconography. When used in dance it is called *sūcī*. See Plate 9 cc
torque: a necklace often worn by Gupta images
tribhaṅga: literally, 'three bends'; a triple-bend position of the body used in both dance and iconography; see Plates 8 d,e
tripuratāṇḍava: a dance pose of Śiva according to the Śilaparatna. See Table 1
triśula: a hand sign, see Plate 9 ii; also one of Śiva's weapons, the trident
tryaśra: the name of a foot position, see Plate 7b
udvāhita: literally, 'raised'; usually refers to a raised position of the torso in the *tribhaṅga* body position. See Plates 8d,e
ūrdhvajānu: literally, 'knee up'; a *karaṇa*; see Table 1
ūrdhvatāṇḍava: literally, 'raised *tāṇḍava*, or raised vigorous dance'; *āgamic* name given to one of Śiva's dances, usually the dance at Tiruvalangadu in which he raised his leg over his head in order to defeat Pārvatī in a dance competition. *Ūrdhvatāṇḍava* is often used interchangeably with the *lalāṭa tilaka karaṇa* by many writers when describing images of dancing Sivas. See Table 1
urnanabha; hand sign; see Plate 9jj
vāhana: vehicle or mount of a god
vaiṣṇava sthāna: literally, 'Viṣṇu stance'; a particular standing position; see Table 1
varada: iconographic name of a hand sign; see Plate 9c
varṇa: literally, 'colour', caste
vimāna: towered sanctuary containing cell in which the deity is enshrined
vīṇā: an Indian lute
vismaya: literally, 'wonder'; iconographic term used to describe that hand position which in

dance is called *alapadma*. See Plate 9a

vṛcika: literally, 'scorpion'; a position of the leg(s), also the name of a *karaṇa*. See Table 1

vyakhyanamudrā/cinmudra/sandarsanamudrā: iconographic name of a hand sign; see Plate 9i

yagñopavīta: sacrificial or sacred thread; one of Śiva's attributes when depicted in sculpture; also permanently worn by high-caste Hindus

yoni: the female sex organ

Bibliography

This list includes some works not referred to in the text, but which were consulted and used in formulating general ideas.

Abhinayadarpaṇam by Nandikeśvara; ed. and trans. M. Ghosh; 2nd edition; Calcutta, 1957.

Acharya, P.K., *A Dictionary of Hindu Architecture,* London, 1927.

Adiceam, M.E., 'Les Images de Śiva dans l'Inde du Sud, II, Bhairava', *Arts Asiatiques,* Vol. XI, 1965, pp. 23–44.

—— 'Les Images de Śiva dans l'Inde du Sud, III et IV, Bhikṣāṭanamūrti, et Kaṅkālamūrti', *Arts Asiatiques,* Vol. XII, 1965, pp. 83–112.

—— 'Les Images de Śiva dans l'Inde du Sud, VI, Ardhanārīśvara', *Arts Asiatiques,* Vol. XVII, 1968, pp. 143–72.

—— 'Les Images de Śiva dans l'Inde du Sud, VII, Vṛṣavāhanamūrti VII', *Arts Asiatiques,* Vol. XIX, 1969, pp. 85–106.

Agni Purāṇa, trans. M.N. Dutt Shastri, 2 Vols., Chowkhamba Sanskrit Series, No. 54, Varanasi, 1967.

Agrawala, P.K., *Gupta Temple Architecture,* Varanasi, 1968.

Agrawala, R.C., 'Mediaeval Sculpture: Sirkar', *Mārg,* Vol. 12, No. 2, March, 1959, pp. 69–71.

—— 'Unpublished Kaṭārmal Wood Reliefs', *East and West,* Vol. 17, Nos. 1–2, March–June, 1967, pp. 83–95.

—— 'Notes Iconographiques, III, Une Réprésentation Insolite des Mātṛkā provenant de Ābānerī (Rajasthān). *Arts Asiatiques*. XXIII. 1971. pp. 147–50.

Agrawala, V.S., 'A Survey of Gupta Art and Some Sculptures from Nachna Kuthara and Khoh', *Lalit Kalā,* 10 April 1961, pp. 16–26.

——*Śiva Mahādeva: The Great God,* Varanasi, 1966.

Aiya Nagam, *The Travancore State Manual,* Vol. II, Trivandram, 1906.

Altekar, A.S., *The Position of Women in Hindu Civilization,* New Delhi, 1962.

Annual Progress Report of the Archaeological Survey of India for the year ending March 31, 1919.

Ancient Sculpture from India, A Catalogue of the Exhibition at the Cleveland Museum, Cleveland, 1964.

Archer, W.G., *Indian Paintings from the Punjab Hills,* London, 1973.

Ashton, M.B., and Christie, B., *Yakṣagāna—A Dance Drama of India,* New Delhi, 1977.

Auboyer, J., *La Vie Publique et Privée dans l'Inde Ancienne,* Fasc. VI, Paris, 1955.

——*Daily Life in Ancient India, from approximately 200 BC–700 AD* trans. S.W. Taylor, London, 1965.

Ayyar, C.V. Narayana, *Origins of Early Śaivism in South India,* Madras, 1936.

Ayyar, Jagadisa, P.V., *South Indian Shrines,* Madras, 1920, revised and enlarged edition, Madras, 1922.

Ayyar, Ramakrishna, *Economy of a South Indian Temple,* Annamalainagar, 1946.

Bajpai, K.D., 'Some Interesting Gaṇa Figures from Panna', *Lalit Kalā,* No. 10, Oct. 1961, New Delhi, pp. 21–4.

Balakrishnan, Shyamala, 'Folk Music in the Life of Tamil Nadu', *Sangeet Natak* 12, April–June 1969, New Delhi, pp. 40–9.

Balasubrahmanyam, S.R., 'The Oldest Chidambaram Inscriptions', *Journal of the Annamalai University,* No. 2/3 xii, April 1943, pp. 106–18, and xiii, March 1944, pp. 55–91.

—— 'Labelled Sculptures of the Western Tower of Chidambaram Temple', *Lalit Kalā,* No. 9, April 1961, pp. 27–9.

—— *Four Chola Temples,* Bombay, 1963.

—— *Early Chola Temples, AD 907–985,* New Delhi, 1971.

Banaji, D.R., *Slavery in British India,* Bombay, 1933.

Banerjea, J.N., *Development of Hindu Iconography,* Calcutta, 1941.

Banerji, Adris, 'Three Temples of Ranakpur', *Journal of the Oriental Institute,* Vol. XVI, No. 2., Dec. 1966, Baroda, pp. 170–5.

Banerji, P., 'The Dancing Body', *Journal of the Indian Society of Oriental Art,* VII, 1939, pp. 116–31.

Banerji, R.D., The Temple of Śiva at Bhumara', *Memoirs of the Archaeological Survey of India,* No. 16, 1924, Calcutta, pp. 1–14.

—— 'The Haihayas of Tripurī and their Monuments', *Memoirs of the Archaeological Survey of India,* No. 23, 1931, Calcutta, pp. 1–152

—— 'The Naihati Grant of Vallalasena', *Epigraphia Indica*, Vol. XIV, 1917–18, pp. 156–63.

—— *History of Orissa,* 2 Vols., Calcutta, 1930.

Barrett, D., *Sculptures from Amaravati in the British Museum,* London, 1954.

—— *Temples at Mukhalingam*. Bombay, 1960.

—— 'Sculptures of the Shāhi Period', *Oriental Art,* Vol. III, No. 2, summer 1957, pp. 54–9.

——*Early Cola Bronzes*, Bombay, 1965.

—— *Early Çola Architecture and Sculpture, 866–1014 AD*, London, 1974.

Barua, Benimadhab, *Aspects of Life and Art,* Calcutta, 1937.

Bazaz, P.N., *Daughters of the Vitasta,* New Delhi, 1959.

Begley, W.E., *Viṣṇu's Flaming Wheel, The Iconography of the Sudarśana Chakra,* New York, 1973.

Bhandarkar, D.R. 'The Chahamanas of Marwar', *Epigraphia Indica,* Vol. XI, 1911–12, pp. 26–30.

Bhattacharji, S., *The Indian Theogony,* Cambridge, 1970.

Bhattacharya, B., *Indian Buddhist Iconography,* 2nd edition.

Bhattacharyya, A., *Chhau Dance of Purulia,* Calcutta, 1972.

Bhattacharyya, A.K., 'A Set of Kulū Folk Paintings in the National Museum of India', *Artibus Asiae,* Vol. XX, 2/3, 1957, pp. 165–83.

Bhattasali, Nalinikantha, M.A., *Iconography of the Buddhists and Brahmanical Sculptures in the Dacca Museum,* Dacca, 1929.

—— 'The Bhārellā Nartteśvara Image Inscription', *Epigraphia Indica,* Vol. XVII, 1923, pp. 349–52.

Bhavnani, E., *The Dance in India,* Bombay, 1965.

Bhoothalingam, M., *Movement in Stone,* Delhi, 1969.

Boner, A. 'The Symbolic Aspect of Form', *Journal of the Indian Society of Indian Art,* Vol. XVII, 1949, pp. 42–50.

——*Principles of Composition in Hindu Sculpture, (Cave Temple Period)*, Leiden, 1962.

——*New Light on the Sun Temple at Konarak,* Varanasi, 1972.

Boner, A. and Ramachandra, K., *Śilpa Prakāśa,* Leiden, 1968.

Bose, L., The Female Figures on the Railing Pillars from Mathurā of the Kushāna Period, B. Litt. thesis, Oxford University, (M.S.S. B. Litt. c. 261) 1973.

Bose, M., A Critical and Comparative Study of Sanskrit Texts Dealing with Dancing, B. Litt. thesis, Oxford University, (M.S.S. B.Litt.d.1008), 1964.

——*Indian Classical Dancing: A Glossary,* Calcutta, 1970.

Bowers, F., *Theatre in the East,* New York, 1956.

Brown, P., *Indian Architecture, (Buddhist and Hindu Periods),* Bombay, 1965.

Buchanan, F., *Journey from Madras through Mysore, Kanara and Malabar,* Vol. I, Madras, 1870.

Buitenen, Johannes A.B. Van, *Two Plays of Ancient India,* London, 1968.

Burgess, J., *The Ancient Monuments, Temples, and Sculptures of India,* London, 1897.

Bushan, V.N., 'Nritya Nirajan', *Roopa Lekha,* Vol. I, serial No. I, July 1939, New Delhi, pp. 47–64.

Butterworth, A. and Aiyangar, S. Krishnaswami, 'Two Tamil Hymns for the Margazhi Festival', *The Indian Antiquary,* Vol. LV, 1926, pp. 161–7 and pp. 186–91.

Carmichael, Amy-Wilson, *Things as They Are,* London, 1904.

—— *Lotus Buds,* London, 1910.

Caton, A.R., *The Key of Progress,* London, 1930.

Census of India, Vol. XIII, *Madras Report, 1891;* Vol. XV, *Madras Report,* Part 1, 1901.

Chakladar, H.C., *Social Life in Ancient India,* Calcutta, 1929.

Chandra, Moti, *The World of Courtesans,* Delhi, 1973.

Chandra, Pramod, *Stone Sculptures in the Allahabad Museum,* Poona, 1971.

Chandra, Ramaprasad, *Medieval Sculptures in the British Museum,* London, 1936.

Chattopadhyay, Aparna, 'The Institution of "Devadasis" according to the Kathasaritsagara', *Journal of the Oriental Institute, Baroda,* Vol. XVI, No. 3, March 1967, Baroda, pp. 216-22.

Chattopadhyay, Sudhakar, *Social Life in India,* Calcutta, 1965.

'Chhau', *Mārg,* Special edition, Vol. XXIII, No. I, Dec. 1968, Bombay.

Chhavi, Golden Jubilee Volume, 1920-70. Bharat Kala Bhavan, Banares.

Classical and Folk Dances of India, a special edition of *Mārg.*

Coomaraswamy, A., *A History of Indian and Indonesian Art,* London, 1927.

—— *Yakṣas.* Washington, 1928.

—— *The Dance of Śhiva*, Bombay, 1948.

—— *Transformation of Nature in Art,* New York, 1956.

Cousens, H., *The Chālukyan Architecture of the Kanarese Districts,* Archaeological Survey of India, xlii, New Imperial Series, 1926.

Cox, A.F. *A Manual of the North Arcot District in the Presidency of Madras,* Madras, 1881.

Dalal, M.L., *Conflict in Sanskrit Drama,* Bombay, 1973.

Dandin, *Dasha-Kumara-Charita, The Ten Princes,* trans. by A.W. Rider, 3rd imp., Chicago, 1960.

Daniélou, A., *Hindu Polytheism,* London, 1963.

Das Gupta, H.C., *History of the Indian Stage,* Vols. I and II, Calcutta, 1946.

Daśarūpa, a Treatise on Hindu Dramaturgy, trans. G.C. Haas, New York, 1912.

Dass, R.K., *Temples of Tamilnad,* Bombay, 1964.

Dass, R.M., *The Women in Manu, and his Seven Commentators,* Varanasi, 1961.

De, S.K., *Aspects of Sanskrit Literature,* Calcutta, 1959.

De Mallmann, M.T., *Les Enseignements Iconographiques de l'Agni-Purāṇa*, Paris, 1963.

Deo, Singh Juga Bhanu, *Chhau (Mask Dance of Seraikela),* Cuttack, 1973.

Desai, Neera, *Women in Modern India,* Bombay, 1957.

Desikan, V.N. Srinivasa, *The Bronze Gallery, A Guide,* Madras, 1972.

Devi, Ragini, *Dance Dialects of India,* London, 1972.

Devi, Rukmini, 'Spiritual Background of Bharata Natyam', *Mārg,* 1963, Special Edition on Dance, pp. 5–6.

De Zoete, B., *The Other Mind: A Study of Dance and Life in South India,* London, 1953.

Dhar, Somnath, *Kalhaṇa, Poet Historian of Kashmir,* Bangalore, 1956.

Dhavamony, M., *Love of God According to Śaiva Śiddhānta, (A study in the mysticism and theology of Śaivism),* Oxford, 1971.

Dikshitar, Ramachandra, V.R., *Studies in Tamil Literature,* Madras, 1936.

Dimock, E.C., *The Place of the Hidden Moon,* Chicago, 1966.

Divakaran, O., 'Le Temple de Jambulinga (Date de 699 ap. J.C.) à Badami', *Arts Asiatiques,* Vol. XXI, 1970, Paris, pp. 15–40.

Divakaran, Odile, 'Les Temples d'Ālampur et de ses Environs au Temps des Cāḷukyas de Bādāmi', *Arts Asiatiques,* Vol. XXIV, 1971, pp. 51–101.

Donaldson, T., 'Doorframes on the Earliest Orissan Temples', *Artibus Asiae,* Vol. XXXVIII, 2/3, 1976, pp. 189–218.

Dubois, Abbé J.A., *Hindu Manners, Customs and Ceremonies,* trans. H.C. Beauchamp, Vol. II, Oxford, 1897; also new ed. Oxford, 1972.

Elliott, H.M., *History of India,* Vol. 4, London, 1872.

Enthovin, R.E., *The Tribes and Castes of Bombay,* Vol. I, Bombay, 1920.

Fawcett, F., 'On Basivis: Women, who through Dedication to a Deity, Assume Masculine Privileges', *Journal of the Anthropological Society of Bombay,* Vol. II, No. 6, 1891, Bombay, pp. 322–45.

Fergusson, J., *History of Indian and Eastern Architecture,* 3 Vols., London, 1910.

Fleet, J.F. 'Sanskrit and Old Canarese Inscriptions', *Indian Antiquary,* III, 1874; V, 1876; VI, 1877; VII, 1878; VIII, 1879; IX, 1880; X, 1881; XI, 1882.

Francis, W., *Gazetteer of the Bellary District,* Madras, 1904.

Frederic, L., *Indian Temples and Sculpture,* London, 1960.

Ganesan, S., 'Some Iconographic Concepts', *Proceedings of the First International Conference Seminar of Tamil Studies, April 1966,* Vol. II, Kuala Lumpur, 1969, pp. 402–16.

Gangoly, O.C., *South Indian Bronzes,* Calcutta, 1915.

—— 'A New Contribution to Śaivite Art', *Rūpam,* No. 5, Jan. 1921, pp. 1–9.

—— *Orissan Sculpture and Architecture,* New Delhi, 1956.

—— *The Art of the Pallavas,* Bombay, 1957.

—— *The Art of the Rashtrakutas,* Bombay, 1958.

Ganhar, J.N., *Jammu Shrines and Pilgrimages,* New Delhi, 1973.

Gargi, B.G., *Folk Theatre of India,* London, 1966.

Gaston, A.M., 'Encounter with Indian Dance', *Sangeet Natak,* No. 19, January-March 1971, pp. 24–33.

Ghurye, G.S., *Rajput Architecture,* Bombay, 1968.

Gnoli, Raniero, *The Aesthetic Experience according to Abhinavagupta,* Rome, 1956.

Goetz, H., *Five Thousand Years of Indian Art,* 2 Vols., London, 1959.

—— *Studies in the History and Art of Kashmir and the Indian Himalaya,* Wiesbaden, 1969.

Gonda, Jan, *A History of Indian Literature, Vedic Literature,* Wiesbaden, 1975.

Gordon, A., *Iconography of Tibetan Lamaism,* 2nd ed., Vermont, 1939.

Goswami, A. *Indian Temple Sculpture,* Calcutta, 1956.

Gravely, F.H., *The Gopuras of Tiruvannamalai,* Government of Madras, New Series, Vol. VII, No. 5, Madras, 1959.

Grünwedel, A., *Buddhist Art in India,* trans. A.C. Gibson, Rev. J. Burgess, London, 1901.

Gupta, R.S., *Iconography of the Hindus, Buddhists and Jains,* Bombay, 1972.

Haque, M.E., 'The Iconography of the Hindu Sculpture of Bengal, up to 1250 AD', D. Phil. thesis, Oxford University, M.S.S.D.Phil. 5825–26, 1973.

Harle, J.C., *The Brahmapurisvara Temple at Pullamangai,* Bombay, 1958.

—— 'The Early Cola Temple at Puḷḷamaṅgai', *Oriental Art,* Vol. IV, No. 3, Autumn 1958, pp. 96–108.

—— The Architecture and Iconography of the Cidambaram Gopuras, D. Phil. thesis, Oxford University, M.S.S.D. Phil. c. 370–1, 1959.

—— *Temple Gateways in South India,* Oxford, 1963.

—— *'Ālīḍha', Mahayanist Art after AD 900 (Colloquies on Art and Archaeology in Asia,* No. 2), 1971, University of London, pp. 10–14.

—— *Gupta Sculpture,* Oxford, 1974.

Hart, G.L., *The Poems of Ancient Tamil; Their Milieu and their Sanskrit Counterparts,* Berkeley, 1975.

Havell, E.B., *Benares: The Sacred City, Sketches of Hindu Life and Religion,* London, 1905.

Havers, G., *The Travels of Pietro Della Valle, from the old English translation of 1664,* Vol. II, London, 1892.

Heimann, B., 'Concept of Deva in Hindu Thought', *Journal of Indian Society of Oriental Art,* Vol. XVII, 1949, pp. 42–50, Calcutta.

Hemingway, F.R., *Madras District Gazetteer, Tanjore,* Vol. I, Madras, 1906.

—— *Gazetteer of the Godavari District,* Madras, 1907.

Hopkins, E.W., *Epic Mythology,* Strassburg, 1915.

Horner, I.B., *Women Under Primitive Buddhism,* London, 1930.

Ingalls, D.H., *An Anthology of Sanskrit Court Poetry,* Harvard, 1965.

Ions, V., *Indian Mythology,* London, 1967.

Iyengar, Srinivasa, C.R., *Indian Dance,* Madras, 1948.

Iyer, Bharata, *Kathakali,* London, 1955.

Iyer, K. Bharata, 'Śiva the Benign', *The Times of India Annual,* 1971, Delhi, pp. 77, 86.

Iyer, Krishna, E., 'Bhagavata Mela, Dance-Drama of Bharata Natyam', *Sangeet Natak,* No. 13, July-Sept. 1969, pp. 46–7.

Iyer, Sarvesvara P., 'Purāṇic Śaivism in Ceylon during the Polonnaruwa Period', *Proceedings of the First International Conference of Tamil Studies,* April 1966, Vol. I, Kuala Lumpur, 1968, pp. 462–74.

Jain, Jagdish Chandra, *Life in Ancient India, as depicted in the Jain Canons,* Bombay, 1947.

Jayal, Shankambari, *The Status of Women in the Epics,* Delhi, 1966.

Jouveau-Dubreuil, G., *Iconography of Southern India,* trans. A.C. Martin, Paris, 1937.

Journal of the Madras Music Academy, 1932, Debate held on the sixth day of the annual Conference, Dec. 28, 1932, on the encouragement of the art of Bharata Natyam, Madras, pp. '13–23.

Kalavikash Kendra Souvenir, Cuttack, 1958.

Kalhaṇa, *Rājataraṅginī—A chronicle of the kings of Kaśmīr,* trans. M.S. Stein, 2 Vols., Westminster, 1900.

Kālidāsa, *Mālavikāgnimitra,* ed. and trans. C.R. Devadhar, Delhi, 1966.

——*The Birth of the War-God (Kumārasambhava),* trans. R.T.H. Griffith, London, 1853.

——*The Cloud Messenger (Meghadūta),* trans. F. and E. Egerton, Michigan, 1964.

Kambar, C., 'Ritual in Kannada Folk Theatre', *Sangeet Natak,* No. 25, July–Sept. 1972.

Kane, P.V., *History of Dharma Sāstra,* Vol. II, Part I, Government Oriental Series, Class B, No. 6, Poona, 1941.

Kauṭilya, *Arthaśāstra,* trans. K.P. Kangle, Bombay, 1961.

——*Arthaśāstra,* trans. R. Shamasastry, 8th ed., Mysore, 1967.

Keith, A.B., *Classical Sanskrit Literature,* Oxford, 1928.

Kennedy, Vans, Lieutenant Colonel, *Researches into the Nature and Affinity of Ancient and Hindu Mythology,* London, 1831.

Khan, A.W., *Stone Sculptures in the Alampur Museum,* Hyderabad, 1973.

Khokar, Mohan, 'Kanchi Kailasa', *Sangeet Natak,* I, 1965, New Delhi, pp. 68–81.

Kosambi, D.D., *Myth and Reality, Studies in the Formation of Indian Culture,* Bombay, 1962.

Kothari, S., 'Gotipua Dancers of Orissa', *Sangeet Natak,* 8, April–June 1968, pp. 31–43.

——'Chhau Dances of Saraikella', *Mārg,* Vol. XXII, No. 1, Dec. 1968, pp. 5–10.

Kramrisch, S., *The Hindu Temple,* 2 Vols., Calcutta, 1946.

—— *The Art of India,* London, 1954.

—— Cousens, J., and Poduval, R.V., *The Arts and Crafts of Travancore,* Oxford, 1952.

—— 'Review of Naṭarāja, in Art, Thought and Literature' by C. Sivaramamurti, *Artibus Asiae,* XXXVII_4, 1975, pp. 311–13.

—— 'Pāla and Sena Sculpture', *Rūpam,* No. 40, Oct. 1929, Calcutta, pp. 107–26.

—— 'The Vishnudharmottaram', *Journal of the Department of Letters,* Vol. XI, 1924, University of Calcutta, pp. 1–56.

Krishnamurti, Y., 'Satya Bhama, The Aesthetic Ideal of Womanhood', *The Times of India Annual,* 1973, pp. 19–24.

Krishnan, Y., 'The Erotic Sculptures of India', *Artibus Asiae,* Vol. XXXIV_4, 1972, Switzerland, pp. 331–43.

Kulārṇava Tantra, ed. A. Avalon, and T. Vidyaratna, London, 1913.

Kūrma Purāṇa, trans. a board of scholars and ed. Anand Swarup Gupta, All-India Kashiraj Trust, Varanasi, 1972.

Lal, Kanwar, *Miracle of Konarak,* Delhi, 1967.

——*Temples and Sculptures of Bhubaneswar,* Delhi, 1970.

Larson, A.J., *Classical Sāṃkhya, An Interpretation of its History and Meaning,* Delhi, 1969.

Laws of Manu, trans. G. Buhler, *Sacred Books of the East,* Vol. 25, Delhi, 2nd reprint, 1967.

Legislative Assembly Debates of India, 2nd session, 'Resolution Re Prohibition of Traffic in Minor Girls', pp. 2599–615, 27 Feb. 1922.

Liebert Gösta, *Iconographic Dictionary of the Indian Religions,* Vol. V, *Studies in South Asian Culture,* Leiden, 1976.

Liṅga Purāṅa, trans. a board of scholars, Ancient Indian Tradition and Mythology series, Vol. 5, Part I; Vol. 6, Part 2; Delhi, 1975.

Madras Epigraphy, GO No. 920, 4th August, 1914.

Madras Epigraphy, GO No. 1260, 25th August, 1915.

Madras Legislative Debates, Nov. 4, 1927.

Mahalingam, T.V., *Kancipuram in Early South Indian History,* London, 1969.

Lippe, A., *The Art of India, Stone Sculpture,* Japan, 1962.

—— 'Early Calukya Icons', *Artibus Asiae,* Vol. XXXIV_4, 1972, pp. 273–330.

—— 'Some South Indian Icons', *Artibus Asiae,* Vol. XXXVII_3, 1975, pp. 169–208.

Lohuizen-de-Leeuw, J.E. Van, 'The Protector of the

Mountain of Truth', *Artibus Asiae,* Vol. XX, 1967, pp. 9–17.

Mahābhārata, trans. P.C. Roy, Vols. 1–11, Calcutta, 1927–32.

Majumdar, A.K., *Calukyas of Gujarat,* Bombay, 1956.

Majumdar, R.C., *History and Culture of the Indian People,* Vol. V, Bombay, 1957.

Manikam, V.T. 'Harlots in Ancient Tamil Literature', *International Conference Seminar of Tamil Studies,* Kuala Lumpur, 1968.

Mārg, Special Edition on the Classical & Folk Dances of India, Bombay, 1963.

Marshall, Sir J., Havell, E.B., and others, *The Bagh Caves,* London, 1927.

Marshall, Sir, J., *Mohenjo-daro and the Indus Civilization*, Vol. I, London, 1931.

Marshall, Sir John, and Foucher, A., *The Monuments of Sāñchi,* 3 Vols., Calcutta, 1946.

Mathur, J.C., *Drama in Rural India.* New Delhi, 1964.

Matsya Purana, trans. a board of scholars, ed. Jamna Dass Akhtar, *The Sacred Books of the Aryans,* Vol. I, 1972.

Menon, Narayana, *Balasareswati,* New Delhi, 1970.

Meyer, J.J., *Sexual Life in Ancient India,* Vol. II, London, 1930.

Mitchell, G., 'The Sangamesvara Temple at Pattadakal', *Art and Archaeological Research Papers,* (AARP) I, London, 1972.

Mitra, D., *Bhubaneswar*, 3rd edition, Dept. of Archaeology, New Delhi, 1966.

—— 'No. 50—Ratnagiri Plates of Somavamsi Karna', *Epigraphia Indica,* XXXIII, 1959–60, pp. 263–8.

—— *Buddhist Monuments,* Calcutta, 1971.

Mitra, R., *Antiquities of Orissa*, 2 Vols, Calcutta, 1875.

Mizuno, S., *Haibik and Kashmir Smast Buddhist Cave Temples in Afghanistan and Pakistan, surveyed in 1960,* Kyoto, 1962.

Monier-Williams, Sir Monier, *A Sanskrit-English Dictionary,* Oxford, 1899.

Mukhopadhyay, Samir K., 'Terracottas from Bhīṭā', *Artibus Asiae,* Vol. XXIV, 1972, pp. 71–94.

Nagaswamy, R., 'Rare Bronzes from the Kongu Country', *Lalit Kalā,* No. 9. April 1961, pp. 7–10.

—— 'Some Adavallān and other Bronzes of the Early Chola Period', *Lalit Kalā,* No. 10, Oct. 1961, pp. 34–40.

—— *Gangaicondacholapuram,* Madras, 1970.

Naidu, B.V.N. and Naidu, P.S. 'A Note on the Occurrence of Certain Sculptures in the Chidambaram Temple', *Journal of the Annamalai University,* Vol. III, No. 2, Oct. 1934, p. 276.

—— 'A Note on Some Sculptural Dance Poses in the Inner Precincts of the Chidambaram Temple', *Journal of Annamalai University,* Vol. IV, No. I, Jan. 1935, p. 165.

Nannithamby, Loganayaky, 'The Fine Arts and Recreation during the Cola Period', *Journal of Tamil Studies,* Vol. I, No. 1, Oct. 1969, pp. 59–71.

Nārada and Mahāthera, and Kassapa Thera, *The Mirror of the Dhamma,* Colombo, 1961.

Nātya Śāstra, by Bharata, Vol. 1, trans. M. Ghosh, Calcutta, 1967; Vol II, text ed. M. Ghosh, 1967.

Nṛttaratnāvalī by Jaya Senāpati, trans, V. Raghavan, Madras, 1965.

O'Flaherty, W.D., *Asceticism and Eroticism in the Mythology of Śiva,* London, 1973.

—— *Hindu Myths,* Harmondsworth, 1975.

Pal, H.P., *The Temples of Rajasthan,* Jaipur, 1969.

Pani, Jivan, 'Chhau Dances of Mayurbañj', *Mārg,* Vol. XXII, No. 1, Dec. 1968. pp. 31–4.

—— 'Chhau, A Comparative Study of Seraikela and Mayurbhañj Forms', *Sangeet Natak,* No. 13, July–Sept. 1969, New Delhi, pp. 35–45.

Panigrahi, K.C., *Archaeological Remains at Bhubaneswar,* New Delhi, 1962.

Patnaik, D.N., 'History and Technique of Odissi Dance', *Sangeet Natak,* No. 5, July–Sept. 1967, pp. 59–68.

—— *Odissi Dance,* Bhubaneswar, 1971.

Pattabiramin, P.Z., *Trouvailles de Nedoungādou, (Tāṇḍavas de Śiva)*, Pondicherry, 1956.

Penzer, N.M., 'Sacred Prostitution', Appendix IV in Somadeva's *Kathāsaritsāgara,* trans. C.H. Tawney, Vol. I, London, 1924, pp. 231–280.

Pereira, Jose, 'The Naṭarāja Theme; a new interpretation', *Journal of the Asiatic Society of Bombay,* Vol. 30, Part I, 1955, pp. 71–86.

Pillai, J.M. Somasundaram, *The Great Temple at Tanjore,* Tanjore, 1958.

—— *Two Thousand Years of Tamil Literature,* Madras, 1959.

—— *The University's Environs, Cultural and Historical,* Annamalainager, 1963

—— *Śiva Naṭarāja—the Cosmic Dancer in Cidambaram,* Cidambaram, 1970.

Pillai, S.S., 'Kāraikkāl Ammaiyar' in Ghananda, S. and Stewart-Wallace, Sir John (eds.), *Women Saints of East and West,* London, 1955, pp. 15–22.

Pillay, K.K., *The Sucindram Temple,* Madras, 1953.

—— *Social History of the Tamils* Part I, Madras.

—— 'The Temple as a Cultural Centre', *Journal of Oriental Research Madras,* Vol XXIX, Parts I–IV, 1963, pp. 83–94.

Pope, U.G., *Tiruvāçagam.* Oxford, 1900.

Prasad, Prakash Charan, 'Dancing Figures in the Patna Museum', *Journal of the Bihar Research Society,* Vol. LIII, Parts I–IV, Jan.–Dec. 1967, pp. 130–6.

Prasad, Rajendra B., 'Rāstrakuta Temples at Bhavanāsi Sangam', *Artibus Asiae,* Vol. XXXIV$_1$, 1972, pp. 211–24.

Pudukkottai State Inscriptions, Chronological List of Inscriptions of the Pudukkottai State, 1929.

Punekar, S.D. and Rao, K., *A Study of Prostitutes in Bombay,* Bombay, 1962.

Raghavan, V., *The Number of Rasas,* Madras, 1940.

—— *Śriṅgāra Mañjarī of Saint Akbar Shah,* Hydrabad, 1951.

—— 'Book Review of the Śilpa Prakaśa by A. Boner', *Journal of Oriental Research,* Vol. XXXIII, Parts I–IV, 1963, pp. 62–6.

—— *The Great Integrators, The saint singers of India,* Delhi, 1966.

Raikar, Y.A., 'Prostitution during the Yadava Period', *Journal of the Oriental Institute, Baroda,* Vol. XIII, No. 2, Dec. 1963.

Rajan, Soundara K.V., *Early Temple Architecture in Karnataka and its Ramifications,* Dharwar, 1969.

—— *Indian Temple Styles,* New Delhi, 1972.

Ramachandran, Nirmala, 'Classical Dance of the Ancient Tamils', *Proceedings of the First International Conference of Tamil Studies in 1966,* Vol. II, Kuala Lumpur, 1969, pp. 379–88.

Ramachandran, T.N., 'Śiva Temple at Cidambaram', *Journal of the Andhra Historical Research Society,* Vol. XIX, 1948, pp. 85–7.

Rangacharya, Adya, *Introduction to Bharata's Nāṭya Sāstra,* Bombay, 1966.

Ranganath, H.K., *The Karnatak Theatre,* Dharwar, 1960.

Rao, Gopinath, *Elements of Hindu Iconography,* 2 Vols. and 2 parts, Madras, 1916, reprinted New Delhi, 1971.

Rao, S.R., 'A Note on the Chronology of Early Calukyan Temples', *Lalit Kalā,* No. 15, 1972, pp. 9–18.

Rawson, P., 'Indian Art at Essen', *Oriental Art,* Vol. 5, No. 3, Autumn, 1959, pp. 106–9.

—— *The Art of Tantra,* London, 1973.

Rele, K. 'Myth', *Mārg,* Vol. XXVI, No. 2, March 1973, p. 6.

Ṛg Veda, trans. H.H. Wilson, London, 1886.

—— trans. R.T.H. Griffith, 4th ed., Chowkamba Sanskrit Series, 35, 2 Vols., Varanasi, 1963.

Rosenfield, J.M., *The Dynastic Arts of the Kushans,* Berkeley, 1967.

Sachau, C.E., *Alberuni,* Vol. I, London, 1887.

Saletore, B.A., *The Social and Political Life in the Vijayanagara Empire,* Vol. II, Madras, 1934.

Sarabhai, M., *Understanding Bharata Nāṭyam,* Baroda, 1965.

Sareswati, S.K., *Early Sculpture of Bengal,* Calcutta, 1962.

Sarkar, S.C., *Some Aspects of the Earliest Social History of India,* London, 1928.

Sarma, M.R., *Temples of Teliṅgāṇa,* Hyderabad, 1972.

Sarma, Mallampalli Somasekhara, *Corpus of Inscriptions in Telangana District,* Archaeological Series, No. 32, Part IV, Hyderabad, 1973.

Sastri, K.A. Nilakantha, *The Cōḷas,* 2nd edition, Madras, 1955.

—— *A History of South India,* 2nd edition, Oxford, 1958.

Sastri, Krishna H., *South Indian Images of Gods and Goddesses,* Madras, 1916.

—— 'Miscellaneous Inscriptions from the Tamil Country', *South Indian Inscriptions,* Vol. III, Part III, Madras, 1920.

Seshadri, M., 'Sandhyā Tāṇḍava', *Artibus Asiae,* Vol. XVIII$_2$, 1955, pp. 116–20.

Sewell, Robert, *A Forgotten Empire, Vijayanagar,* London, 1900.

Shah, U.P. 'Sculptures from Śāmalājī and Roḍā', *Bulletin of the Museum and Picture Gallery,* Baroda, Vol. XIII, Special No., 1960, Baroda.

Shankaranarayanan, 'New Light on the Genealogy and Chronology of the Visnukundins', *Journal of the Oriental Institute M.S. University, Baroda,* Vol. XVI, No. 4, June 19, 1967, pp. 375–81.

Sharma, Dasharatha, *Early Chauhan Dynasties,* Delhi, 1959.

Shilappadikaram, trans. A. Daniélou, London, 1965.

Śilappadikāram, trans. V.R.R. Dikshitar, Oxford, 1939.

Singh, Bahadur, Deo, 'The Icons of Naṭarāja in Uttar Pradesh', *Lalit Kalā,* No. 16, 1974, p. 48.

Sinha, Chitta Ranjan Prasad, 'Some Important Sculptural Acquisitions of the Patna Museum', *Journal of the Bihar Research Society,* Vol. LIII, Parts I–IV, Jan.–Dec. 1967, pp. 155–60.

Śiva Purāṇa, trans. a board of scholars, 4 Vols., Ancient Indian Tradition and Mythology Series, Delhi, 1970.

Sircar, D.C., No. 51, 'Note on Ratnagiri Plates of Somavamsi Karna', *Epigraphia Indica,* Vol. XXXIII, 1959–60, pp. 269–74.

—— 'Devadādasīs in Buddhist Temples', *Epigraphia Indica,* Vol. XXXV, No. 12, 1963, pp. 97–9.

Sivaramamurti, C., 'Three New Naṭeśas in the Madras Museum', *Roopa Lekha,* Vol. 2, No. 3. 1940, New Delhi, pp. 6–8.

—— *Early Eastern Calukya Sculpture,* Bulletin of Madras Government Museum, Vol. 7, No. 2, Madras, 1954.

—— 'The Weapons of Viṣṇu', *Artibus Asiae,* No. 18, 1955, pp. 128–37.

—— 'Geographical and Chronological Factors in Indian Iconography', *Ancient India,* No. 6, Jan. 1950, pp. 21–63.

—— *Royal Conquests and Cultural Migrations in South India and the Deccan,* Calcutta, 1955.
—— *Kalugumalai and Early Pandyan Rockcut Shrines,* Bombay, 1961.
—— *Indian Sculpture,* New Delhi, 1961.
—— 'Nolamba Sculptures in the Madras Government Museum', *Bulletin of the Madras Government Museum,* New Series, Vol. 9, No. 1, 1964, Madras.
—— *Le Stupa du Barabudur,* Paris, 1961.
—— *South Indian Bronzes,* New Delhi, 1963.
—— *South Indian Painting,* New Delhi, 1968.
—— *Sanskrit Literature and Art—Mirrors of Indian Culture,* New Delhi, 2nd edition, 1970.
—— *Mahābalipuram,* New Delhi, 1972.
—— *The Cola Temples Thanjavur, Gangaikondacolapuram and Darasuram,* New Delhi, 1973.
—— *Naṭarāja in Art, Thought and Literature,* New Delhi, 1975.
—— *Śatarudriva Vibhūti of Śiva's Iconography,* New Delhi, 1976.
Somadeva, *Kathāsarıtsagara,* trans. C.H. Tawney, Vols. I & V, London, 1924.
South Indian Epigraphy, Annual Report for the year ending 31st March, 1923.
South Indian Inscriptions, Vols. I–IV, Archaeological Survey of India, New Imperial Series, 1890–1924; Vol. X, Archaeological Survey of India, 1948.
Spink, W., 'Ajanta to Ellora', *Mārg,* XX, 2, 1967, Bombay.
Srinivasan, K.R., *Cave Temples of the Pallavas,* Archaeological Survey of India, New Delhi, 1964.
—— *Temples of South India,* New Delhi, 1971.
—— 'Some Aspects of Religion as Revealed by Early Monuments and Literature of the South', *Journal of Oriental Research,* Vol. XXXII. No. I, July, 1960.
Srinivasan, P.R., *Bronzes of South India,* 1963, Bulletin of the Madras Government Museum, No. 8, New Series, Madras.
—— 'The Naṭarāja Concept in Tamil Nad Art', *Roopa Lekha,* Vol. XXVII, No. I, summer, 1956, pp. 24–35.
—— 'The Naṭarāja Theme in Cōḷa and Subsequent Period', *Roopa Lekha,* Vol. XXVII. No. 2, winter, 1956, pp. 4–11.
Subramaniam, K.R., *Origin of Śaivism and its History in the Tamil Land,* Madras, 1941.
Tāṇḍava Lakṣaṇam, trans. B.V.N. Naidu and others, Madras, 1936.
Tarr, G., 'The Śiva Cave Temple of Dhokesvara', *Oriental Art,* Vol. 15, No. 4, winter, 1969, pp. 269–80.
Tavernier, Jean-Baptiste, *Travels in India,* trans. V. Ball, Vol. I, London, 1925.
Thomas, P., *Indian Women through the Ages,* Bombay, 1964.
Thurston, E., *Castes and Tribes of Southern India,* Vol. II, Madras, 1909.
Travancore State Manual, 1906, Trivandrum.
Tripathi, Narayana, 'An Incomplete Charter of a Somavamsi King Found at Ratnagiri', *Journal of the Bihar and Orissa Research Society,* Vol. XVI, 1930, pp. 206–10.
Travels of Fray Sebastien Manrique, 1629–43, trans. C. Eckford Luard, Vol. I, The Hakluyt Society, Oxford, 1927.
Vāmana Purāṇa, trans. a board of scholars, All India Kashiraj Trust, Varanasi, 1968.
Vats, M.S., 'Mediaeval Śaiva Sculptures from Jagatsukh and Jogesvara', *Annual Report of the Archaeological Survey of India for 1926–7,* pp. 234–6.
Vatsyayan, *Kāmasūtra,* trans. S.C. Upadhyaya, Bombay, 1961.
Vatsyayan, K., 'Classical Indian Sculpture and Dance', *Journal of the Oriental Institute, Baroda,* Vol. XI, March, 1962, Baroda, pp. 45–59.
—— 'The 108 Karaṇas', *Sangeet Natak,* No. 3, Oct. 1966, New Delhi, pp. 51–62.
—— *Indian Classical Dance in Literature and the Arts,* New Delhi, 1968.
—— 'Common Errors in Dance', *Sangeet Natak,* No. 24, April–June 1972, New Delhi, pp. 24–38.
Venkatachalam, G., *Dance in India,* Bombay, 1948.
Venkatarana Raju, 'Coḷa Temples at Pudukkoṭṭai', *Journal of the Indian Society of Oriental Art,* Vol. V, June–Dec. 1937, pp. 78–90.
Viṣṇudharmottara Purāṇa, (*Third Khaṇḍa*) Vol. II, trans. Priyabala Shah, Gaekwad's Oriental Series, No. 137, Baroda, 1961.
Walker, B., *Hindu World,* London, 1968.
Warder, A.K., *Kāvya,* Vol. I, New Delhi, 1972.
Watson, J.F. and Kaye, J.W. *The People of India,* Vols. 1–8, London, 1968–75.
Winternitz, M., *A History of Indian Literature,* 3 Vols., Calcutta, 1927.
Yazdani, G. *Ajanta,* text, Part III, London, 1946.
—— *Ajanta, The Colour and Monochrome Reproductions of the Ajanta Frescoes Based on Photography* London, 1946.
Yule, Colonel Henry, *The Book of Ser Marco Polo The Venetian,* London, 1875.
Zarina, Xenia, *Classical Dances of the Orient,* New York, 1967.
Zimmer, H., *Myths and Symbols in Indian Art and Civilization,* New York, 1946.
—— *The Art of Indian Asia (Its Mythology and Transformations*), 2 Vols., New York, 1955.
Zvelebil, K.V., *The Smile of Murugan, on Tamil Literature of South India,* Leiden, 1973.
—— *Tamil Literature,* History of Indian Literature Series, Vol. X, fasc. I, Wiesbaden, 1974.

Notes

Introduction

1. Patnaik, D., 'History and Technique of Odissi Dance', *Sangeet Natak*, No. 5, July–Sept. 1969, p. 68.
2. *VDP*, P. Shah trans., pp. 1–5.
3. For a brief introduction to the various regional Indian dance styles referred to in the text see Appendix A.
4. *NŚ*, Vol. I, trans. Ghosh, M., pp. 33–4; III. 1–10; p. 44; III, pp. 96–7.

Chapter 1. Dance in Indian Society

1. Larson, A. J. *Classical Sāṃkhya*, p. 278: 'As a dancer ceases from the dance after having been seen by the audience; so also *prakṛiti* ceases after having manifested herself to the *puruṣa*.' See also Agrawala, V. S., *Śiva Mahādeva*, p. 9. Śiva is not always the dancer and it is Pārvatī, the great mother, *Prakṛti* who performs her dance on Śiva's chest while Śiva remains in the background or immersed in eternal passivity. See also Boner, A., *Principles of Composition in Hindu Sculpture*, pp. 167–72.
2. Ibid., p. 168. Coomaraswamy, A., *The Dance of Shiva*, pp. 87–8.
3. Rao, G., *Elements of Hindu Iconogrcphy*, Vol.II, Part I, pp. 22–3: '*Vidhi* or the rules of conduct of the *Pāśupatas* is the most interesting part of their religion ... Singing loudly the praises of their god, dancing either according to the science of dancing or in any manner, curling the tongue and roaring like bulls.... this noise is called *huḍukkāra*'; pp. 31–2: ... At the present time all the Vaidika or Smārta Brāhmaṇas are worshipping the *liṅga* and even seen dancing and making the *huḍukkāra* noise while worshipping in temples, a strange survival of the Pāśupata customs.' See also Hart, G. L. *The Poems of Ancient Tamil*, p. 29.
4. Bose, M., *Indian Classical Dance*, p. 9; Bhattacharyya, A., *Chhau Dance of Purulia*, p. 59.
5. Sharma, Radha Sadashiva, 'The Mahari', pp. 104–8; Kothari, Sunil, 'Gotipua Dancers of Orissa,' in *Lesser Known Performing Arts in India*, Sterling Publishers, New Delhi, pp. 93–9.
6. *Madras Census Report* for 1901, p. 151. See also Punekar and Rao, *A Study of Prostitutes in Bombay*, p. 3.
7. *Madras Legislative Debates*, 4 Nov. 1927, speech of Mrs Muthulakshmi Reddy.
8. Thurston, E., *Castes and Tribes of Southern India*, Vol.11, pp. 124–53.
9. *1901 Census Report of India*, p. 151.
10. *Legislative Assembly Debates*, 27 Feb. 1922, p. 2600–1.
11. Ibid., p. 2604.
12. Ibid., p. 2602.
13. Dubois, Abbé, J. A., 1897, *Hindu Manners, Customs and Ceremonies,* p. 593.
14. *Legislative Debates of India*, 27 Feb. 1922, p. 2600.
15. Ibid., p. 2600.
16. Penzer, N. M., 'Sacred Prostitution', p. 257.
17. *Legislative Debates of India*, 27 Feb. 1922, pp. 2600–1. Penzer, 'Sacred Prostituion', pp. 257, 260.
18. *Legislative Debates of India*, 27 Feb. 1922, p. 2600.
19. Pillay, K. K., *Śucindram Temple*, p. 281.
20. Ibid., p. 282.
21. *Legislative Debates of India*, 27 Feb. 1922, p. 2600.
22. Ibid., p. 2601, quotes *Madras Census Report* of 1911.
23. Pillay, *Śucīndram Temple*, p. 282. Dubois, 1897. *Hindu Manners*, p. 595.
24. *Ṛg Veda*, trans. Wilson, H. H., Vol. I, p. 237, 1.xxc11, fn.a. Auboyer, J., *Daily Life in Ancient India*, p. 237. She states that the early dancers were courtesans: *Veśyā-gaṇikā*, not temple dancers.
25. Kautilya, *Arthaśāstra*, trans. Shamasastry, R., p. 141.
26. *Laws of Manu*, trans. Buhler, G., IX.225, p. 381.
27. Horner, I. B., *Women Under Primitive Buddhism*, pp. 89–90.
28. De Zoete, B., *The Other Mind*, p. 166, fn.1.
29. Sewell, R., *The Forgotten Empire*, p. 242.
30. Auboyer, J., *Daily Life in Ancient India*, pp. 269–70.
31. Vatsyayan, K., *Indian Classical Dance in Literature and the Arts*, p. 232.
32. Dandin, *Dasha-Kumara-Charita, The Ten Princes*, trans. Rider, A., p. 73.
33. Kalidasa, *Meghadūta*, trans. Egerton, F. & E., 1.35.
34. Altekar, A. S., *The Position of Women in Hindu Civilisation*, p. 183.
35. *Vāmana Purāṇa*, trans. a board of scholars, p. 13: 3.36.31.
36. *Pañchama gata*, or the highest key, is considered erotic.
37. Rambhā was one of the heavenly dancers in Indra's

court. Bhāvanī is a local name for a temple dancer.
38. Sircar, D. C., 'Devadāsīs in Buddhist Temples', *Epigraphia Indica*, XXXV, No.12, 1963, p. 97.
39. **Somadeva, *Kathāsaritsāgara*, trans. Tawney, C.H.,** Vol. V., p. 7.
40. Sharma, Dasharatha, *Early Chauhan Dynasties*, p. 225.
41. Kauṭilya, *Arthaśāstra*, trans. R. Shamasastry, p. 139.
42. Dubois, 1972, *Hindu Manners*, p. 585.
43. Kalhaṇa, *Rājataraṅgiṇī*, trans. Stein, M. A., Vol.1,1.151; p. 28.
44. Sircar, D. C., 'Devadāsīs in Buddhist Temples', *Epigraphia Indica*, XXXV, No.12, 1963, p. 97.
45. *South Indian Inscriptions*, Vol.II, Part II; 1895, pp. 259–60.
46. Iyengar, Srinivasa C. R., *Indian Dance*, p. 1.
47. Zvelebil, K., *The Smile of Murugan*, p. 178.
48. **Śilippaḍikāram**, trans. Dikshitar, V. R. R., p. 105.
49. Sastri, K. A. Nilakantha, *A History of South India*, p. 179.
50. **Ayyer, P.V. Jagadisa, *South Indian Shrines*, No.** 128 of 1912.
51. Sastri, *History of South India*, p. 172.
52. *South Indian Inscriptions*, Vol.III, Part III, 1920, p. 379.
53. Sastri, *History of South India*, p. 201.
54. ***Madras Epigraphical Report*, 25 August 1915**, p. 16, No. 65 of 1914. Butterworth, A., and Aiyangar, S. Krishna Swami, 'Tamil Hymns of the Margazhi Festival,' *Indian Antiquary*, Vol. LV, 1926, p. 188, verse 12.
55. *Pudokkottai State Inscriptions*, 1929, No. 138.
56. Saletore, B. A., *Social and Political Life in the Vijayanagara Empire*, Vol.II, pp. 409–10; Bazaz, P. N., *Daughters of the Vitasta*, p. 109.
57. Saletore, *The Vijayanagara Empire*, Vol.II, p. 411.
58. Ibid.
59. *Mārg*, Special Edition on the Classical and Folk Dances of India, 1963, Part VI, p. 8. *Kollatam* is a folk dance of Andhra Pradesh and Tamil Nadu. The dancers strike small sticks which they hold in their hands. See also Bowers, F., *Theatre in the East*, p. 53.
60. Saletore, *The Vijayanagara Empire*, p. 410.
61. Vatsyayan, *Kāmasūtra*, trans. Upadhyaya, S. C., v.25, p. 214.
62. Fleet, J. B., 'Sanskrit and Old Canarese Inscriptions', *Indian Antiquary*, Vol.X, April 1881, p. 103.
63. *South Indian Inscriptions*, Vol.X, 1948, No.249.
64. Sastri, *History of South India*, pp. 213–14.
65. *South Indian Epigraphy*, 1923, **year ending 31st** March, p. 106, No.172 of 1923.
66. Kalidasa, *Megadūta*, trans Egerton, F. & E., 1.35.
67. Boner, A., *Śilpa Prakāśa*, p. 51.
68. Ayyer, Jagadisa, P. V. *South Indian Shrines*, p. 168.
69. *Viṣnudharmottara Purāṇa*, trans. Shah, P., p. 191. 'After the procession of the king through the city with a small image of the deity . . . then a festival should commence beginning from the second day. One should hold performances of actors, male and female dancers . . . and give them money.'
70. Bhadarkar, D. R., 'The Chahamanas of Marwar', ***Epigraphia Indica*, Vol. XI, 1911–12, p. 27.**
71. Saletore, *The Vijayanagara Empire*, p. 412.
72. *The Travels of Fray Sebastien Manrique*, trans. Eckford Luard, C., Vol.1, p. 71.
73. Dubois, 1972, *Hindu Manners*, p. 136.
74. Thurston, E., *Castes and Tribes of Southern India*, Vol.II, p. 136.
75. Dubois, 1972, *Hindu Manners*, p. 574.
76. Carmichael, A., *Lotus Buds*, p. 338.
77. **Vatsyayan, *Classical Indian Dance*, p. 221.**
78. Kalidasa, *Kumārasambhava*, trans. Griffith, R., p. 79.
79. In fact in 1971, I was one of many Indian classical dancers who presented solo recitals during the week-long marriage celebrations at Mathura for the Raja of Nathadwara.
80. Sachan, C. E., ***Alberuni*, Vol. I, p. ix; Vol. II, p. 157.**
81. *Travels of Jean Baptiste-Tavernier*, trans. Ball, V Vol.I, pp. 127–8.
82. Pillay, *Sucīndram Temple*, p. 285.
83. Dubois, 1972, *Hindu Manners*, p. 585.
84. Buchanan, F., *Journey from Madras through Mysore, Kanara, and Malabar*, Vol.1, pp. 12–13.
85. *Legislative Debates of India*, 27 February 1922, p. 2610.
86. *Journal of the Madras Music Academy*, 1932, Debate held on the sixth day of the annual conference, 28 Dec. 1932, on 'The encouragement of the art of Bharata Nāṭyam', p. 122.
87. Sastri, Krishna, H., *South Indian Gods and Goddesses*, p. 3.
88. Dubois, 1887, *Hindu Manners*, p. 595; See also Dubois, A., 1972, *Hindu Manners*, p. 149.
89. Pillay, *Sucīndram Temple*, p. 284.
90. Ayyar, P. V. Jagadisa, *Southern Shrines*, p. 193.
91. Nannithamby, Loganayaky, 'Fine Arts and Recreation during the Cola Period', *Journal of Tamil Studies*, Vol.1, No.2, Oct. 1969, p. 59. See also **Kane, P. V., *A History of the Dharma Śāstras*.** Vol.II, Part I, pp. 705–40.
92. Sastri, *History of South India*, p. 211.
93. *State Inscriptions of Pudukkottai*, 1929, p. 20, No.162.
94. Yule, Henry, *The Book of Ser Marco Polo the Venetian*, Vol. II, pp. 335, 329, Tanjore is caled Malabar

by Marco Polo.

95. Ibid., p. 329.
96. Saletore, *The Vijayanagara Empire*, p. 411; see also p. 409 where Nuñiz, who was also writing about Vijayanagar in the 16th c. states that Saturday was the day for the dancing girls to perform before the royal deities.
97. Dubois, 1972, *Hindu Manners*, p. 585. See also Penzer, 'Sacred Prostitution'; appendix IV in Somadeva's *Kathāsaritsāgara*, trans. Tawnev, C. H., Vol. 1, p. 253.
98. Aiya Nagam, *Travancore State Manual*, Vol. II, p. 385.
99. Ayyar, P. V., Jagadisa, *Southern Shrines*, 1920, p. 193.
100. Pillay, *Sucīndram Temple*, p. 283.
101. Ibid., pp. 282–3.
102. Ibid., p. 289.
103. Aiya, Nagam, *Travancore State Manual*, Vol. II, 1906, p. 383.
104. Menon, Narayana, *Balasareswati*, p. 17.
105. Pillay, *Sucīndram Temple*, p. 286.
106. Thurston, E., *Tribes and Castes of Southern India*, p. 141. See also penzer, 'Sacred Prostitution,' p. 262.
107. Dubois, 1972, *Hindu Manners*, p. 602.
108. Pillay, *Sucīndram Temple*, p. 285.
109. De Zoete, *The Other Mind*, p. 167.
110. Hemingway, F. R., *Gazetteer of the Godaveri District*, 1907, p. 208.
111. Dhar, Somnath, *Kalhana, Poet Historian of Kashmir*, P. 9.
112. Kalhana, *Rājataranginī*, trans. Stein, M. A., Vols. 1, IV, pp. 265–71.

Chapter II. The Formalization of Indian Dance

1. Bose, M., *A Critical and Comparative Study of Sanskrit Texts dealing with Dancing*, B. Litt Thesis. p. 1. The *Pāraskara Grya-Sūtra* 2.7.3. disapproved of the pursuit of dance by the higher castes.
2. Gnoli, Raniero, *The Aesthetic Experience according to Abhinavagupta*, p. xix.
3. Buitenen, J.A.B. Van, *Two Plays of Ancient India*, p. 5.
4. Bhattacharyā, A., *Purulia Chhau*, p. 59. Mathur J.C., *Drama in Rural India*, p. 51. In the Kuchipudi style of dance, the spoken word often alternates with the music.
5. *AD*, trans. Ghosh, M., p. 38. This differentiation is gone into in some detail because Kalakshetra, a dance school in Madras that teaches theory uses the *AD*. Many of the graduates of this school become dance teachers.
6. Ibid., p. 41.
7. Kramrisch, S., 'The Vishnudharmottaram', *Journal of the Department of Letters*, Vol.XI, 1924, p. 4. She dates the *VDP* no earlier than the 5th c.
8. *VDP.*, GOS.II, trans. Shah, P., pp. 216–17.
9. Ibid., p. 217
10. Dimock, E.C., *The Place of the Hidden Moon*, p. 21.
11. *Journal of the Madras Music Academy*, 1932, p. 114. See also Kane, P.V., *History of the Dharma Sāstras*, p. 904. Female dancers in Maharashtra are called *Bhāvins*, women having *bhāva* or love of God. See also Enthovin, R.E., *The Tribes and Castes of Bombay*, Vol.I, pp. 145–6.
12. The Sanskrit word is *pada* and the Tamil word *padam*. See also Bowers, F., *Theatre in the East*, pp. 38–9; Bhavnani, Enakshi, *The Dance in India*, p. 34.
13. Gnoli, R., *The Aesthetic Experience according to Abhinaragupta*, p. 36. 'Representation (*abhinayana*), indeed, is nothing but a power of communication (*avagamanaśakti*)—this power differing from the one of verbal expression.'
14. Personal communication, Balasareswati, a former *devadāsī*, speaking at the Madras Music Conference in December 1973, stated that the items most commonly presented before the deity were the highly religious songs or *padams* of Kśetragña. See also Iyengar, Srinivasa, C.R., *Indian Dance*, p. 42.
15. *VDP*, GOS. II., p. 216. Banerjea, J.N., *Development of Hindu Iconography*, p. 72.
16. Hart, G.L., *The Poems of Ancient Tamil*, p. 29.
17. Zvelebil, K., *The Smile of Murugan*, p. 197, for Appar's date as 7th c. A.D.
18. Ibid., p. 186.
19. Ibid., pp. 185–206.
20. Banerjea, *Development of Hindu Iconography*, p. 78. He considers the study of the *bhakta* tradition is necessary in the study of the origin of attributes shown in images.
21. *Rg Veda*, trans. Wilson, H.H., p. 153, book I, hymn CXIV, verse 5. Here Rudra, the Vedic counterpart of Śiva has *jatā* or matted hair, and these are later eulogized in song by the Śaiva *bhaktas* such as Kāraikkālammaiyār. See Dhavamony, M., *Love of God According to Saiva Siddhānta*, pp. 132–8
22. *Śilappadikāram*, trans. Dikshitar, V.R.R., p. 124, lists the various occasions on which Śiva danced. Zvelebil, *Smile of Murugan*, p. 178, dates the *Śilappadikkāram* at 4–6th c. A.D.
23. Zvelebil, *Smile of Murugan*, p. 185.
24. Devi, Rukmini, 'Spiritual Background of Bharata Nātyam', *Mārg*, 1963, Special Edition on Dance, p. 5. Iyengar, *Indian Dance*, p. 42.
25. *VDP*, p. 216. Vatsyayan, *Indian Classical Dance*,

pp. 302–3.

26. **NŚ, trans. Ghosh, M., IV. 30–4, p. 48.**
27. Bose, M., *Indian Classical Dancing*, p. 107.
28. Ibid., p. 107.
29. *VDP*, pp. 42–3.
30. Sivaramamurti, C., *Naṭarāja*, p. 348.
31. Srinivasan, K.R., *Cave Temples of the Pallavas*, p. 22, gives the date for Dantivarman Pallava as A.D. 796–846.
32. Sivaramamurti, *Naṭarāja*, pp. 348–9. However, Barrett, D., *Early Cola Architecture and Sculpture*, pp. 86–7, dates the Mulesvara Temple at Bahur at 10th c.
33. Sivaramamurti, *Naṭarāja*, pp. 348–9. Coomaraswamy, A., *A History of Indian and Indonesian Art*, p. 202. *Chaṇḍi* = temple; p. 303, Prambanam indicates a group of 30 temples of differing periods and types, both Buddhist and Jain.
34. *Nṛttaratnāvalī*, ed. and notes, Raghavan, V. p. 88.
35. Ibid., pp. 87, 89.
36. Ibid., p. 88. Sivaramamurti, *Naṭarāja*, p. 42.
37. Harle, J.C., *Temple Gateways in South India*, p. 67; *The Architecture and Iconography of the Cidambaram Gopuras*, fig.71.
38. Harle, *Temple Gateways in South India*, p. 67; *The Cidambaram Gopuras*, fig. 64.
39. Harle, *Temple Gateways in South India*, p. 67.
40. Brown, P., *Indian Architecture (Buddhist and Hindu Periods)*, p. 89.
41. Sivaramamurti, *Naṭarāja*, p. 348; *Nṛttaratnāvalī*, p. 87.
42. Brown, *Indian Architecture (Buddhist and Hindu Periods)*, p. 108.
43. *TL*, trans. Naidu B.V.N., p. 8.; Harle, *Temple Gateways in South India*, p. 157.
44. *VDP*, p. 45. The first sixty *karaṇas* on the east and west *gopuras* of the Naṭarāja temple at Cidambaram are in the order given in the *NS*.
45. Vatsyayan, *Indian Classical Dance*, p. xiii, figs. 107–21.
46. Ibid., p. 363.
47. Fergusson, J., *History of Indian and Eastern Art*, Vol.I, p. 374. Naidu, B.V.N., 'A Note on Some Sculptural Dance Poses in the Inner Precincts of The Cidambaram Temple', *Journal of Annamalai University*, Vol. IV, No.1, January 1935, p. 165.
48. Sivaramamurti, *Naṭarāja*, p. 42. *Nṛttaratnāvalī*, p. 87.
49. Ibid., p. 54, fig. 37; p. 57, fig, 45; p. 59, fig. 45.
50. Sivaramamurti, *Naṭarāja*, p. 60.
51. *Nṛttaratnāvalī*, p. 89
52. Ibid., p. 90.
53. Brown, *Indian Architecture* (*Buddhist and Hindu Periods*), p. 108. *Nṛttaratnāvalī*, p. 88.
54. Sivaramamurti, *Naṭarāja*, p. 65, fig.13.
55. *Nṛttaratnāvalī*, p. 87.
56. Ibid., p. 90.
57. Brown, *Indian Architecture* (*Buddhist and Hindu Periods*), p. 108. *Nṛttaratnāvalī*, p. 88.
58. The *gopuras* leading into the temples at Darasuram, Tribhuvanam, Madurai and Tiruchirapalli are examples of *gopuras* without *karaṇa* figures.
59. Zimmer, H., *The Art of Indian Asia*, pp. 281–2.
60. Sewell, R., *A Forgotten Empire* (*Vijayanagar*), Vol.1, p. 289.
61. Zimmer, *Art of Indian Asia*, Plate 440.
62. Sivaramamurti, *Naṭarāja*, pp. 43–58.
63. Patnaik, D.N., *Odissi Dance*, p. 75.

Chapter III. A Classification of Naṭarāja Images

1. Coomaraswamy, A., *The Dance of Śiva*, pp. 83–5. Rao, G., *Elements of Hindu Iconography*, Vol. II, Part I, pp. 231–52. He quotes A. Coomaraswamy's article in *Siddhānta Dipikā*, Vol. XIII, July 1912.
2. Ibid., pp. 259–68.
3. *NŚ*, trans. M. Ghosh, IV, 30–4, p. 48.
4. *Madras Epigraphical Report* of 1914, G. O. No. 920, 4 of August 1914, pp. 82–3. Note that in some instances the inscription does not describe the sculpture above it.
5. Vatsyayan, K., 'Classical Indian Sculpture and Dance', *Journal of the Oriental Institute*, Baroda, Vol. XI, No. 3, March 1962, pp. 258–9.
6. Rao, G., *Elements of Hindu Iconography* Vol. II. Part I, p. 258.
7. Gupte, R. S., *Iconography of the Hindus, Buddhists and Jains*, fig. 140. Sivaramamurti, C.. *Naṭarāja*, pp. 293,296,244, etc. Banerjea, J.N., *The Development of Hindu Iconography*, p. 280. Vatsyayan, K., *Indian Classical Dance in Literature and the Arts*, pp. 342, 354, etc.
8. Banerjea, *Hindu Iconography*, p. 452.
9. Ayyar, Narayana, *Śaivism in South India*, p. 249.
10. Winternitz, M., *A History of Indian Literature*, Vol. I, p. 588, fn. 2.
11. Rao, *Hindu Iconography*, Vol. II, Part I, p. 58.
12. Raghavan, V., in Pattabiramin, P. Z., *Trouvailles de Nedoungadou*, p. 21.
13. Rao, *Hindu Iconography*, Vol. II, Part I, p. 58.
14. Ibid., Vol. II, Part I, pp. 252–7.
15. Raghavan, in Pattabiramin, *Trouvailles de Nedoungadou*, pp. 20–7.
16. Boner, A., *Principles of Composition in Hindu Sculpture*, pp. 174, 175, 180; *Śilpa Prakāśa*, p. 80.
17. *AD*, v. 2–11, pp. 39–40. *NŚ*, IV. 1–29, pp. 45–6. According to the myth in the *VDP*, however, *nṛtta*

originated with Viṣṇu, and not with Śiva. *VDP*, pp. 38–9.

18. Banerjea, *Hindu Iconography*, p. 246.
19. *VDP*, p. 76.
20. *VDP*, p. 77.
21. Ibid.
22. Grünwedel, A., *Buddhist Art in India*, trans. Gibson, A. C., p. 177.

Chapter IV. Varieties of Naṭarāja Image

1. Zvelebil, K., *Tamil Literature*, p. 170. Pope, U. G., *Tiruvāçagam*, pp. lx–vii.
2. The Tamil song on the theme, *Natanam Adinar*, is a favourite piece and is considered by many dance enthusiasts to be an integral part of any Bharata Nāṭyam recital.
3. Sivaramamurti, C., *Naṭarāja*, figs. 239, 240.
4. Goetz, H., *Studies in the History and Art of Kashmir and the Indian Himalaya*, p. 96, fn. 16: 'Mukha-Liṅgas were common under the Guptas; after the 7th c. they became rare.'
5. Harle, J. C., *Gupta Sculpture*, Plate 50.
6. Ibid., Plate 149 for an illustration of an emaciated Śiva with a moustache, also from the Gupta period (see also Plate 33).
7. Ibid., Plate 9. In Bharata Nāṭyam, the third eye is important as one of Śiva's attributes, and in the Seraikella Chhau tradition a vertical third eye is painted on the dancer's mask as one of Śiva's distinctive characteristics. See Plates 66c, 67.
8. Barrett, D., *Early Cola Bronzes*. Plates 57, 61, 63, 87.
9. Zimmer, H., *The Art of Indian Asia*, Vol. II, Plate 232. In Bharata Nātvam, Naṭarāja's hair is depicted as flowing outwards. This attribute is important and is usually included when the form of Naṭarāja is being described (Plates 64g, h).
10. Zvelebil, *Tamil Literature*, p. 170. Pope, U. G., *Tiruvāçagam*, pp. lx–vii. Kramrisch, S., 'The Religious and the Grotesque in Indian Art', *Modern Review*, November 1928, pp. 569–79.
11. Vatsyayan, K., *Indian Classical Dance in Literature and the Arts*, pp. 168–72. See O'Flaherty, W. D., *Asceticism and Eroticism in the Mythology of Śiva*, pp. 81–9, for other attributes of Indra that are assimilated by Śiva.
12. Banerji, R. D., 'The Temple of Śiva at Bhumara', *Memoirs of the Archaeological Survey of India*, No. 16, 1924, Plate XIIIb. Śiva dancing in a *kūḍu* is identified as Śiva *tāṇḍava*.
13. Srinivasan, K. R., *Cave Temples of the Pallavas*, Avanībhajana's Cave Temple at Siyamangalam, Plate XXIII.
14. Barrett, D., *Early Cola Architecture and Sculpture*, for illustrations in stone, figs. 49a, 56, 70. For illustrations in bronze see Sivaramamurti, C., *Naṭarāja*, figs. 78, 79, 80, 82.
15. Banerji, R. D., 'The Temple of Śiva at Bhumara', Plate X. The *gaṇas* are of Types A, C, and E. Sivaramamurti, *Naṭaraja*, p. 170, p. 114, fig. 12. Other dancing *gaṇas* from Nachna are illustrated in the *Annual Progress Report of the Archaeological Survey of India* for the year ending 31 March 1919, Plate XV. Here the *gaṇa* is a niche figure with the right leg lifted up and across the body.
16. Sivaramamurti, *Naṭarāja*, p. 171, fig. 6.
17. Ibid., p. 172, fig. 9.
18. *NŚ*, trans. M. Ghosh, Vol. I., Book IV. 17–18, p. 47.
19. Shah, Umakant Premanand, 'Sculptures from Samalaji and Roda (North Gujarat)', *Bulletin of the Baroda Museum and Picture Gallery*, Vol. XIII, Special Number, 1960, Plate 1. In Bharata Nāṭyam Naṭarāja tearing the skin from a tiger and tying it about his loins is frequently shown and is no doubt also connected with the story in the *Kōyil Purāṇam* (Plates 62c–e).
20. Sivaramamurti, *Naṭarāja*, p. 177, fig. 15.
21. Ibid., pp. 7, 66, 72, 95.
22. In fact Type A.IV is not usually found in images of Naṭarāja, only in decorative dancing figures.
23. See also Sivaramamurti, C., *Naṭarāja*, p. 174, fig. 11.
24. Ibid., p. 193, fig. 38.
25. Ibid., p. 174, fig. 16.
26. Khokar, Mohan, 'Kanchi Kailasa', *Sangeet Natak*, No. I, 1965, Plates 6, 7, 8.
27. Ibid., pp. 68–81.
28. Sivaramamurti, *Royal Conquests and Cultural Migrations in South India and the Deccan*, pp. 8–9.
29. See also Sivaramamurti, *Naṭarāja*, pp. 336–7.
30. Panigrahi, K. C., *Archaeological Remains of Bhubaneswar*, pp. 6–12.
31. Boner, A., *Silpa Prakāśa*, pp. 80–2.
32. See Sivaramamurti, *Naṭarāja*, p. 191, fig. 36 for a rare example from the Deccani region from Biccavolu of an *ūrdhvaliṅga* Naṭarāja.
33. Bhattasali, Nalinikantha M. A., 'The Bhārellā Narteśvara Image Inscription', *Epigraphia Indica*, Vol. XVII, 1923, p. 349. Haque, E., *The Iconography of the Hindu Sculpture of Bengal (up to c 3250* A.D.*)*, Appendix A, pp. 618–19 for a list of all the Naṭarāja images in Bengal.
34. Haque, E., *Hindu Sculpture of Bengal*, p. 221.
35. Ibid., pp. 222–3.
36. Bhattasali, Nalinikantha M. A., 'The Bhārellā Narteśvara Image Inscription', p. 350.
37. Ibid., p. 352.

38. *MP*. CCLIX. 5–10, p. 306.
39. Haque, *Hindu Sculpture of Bengal*, p. 221–2.
40. Śivaramamurti, *Naṭarāja*, p. 137. Fig. 6.
41. Ibid., p. 193. Fig. 38.
42. Ibid., p. 171, Fig. 6.
43. Patnaik, D. N., *Odissi Dance*, no pagination, see *hasta* section as *bastra* is a specific *hasta* for Oḍissi.
44. Harle, *Gupta Sculpture*, Plate 88.
45. Sivaramamurti, *Naṭarāja*, p. 309, Fig. 188.
46. Ibid., p. 336, Fig. 228.
47. Ibid., p. 335.
48. Harle, *Gupta Sculpture*, Plate 149.

Chapter V. Components of the Naṭarāja Image

1. *AD*., V. 88–92, p. 52; V. 248–9, p. 66.
2. *Mārg*, 1963 special edition on 'Classical and Folk Dances of India', Bharata Naṭyam section, pp. 16–23.
3. Pattabiramin, P. Z., *Trouvailles de Nedoungādou (Tāṇḍavas de Śiva)*, p. 34.
4. Boner, A., *Śilpa Prakāśa*, p. 80, fig. 14b.
5. Ibid., p. 80, fig. 14b.
6. Hopkins, E. W., *Epic Mythology*, p. 57. For illustrations see Bose, L., *The Female Figures on the Railing Pillars from Mathura of the Kuṣāṇa Period*, Plates 5, 15, 16, 22, 29, 36, 44, 49, 56, 57, 58, 63. Also see Zimmer, H., *The Art of Indian Asia*, Plate 34a.
7. Agrawalla, V. S., *The Glorification of the Great Goddess*, p. 5.
8. Rao, G., *Elements of Hindu Iconography*, Vol. II, Part I, Plate II.
9. Sivaramamurti, C., *Naṭarāja*, p. 194, fig. 39.
10. Pope, U. G., *Tiruvāçagam*, pp. iv–lvii. See also Rao, *Hindu Iconography*, Vol. II, Part I, p. 113. See also Lippe, A., 'Some South Indian Icons', *Artibus Asiae*, Vol. XXXVII$_3$, 1975, fig. 1 and p. 177. Lippe states that this image on the Muktesvara temple (Pallava A.D. 732–46.) at Kancipuram, contains the first example of Apasmāra.
11. Banerjea, J. N., *Development of Hindu Iconograply*, p. 472.
12. *Agni Purāṇa*, trans. Dutt, M. N., Vol. II, pp. 1246–77. Dalal, M. L., *Conflict in Sanskrit Drama*, p. 127. See also *NŚ*, trans. Ghosh, M. VII 73, p. 138.
13. For depictions of Apasmāra from the Deccani region, see Lippe, A., 'Early Chālukyan Icons', *Artibus Asiae*, Vol. XXXIV$_4$, 1972, p. 278.
14. Sivaramamurti, C., *South Indian Bronzes*, Plates 16 and 22.
15. Ibid., Plate 78.
16. Vatsyayan, K., *Indian Classical Dance in Literature and the Arts*, Plate 144. O'Flaherty, W. D., *Asceticism and Eroticism in the Mythology of Śiva*, Plate 7.
17. Sivaramamurti, *Naṭarāja*, p. 206, Plate 54.
18. Sivaramamurti, *South Indian Bronzes*, Plate 9a.
19. Rao, *Hindu Iconography*, Vol. II, Part i, pp. 113, 253–54.
20. Ibid., Plate XXIV and p. 136.
21. Ibid., p. 168.
22. Vatsyayan, K., *Indian Classical Dance in Literature and the Arts*, Plates 148–54. See also Sivaramamurti, *Naṭarāja*, p. 270, fig. 134.
23. Rao, *Hindu Iconography*, Vol. II, Part I, Plate XLV, fig. 2.
24. Ibid., Plate LXXII, fig. 1 and 2; Plate LXXIII.
25. Ibid., Plate XCI.
26. Mūyaḷagan is the southern name of Apasmāra and is depicted as a crouching demon in Bharata Nāṭyam. Bhavnani, E., *The Dance in India*, Plate 34, fig. 11.
27. *MP*., CCLIX. 5–10, p. 306.
28. Sivaramamurti, *Naṭarāja*, p. 36. Bhattacharji, S., *Hindu Theogony*, p. 53. Daniélou, A., *Hindu Polytheism*, p. 220.
29. Haque, E., *The Iconography of the Hindu Sculpture of Bengal up to 1250 A. D.*, Plates 27, 31, 32, 43.
30. Boner, *Śilpa Prakāśa*, p. 79. Panigrahi, K. C., *Archaeological Remains at Bhubaneswar*, Plate 121; pp. 49–50, 175.
31. Sivaramamurti, *Naṭarāja*, p. 305, fig. 182.
32. Ibid., p. 91, fig. 3. (It is the Śiva side of an Ardhanārīśvara image that is dancing on the bull).
33. Ibid., p. 303, fig. 181.
    Haque, *Hindu Sculpture of Bengal*, pp. 221–2. Balasubrahmanyam, S.R., *Four Chola Temples*, pp. 52–3.
34. Sivaramamurti, *Naṭarāja*, p. 274, fig. 137, p. 286, fig. 154. Ingalls, D. H. H., *An Anthology of Sanskrit Court Poetry*, p. 89, v. 84, by Bhavabhuti: 'When to the wild dance of the trident-weaponed god the hand of Nandin gladly beats the drum.' When Naṭarāja's dance is described in the Bharata Nāṭyam *padam, Kalle Tukke*, Nandi is depicted playing the drum. Bhavnani, E., *The Dance in India*, Plate 33, Fig. 8.
35. Rao, *Hindu Iconography*, Vol. I, Part II, p. 323.
36. Sivaramamurti, *Naṭarāja*, p. 172, fig. 9.
37. Ibid., p. 293, fig. 164.
38. Ibid., p. 294, fig. 165.
39. Ibid., p. 258, fig. 119. Barrett, D., *Early Cola Architecture and Sculpture*, Plate 70.
40. Rao, *Hindu Iconography*, Vol. II, Part I, pp. 322–23.
41. Pillai, S. S., 'Kāraikkāl Ammaiyār', in Ghanananda, S., and Stewart-Wallace, John (eds), *Women Saints of East and West*, p. 22.

42. *MP.*, p. 1; CCLX. 66–9 p. 310; CCLXI. 1–22 p. 311 for a description of the *dikpālas*.
43. Ingalls, D. H. H., *An Anthology of Sanskrit Court Poetry*, p. 87, v. 74.
44. *NŚ*, trans. M. Ghosh. V. 23–4, p. 79; V. 95–7, p. 88.
45. Sivaramamurti, *Naṭarāja*, p. 208, fig. 56.
46. Rao, *Hindu Iconography*, Vol. II, Part I, p. 262, Plate LXII.
47. Sivaramamurti, *Naṭarāja*, p. 175, fig. 12.
48. Rao, *Hindu Iconography*, Vol. II, Part I, Plate LXIII.
49. Gupte, R. S., *Art and Architecture of Aihole*, p. 86.
50. Cousens, H., *Chālukyan Architecture*, Plate CXIV, the Kedaresvara Temple at Balagamve; Plate CLIX at Ganjigatti. Here Śiva dances on an elephant's head as well as on Apasmāra.
51. Bhavnani, E., *The Dance in India*, p. 35.

Chapter VI. Other Dancing Images of Śiva

1. Pope, G., *Tiruvāçagam*, for in praise of Śiva which describes his various attributes.
2. Banerji, R.D., *History of Bengal*, p. 430, in Panigrahi, K.C., *Archaeological Remains of Bhubaneswar*, p. 6.
3. *Ṛg Veda*, trans. Wilson, H.H., Vol. II, p. 34.
4. *Mahābhārata*, trans. Roy, P.C., Karna Parva, section XXXIII–IV, pp. 76–88.
5. *NŚ*, trans. Ghosh, M., Vol. I, Book I, 7–12, pp. 3–4.
6. Ibid., Book IV, 9-10, pp. 45–6. The other drama, *Amṛtha-Manthana*, 'The churning of the Ocean of Milk', is also connected with dance as it was at this time that Viṣṇu assumed the form of Mohinī, after which Mohinī Āṭṭam, a classical dance style from Kerala, is named. See *Mārg* (Special edition on Mohinī Āṭṭam), Vol. XXVI, No. 2, March 1973, p. 6. O'Flaherty, W.D., *Hindu Myths*, pp. 274-80.
7. *NŚ*, Book IV. 17–18, p. 47. Bhavnani, E., *The Dance in India*, p. 56.
8. I have seen a full-length Kuchipudi dance drama composed by Chinna Satyam of the Kuchipudi Arts Academy, Madras, in which the Tripurāntaka myth was enacted. This is a modern dance-drama based on a traditional presentation.
9. Buitenen, Van, J.A.B., *Two Plays of Ancient India*, p. 185.
10. *Śilappadikāram*, trans. Diksitar, V.R.R., p. 124.
11. Ayyar, Narayanna, *Origin and History of Early Śaivism in South India*, p. 462.
12. Raghavan, V., in Pattabiramin, P.Z., *Trouvailles de Nedoungādou*, pp. 24–5.
13. *NŚ*, Book XI. 71–2, p. 206.
14. Sivaramamurti, C., *Naṭarāja*, p. 342. See also p. 158. Sivaramamurti states that when Śiva is depicted as Tripurāntaka he should hold the conch, wheel, club, horn, and bell. He gives the *MP* as his reference. The directions, however, are ambiguous, and it seems possible that the dancing posture refers only to images including the elephant hide, which is Śiva as Gajāsurasamhāramūrti. See also *MP*, 259.11.12, p. 306.
15. *NŚ*, Book IX. 67–72, p. 206. See also Banerjea, J.N., *Development of Hindu Iconography*, p. 487, where he refers to *pratyālīḍha* as a pose to be adopted by archers. See also Sivaramamurti, *Naṭarāja*, pp. 211–12. Note that the stage entry used by dancers in the Purulia Chhau style of dance is performed alternatively in *ālīḍha* and *pratyālīḍha*. This dance style was originally performed in the war camps of eastern India.
16. Harle, J.C., 'Ālīḍha', *Mahayanist Art after AD 900 (Colloquies on Art and Archaeology in Asia)* No. 2, 1971, pp. 10–12. Rao, *Hindu Iconography*, Vol. II, Part I, p. 270. He labels an image of Naṭarāja in his *nṛttamūrti* section as similar to *ālīḍhāsana*, but does not discuss it. While it is clear that several of Rao's examples for Tripurāntaka are in a pose which Harle would identify as in *ālīḍha*, Rao's example for *ālīḍha* does not represent it according to Harle and myself.
17. Vatsyayan, K., *Indian Classical Dance in Literature and the Arts*, p. 21.

17b. *NŚ*, trans. M. Ghosh, p. 206, IX. 71-2.

17c. Sivaramamurti, C., *Naṭarāja*, p. 25.

17d. *Agni Purāṇa*, trans. Dutt, CCXLIX, 10, p. 895.

17e. Vatsyayan, K., *Indian Classical Dance in Literature and the Arts*, pp. 21,246,307.

17f. *ŚP*, Vol. II, *Rudrasaṃhitā*, 56, 9-10, p. 1051.

17g. Those authors that consider *ālīḍha* should have the right knee bent and the left stretched out are: Bhattasali, N. *Iconography of the Buddhist and Brahmanical Sculptures in the Dacca Museum*, p. 118; Auboyer, J., *La Vie Publique et Privée dans l'Inde Ancienne*, fasc. VI, Les Jeu et les Jonets, p. 6; Kramrisch, S., 'Pala and Sena Sculpture', *Rupam*, No. 40, Oct. 1929, captions 1 & 30. Those authors that consider that the *ālīḍha* pose has the left knee bent and the right stretched out: Gordon, A.K.G., *Iconography of Tibetan Lamanism*, 2nd ed., p. 24; Bhattacharya, B., *Indian Buddhist Iconography*, 2nd ed. p. 432; Harle, J.C., 'Ālidha', *Colloquies on Art and Archaeology in Asia*, No. 2, 19, pp. 10–11.

17h. *Mārg*, 1963, Special edition on dance, see section under Bharata Nāṭyam where the basic steps or *adavus* are given.

18. The philosophical interpretations of images does

not concern me here; however, the following references are useful: *ŚP*, Vol. I, *Rudrasaṃhitā*, p. 472, note 344: 'The Ardhanārīśvara form symbolizes the union and concord of the spirit and its energy'; Vol. 4, *Vāyavīyasaṃhita* 4.2, note 244, p. 1919: 'Śiva in the half-male and half-female (Ardhanārīśvara) form is the cause of the universe. The concept has its basis in the Puruṣa-Prakṛti doctrine of the Sāṅkhya philosophers.' See also *Kulārṇava Tantra*, ed. Avalon, A., and Taranatha Vidyaratna. The Ardhanārīśvara form is the final stage of reaching the unity within the duality, according to the Śaiva/Tantric religious philosophy. Personal communication, Dr Sanjukta Gupta, Utrecht University, Holland.

19. Agrawalla, V.S., *Śiva Mahādeva*, pp. 47–9; Sivaramamurti, *Naṭarāja*, pp. 47–9.
20. *MP*, trans. Akhtar, Jamna Dass, CCLX. 1–9, p. 307.
21. Kalidasa, *Mālavikāgnimitra,* ed. and trans. Devadhar, C.R., 1.4.p.9.
22. Sivaramamurti, *Naṭarāja*, p. 138, 'The transformation of *tāṇḍava* into *lāsya* is possible in Śiva, who is master of both, with a special preference for *tāṇḍava.'*
23. Warder, A.K., *Indian Kāvya Literature,* Vol. I, p. 148. Also see Bose, M., *Indian Classical Dancing,* p. 10. *AD*, p. 40.
24. Ingalls, D.H.H., *An Anthology of Sanskrit Court Poetry,* p. 81, verse 60. 'A sculpture from the northern region of Śiva and Pārvatī has been identified as Śiva instructing Pārvatī in dance', Sivaramamurti, *Naṭarāja,* p. 115, fig. 13. He describes the image as Calukyan. Kramrisch, S., in her review of Sivaramamurti's book, *Naṭarāja, Artibus Asiae,* Vol. XXXVII4, 1976, p. 313, states that the sculpture is Candella, 11th c.
25. *Shilappadikāram*, trans. Daniélou, A., p. 182.
26. Banerji, R.D., 'The Naihati Grant of Vallala-Sena; The 11th Year'. *Epigraphia Indica,* Vol. XIV, 1917–18, pp. 157, 162.
27. Deo, Juga Bhanu Singh, *Chhau, Mask Dance of Seraikela*, p. 31. Kothari, Sunil, 'Chhau Dances of Saraikella', *Mārg,* Vol. XXII, No. 1, Dec. 1968, p. 6. Bhattacharya, A., *Chhau of Purulia,* p. 82. Bhavnani, *Dance in India,* p. 75.
28. Bhavnani, *Dance in India,* p. 56.
29. *MP*, CCLX. 3–4, p. 307; 12–20, p. 308.
30. Sivaramamurti, *Naṭarāja,* p. 91, fig. 3.
31. Rao, *Hindu Iconography,* Vol. I, Part II, pp. 156–8. See also Dass, R.D., *Temples of Tamil Nad,* pp. 174–85.
32. Rao, *Hindu Iconography,* Vol. II, Part I, pp. 158–61.
33. Ibid., Plate XXXIV, XXXV, fig. 1.
34. Ibid., Plate XXIV; Plate XXV, fig. 1.
35. Ibid., Plate XXXV, fig. 2, Plate XXXV, fig. 1.
36. Ibid., Plate XXXV, fig. 2.
37. Ibid., Plate XXXVI, fig. 1. Dass, R.K., *Temples of Tamil Nad,* p. 174, records that according to the myth associated with the shrine at Tirukkadaiyur, Śiva emerged from the *liṅga* and danced on Yama. Dass records a variation of this myth (p. 190), when an even younger *bhakta* (eight years old) was saved from Yama by clasping the *liṅga,* and after Śiva saved him, Śiva danced seven *tāṇḍavas,* or types of dances: *'ānanda, sandhyā, saṃhāra, tripurānta, urdhva, bhujaṅga,* and *lalita'.*
38. *Kūrma Purāṇa*, 2.3.22, p. 306; 2.5.4, p. 310.
39. Walker, B., *The Hindu World,* Vol. I, pp. 383–4. See also Rele, Kanak, 'Myth', *Mārg,* Vol. XXVI, No. 2, March 1973. A variation on the usual myths in which Śiva dances on the demon. Briefly it concerns Bhasmāsura, a demon who received a boon from Śiva that all whom he touched would be turned to ashes. Thus even Śiva could have been destroyed. Bhasmāsura comes under the spell of Mohinī, the celestial dancer, and destroys himself by placing his hands on his head when he imitates her dance. This story is told in Bharata Nāṭyam in the Tamil song, *Onai Ninainde, Ninainde*.
40. *AD*, 213, p. 63. These differ slightly from the instructions given by traditional dance masters.
41. Zimmer, H., *The Art of Indian Asia,* Vol. I, p. 360.
42. Sivaramamurti, C., *Sanskrit Literature and Art, Mirrors of Indian Culture,* p. 76; *Meghadūta*, line 76.
43. Ingalls, D.H.H., *An Anthology of Sanskrit Court Poetry*, pp. 87–8, verse 76.
44. *MP,* CCLX.11–2, p. 306.
45. Sivaramamurti, *Naṭarāja,* p. 264, fig. 126. Rao, *Hindu Iconography,* Vol. II, Part I, Plate XXX; Plate XXXIII.
46. Singh, Sheo Bahadur, 'The Icons of Naṭarāja in U.P.', *Lalit Kalā,* No. 16, 1974, p. 48, Plate XVIII, fig. 4.
47. Sivaramamurti, *Naṭarāja,* p. 342. He identifies this image as in *ālīḍha sthāna.*
48. *Śiva Purāṇa*, Vol. II, *Rudrasaṃhitā* 30, 26.
49. Ibid., 30.37.
50. Ibid., 30.38.
51. In the *Liṅga Purāṇa,* Part I, it is the women living in the forest who dance on the arrival of the beautiful mendicant. Chapter 29. 18–19, p. 116.
52. O'Flaherty, W.D., *Asceticism and Eroticism in the Mythology of Śiva,* p. 32.
53. Zvelebil, K., *Tamil Literature,* p. 170. The *Kōyil purāṇam*, A.D. 1213, was written by Umāpati.

54. This is the first textual reference to Apasmara or Mūyaḷagan, an iconographic feature that was discussed in Chapter IV.
55. Zvelebil, *Tamil Literature,* p. 171: 'The authors (of the *purāṇas,* and *sthalapurāṇas*) were more concerned with the patterns of events occurring in the world than with the events themselves.'
56. Sivaramamurti, *South Indian Painting,* Plates 78, **79, a Nāyak painting at Cidambaram. Most rep**resentations of Siva as the beggar in stone, bronze or painting, particularly in the south, depict Śiva as a wandering mendicant, with wooden shoes and begging bowl. His erotic nature in this aspect is suggested by his beautifully proportioned body and cobra with erect hood tied about his loins. The treatment of the cobra in this manner is not unique to the Bhikṣāṭana *mūrti,* and is seen in several Naṭarāja images.
57. O'Flaherty, *Śiva,* p. 216. She translates a Tamil *padam* taught me by Swarna Saraswathy. Another Tamil *padam, Peyandi,* is also about Śiva as Bhikṣāṭana.
58. *Śilappadikāram,* trans. Dikshitar, V.R.R. p. 124.
59. *KP.* 2.31.30-31.
60. Ibid., 97-100.
61. Pani, Jivan, 'Chhau Dances of Mayurbanj', *Mārg,* Vol. XXII, No. 1, Dec. 1968, p. 32. See also Deo, Juga Bhanu Singh, *Chhau, Mask Dance of Seraikela,* p. 17. The exercises for the Seraikella style of Chhau are generally performed at or before sunrise in the place consecrated to Bhairava. The Seraikella Chhau dance festival is dedicated to **Ardhanārīśvara; see above.**
62. Chandra, Pramod, *Stone Sculpture in the Allahabad Museum,* p. 107. The image from Bhita (UP, 11th c.) is described but not illustrated. Haque, E., *The Iconography of the Hindu Sculpture of Bengal (up to c. 1250 AD),* Plates 187, 188, illustrate Bhairava from Bengal in *ālīḍha.* Boner, A., *Śilpa Prakāśa,* Plate XLVII(b), also p. 78; the *Saudhikāgama* states that Bhairava should be a *nṛttamūrti.*
63. Dass, R.K., *The Temples of Tamilnad,* p. 180. The town of Mayavaram (TN) is where Śiva assumed his form as Vīrabhadra but there is no mention of dance.
64. Sivaramamurti, *Naṭarāja,* p. 341, fig. 238; p. 342, **fig. 239; p. 343, fig. 240.**
65. O'Flaherty, *Śiva,* p. 214, from the *Padma Purāna,* I.5. 39–44.
66. **Rao, *Hindu Iconography,* Vol. II, Part I, pp. 182–6.** Harle, J.C., *Gupta Sculpture,* an illustration from Ahicchatra of the destruction of Daksa's sacrifice, Plate 137.
67. ***NŚ,* p. 66, IV. 255.**
68. **O'Flaherty, *Śiva,*** p. 31. Rao, *Hindu Iconography,* Vol. II, Part I, Plate XLIV, fig. 2.
69. Rawson, P., 'Indian Art at Essen', *Oriental Art,* Vol. V, No. 3, Autumn 1959, p. 108. See also Rao, *Hindu Iconography,* Vol. II, Part I, Plate XLIV, fig. 2. He illustrates another bronze of Vīrabhadra dancing from Tenkasi (TN).
70. Gangoly, O.C., 'A New Contribution of Śaivite Art', *Rūpam,* No. 5, January 1921, p. 5, fig. A. 'It is the pictorial symbol of a super tragedy, of the destructive energy of nature losing its very soul and essence.'
71. O'Flaherty, *Śiva,* p. 31. See also p. 32 where she describes another occasion in which divine intervention becomes necessary to control the destructive nature of dance. This time it is Śiva who must stop the sage from dancing. 'While Śiva had been away performing his vow of *tapas,* the earth had begun to shake and the gods begged Śiva to discontinue his *tapas.* Śiva complied, but when the earth continued to tremble he went to seek the cause and discovered the sage Maṅkanaka, who was dancing in joy because of a miracle: when he had cut his thumb on a blade of grass, vegetable sap flowed from the wound instead of blood. Śiva then pierced his own thumb, and ashes white as snow flowed from the wound, and Maṅkanaka stopped dancing.'
72. Bhattacharyya, *Chhau Dance of Purulia,* p. 43. Note that the Chhau performed in the Jalda area of Bengal is considered to be the most innovative and modern; ibid., p. 42.
73. Ranganath, H.K., *The Karnatak Theatre,* p. 57. Sivaramamurti, *Naṭarāja,* p. 7.
74. Sivaramamurti, C., *Kalugumalai,* fig. 5. Rao, *Hindu Iconography,* Vol. II, Part I, p. 273. The south wall of the temple is the traditional position for Dakṣināmurti images. The south is also the quarter for Yama, god of death and the *Liṅga Purāṇa* connects this with dance. *Liṅga Purāṇa,* Part I, trans. a board of scholars, p. 481, 91.15. 'If one dreams of going towards the southern direction in a chariot . . . and sings and dances in the meantime, it should be known that death is imminent.'
75. Sivaramamurti, *Naṭarāja,* p. 7. Śiva's/Rudra's association with music is first mentioned in the *Ṛg Veda,* Vol. I, trans. Griffiths, R., p. 601.43.4.
76. Lippe, A., 'Some South Indian Icons', *Artibus Asiae,* Vol. XXXVII3, 1975, figs. 2–10, 13–20. Srinivasan, K.R., 'Some Aspects of Religion as revealed by early Monuments and Literature of the South', *Journal of Oriental Research. Madras*

University, Vol. XXXII, No. 1, July 1960, p. 187. Rao, *Hindu Iconography,* Vol. II, Part I, Plate CXVII (a seated Ardhanārīśvara image with a *vīṇā*).

77. Adiceam, M.E., 'Les Images de Śiva dans l'Inde du Sud, Vṛṣavāhanamūrti VII', *Arts Asiatiques,* Vol. XIX, 1969, fig. 24.
78. Rao, *Hindu Iconography,* Vol. II, Part I, Plate LXXI. Sivaramamurti, *Naṭarāja,* p. 305, fig. 183; p. 177, fig. 14.
79. In this representation Vīṇādhara may be seen in the centre of the seven mothers, or at one end. Gaṇeśa, also dancing, is usually at the other end of the panel.
80. **MP, CCLXI, 39, p. 312.**
81. Sivaramamurti, *Naṭarāja,* p. 319, fig. 198.
82. Ibid., p. 305, fig. 183.
83. Ibid., p. 321, fig. 200.
84. Ibid., p. 175, fig. 12.
85. Ibid., p. 172, fig. 9.
86. Ibid., p. 174, fig. 11.
87. Ibid., p. 319, fig. 198.
88. Sivaramamurti, *Naṭarāja,* p. 356. The image is from Baset, Cambodia, 9th c. AD. Note that the southern Śaiva *bhakta,* Kāraikkal Āmmaiyār, is on the left. Ibid., p. 362, fig. 21.
89. *MP.* CCLXI. 39, p. 312.
90. Bhattasali, N.K., *Iconography of Buddhist and Brahmanical Sculptures in the Dacca Museum,* Plate XLV, 3a(ii)a/2; Plate 94 which is illustrated here is also from Natghar. Ibid., Plate XLV. 3a iia/3. For other illustrations of Vīṇādhara images dancing from Bengal see Haque, *Hindu Sculpture of Bengal,* Plates 31,32,43.
91. *Linga Purāṇa,* Part II, 106.25–8, p. 581. See also Part I, 82.71–3a, p. 407: 'May the celestial damsels and the goddesses engaged in the worship of Śiva dispel my impurities—viz., Urvaśī, Menakā, Rambhā, Rati . . . and other divine Apsaras in all the worlds and the goddesses who are highly purified by doing the *Tāṇḍava* dance for Śiva.'
92. *MP,* CCLXI.39, p. 312. Lippe, A., 'Some South Indian Icons', *Artibus Asiae,* Vol. XXXVII$_3$, 1975, p. 172. 'The form of Śiva which accompanies the seven mothers often in yoga position or playing the ***vīṇā* is generally called Dakṣiṇāmūrti. This *mūrti* is** a variant of Vīrabhadra.' See also de Mallmann, M.T., *Les Enseignements de l'Agni Purāṇa,* pp. 62–3.
93. Chandra, Pramod, *Stone Sculptures,* p. 119, and Plate 301. Agrawala, R.C., 'Notes Iconographiques, III, Une Répresentation Insolite des Mātṛkā Provenant de Ābānerī (Rājasthān)', *Arts Asiatiques,* Vol. XXIII, 1971, p. 151.

Chapter VII. Decorative Dancing Figures

1. Vatsyayan, K., *Indian Classical Dance in Literature and the Arts,* fig. 1.
2. Ibid., fig. 2.
3. Marshall, Sir John, *Mohenjo-daro and the Indus Civilization,* Vol. I, p. 46.
4. Chandra, Moti, *The World of Courtesans,* p. 1.
5. **Yazdani, G., *Ajanta,* Part III, p. 24 and** *Ajanta, Colour Supplement,* Part III, Plate XXIVa.
6. Yazdani, *Ajanta,* p. 26. He believes that the organization of female dancers and musicians attached to the temples was borrowed by Buddhists from the earlier Brahmanical institutions.
7. Mitra, D., *Buddhist Monuments,* Plate 4. See also Marshall, John, and Foucher, A., *The Monuments of Sanchi,* p. 117. Narada and Mahathera and Kassapa Thera, *The Mirror of the Dhamma,* pp. 18–19). 'I undertake to observe the precept to abstain from dancing, singing, music, and unseemly shows.'
8. Havell, E.B., 'Notes on the Paintings', in Marshall, *The Bagh Caves,* Plates D and E.
9. Mukhopadhyay, Samir K., 'Terracottas from Bhita', *Ars Asiatiques,* Vol. XXXIV, 1972, Plate 10.
10. Vatsyayan, *Indian Classical Dance,* Plate 67. For further descriptions of illustrations of dance at Amaravati see *Nṛttaratnāvalī,* ed. and trans. **Raghavan, V., pp. 18–19.**
11. Ibid., Plate 64.
12. *Ancient Sculpture from India,* Plate 41.
13. Vatsyayan, *Indian Classical Dance,* Plate 58.
14. Ibid., Plate 56.
15. Ibid., Plate 59. The central dancer (from Bharhut) has both knees bent and is of Type A.I. The sculptures of dancing girls on the late mediaeval Jain temples in Rajasthan revert to one leg straight and one bent.
16. Banerji, R.D., 'The Temple of Śiva at Bhumara', *Memoirs of the Archaeological Survey of India,* No. 16, 1924, Plate XIIIb, dated at 5th–6th c. A.D..
17. Srinivasan, K.R., *Cave Temples of the Pallavas,* Plate XXIII.
18. Sivaramamurti, C., *Naṭarāja,* pp. 43–58.
19. Ibid., pp. 62–9.
20. Rosenfield, J.M., *The Dynastic Arts of the Kushans,* Plates 3, 8, 12, 13, 22, 24, 28.
21. Panigrahi, K.C., *Archaeological Remains at Bhubaneswar,* fig. 44.
22. Ibid., fig. 43.
23. Vatsyayan, K., *Indian Classical Dance in Literature and the Arts,* Plate 154.

24. Panigrahi, K.C., *Archaeological Remains at Bhubaneswar,* Plate 10.
25. Sivaramamurti, C., *Naṭarāja,* p. 47.17.
26. *NŚ,* GOS, Vol. I., 2nd edition, Plate IV, *karaṇa* no. 24.
27. *TL*, p. 42.
28. Sivaramamurti, C., *Naṭarāja*, p. 193. fig. 38.
29. *TL*, karana number 40.

Appendix A

1. Bhavnani, E., *The Dance in India*, p. 46.
2. Ibid., p. 56.

Index